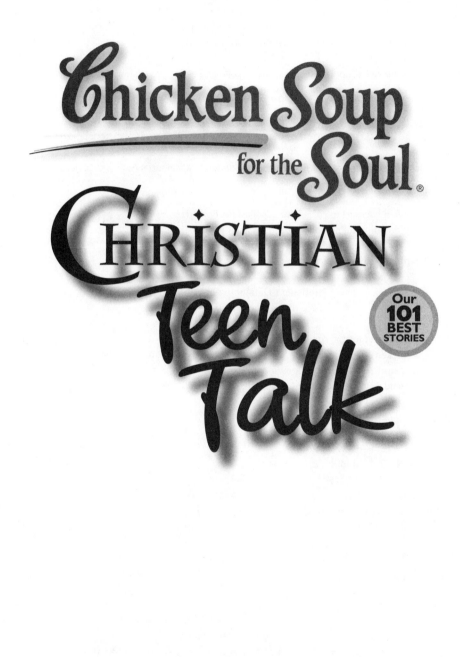

Chicken Soup for the Soul®

CHRISTIAN

Teen Talk

Our **101** BEST STORIES

Chicken Soup for the Soul: Christian Teen Talk
Christian Teens Share Their Stories of Support, Inspiration and Growing Up
by Jack Canfield, Mark Victor Hansen & Amy Newmark

Published by Chicken Soup for the Soul Publishing, LLC   www.chickensoup.com

The publisher gratefully acknowledges the many publishers and individuals who granted Chicken Soup for the Soul permission to reprint the cited material.

Cover photos courtesy of © Radius Images/Alamy, iStockphotos.com/sunnyfrog. Interior illustration courtesy of iStockphoto.com/Vjom

Cover and Interior Design & Layout by Pneuma Books, LLC
For more info on Pneuma Books, visit www.pneumabooks.com

Distributed to the booktrade by Simon & Schuster. SAN: 200-2442

Publisher's Cataloging-in-Publication Data
(Prepared by The Donohue Group)

Chicken soup for the soul. Selections.
   Chicken soup for the soul : Christian teen talk : Christian teens share their stories of support, inspiration and growing up / [compiled by] Jack Canfield [and] Mark Victor Hansen ; [edited by] Amy Newmark.

   p. ; cm.— (Our 101 best stories)

 ISBN-13: 978-1-935096-12-2
 ISBN-10: 1-935096-12-5

1. Christian teenagers--Literary collections. 2. Christian teenagers--Anecdotes. I. Canfield, Jack, 1944- II. Hansen, Mark Victor. III. Newmark, Amy. IV. Title. V. Title: Christian teen talk

PN6071.C57 C5 2008
808.89.283   2008934915

PRINTED IN THE UNITED STATES OF AMERICA
on acid∞free paper
15 14 13 12 11   02 03 04 05 06

Chicken Soup for the Soul. CHRISTIAN Teen Talk

Our 101 BEST STORIES

Christian Teens Share Their Stories of
Support, Inspiration and Growing Up

Jack Canfield
Mark Victor Hansen
Amy Newmark

CSS

Chicken Soup for the Soul Publishing, LLC
Cos Cob, CT

Chicken Soup for the Soul

Contents

❸

~Having Values~

❹

~ The Power of Prayer~

❺

~Family~

❻
~Growing Up~

❼
~Miracles Great and Small~

❽
~Life Lessons~

❾

~Tough Stuff~

❿

~Reaching Out~

⓫
~Not Really Gone~

⓬
~Love Is All You Need~

A Special Foreword

by Jack and Mark

For us, 101 has always been a magical number. It was the number of stories in the first *Chicken Soup for the Soul* book, and it is the number of stories and poems we have always aimed for in our books. We love the number 101 because it signifies a beginning, not an end. After 100, we start anew with 101.

We hope that when you finish reading one of our books, it is only a beginning for you too — a new outlook on life, a renewed sense of purpose, a strengthened resolve to deal with an issue that has been bothering you. Perhaps you will pick up the phone and share one of the stories with a friend or a loved one. Perhaps you will turn to your keyboard and express yourself by writing a Chicken Soup story of your own, to share with other readers who are just like you.

This volume contains our 101 best stories and poems about life as a Christian teenager. We share this with you at a very special time for us, the fifteenth anniversary of our *Chicken Soup for the Soul* series. When we published our first book in 1993, we never dreamed that we had started what became a publishing phenomenon, one of the best-selling series of books in history.

We did not set out to sell more than one hundred million books, or to publish more than 150 titles. We set out to touch the heart of one person at a time, hoping that person would in turn touch another person, and so on down the line. Fifteen years later, we know that it has worked. Your letters and stories have poured in by the hundreds of thousands, affirming our life's work, and inspiring us to continue to continue to make a difference in your lives.

On our fifteenth anniversary, we have new energy, new resolve, and new dreams. We have recommitted to our goal of 101 stories or poems per book, we have refreshed our cover designs and our interior layout, and we have grown the Chicken Soup for the Soul team, with new friends and partners across the country in New England.

We have chosen our 101 best stories and poems for Christian teenagers from our rich fifteen year history to share with you in this new volume. We know that your connection and relationship with God are important to you, and most importantly that you are experiencing all the ups and downs of teenage life, with the attendant joys and sorrows of growing up.

The stories that we have chosen for you were written by other teenagers just like you. They wrote about love, compassion, loss, forgiveness, friends, school, and their faith. We hope that you will find these stories inspiring and supportive, and that you will share them with your families and friends. We have identified the 27 *Chicken Soup for the Soul* books in which the stories originally appeared, in case you would like to continue your journey among our other books. We hope you will also enjoy the additional books for teenagers in "Our 101 Best Stories" series

With our love, our thanks, and our respect,
~*Jack Canfield and Mark Victor Hansen*

An Introductory Poem

When I Say I Am a Christian

When I say, "I am a Christian,"
I'm not shouting "I am saved."
I'm whispering "I was lost!
That is why I chose His way."

When I say, "I am a Christian,"
I don't speak of this with pride.
I'm confessing that I stumble
Needing God to be my guide.

When I say, "I am a Christian,"
I'm not trying to be strong.
I'm professing that I'm weak
And pray for strength to carry on.

When I say, "I am a Christian,"
I'm not bragging of success.

I'm admitting I have failed
And cannot ever pay the debt.

When I say, "I am a Christian,"
I don't think I know it all.
I submit to my confusion
Asking humbly to be taught.

When I say, "I am a Christian,"
I'm not claiming to be perfect.
My flaws are too visible
But God believes I'm worth it.

When I say, "I am a Christian,"
I still feel the sting of pain.
I have my share of heartaches
Which is why I seek His name.

When I say, "I am a Christian,"
I do not wish to judge.
I have no authority.
I only know I'm loved.

~Carol Wimmer
Chicken Soup for the Christian Family Soul

Finding God

God enters by a private door into each individual.
~Ralph Waldo Emerson

Rescue Me

My high school was in a border town, meaning we got new students who came over with their families from Mexico. Sometimes they'd speak English, and sometimes they didn't. We wouldn't normally mingle with these kids. We just sort of stuck with our own group.

Leticia was different. She was one of those girls who walks in a room, and everything gets all fuzzy and slow motion, like in the movies. She had long, dark hair and the greenest eyes I'd ever seen. She smiled as she walked by, and even though it probably wasn't at me, I took it as a sign.

I'm not usually the "lucky" type, but fate seemed to be smiling down on me because it turned out she was in most of my classes. The first time she was called on in U.S. History, she knew the answer (which I didn't), and she spoke in perfect English. I later found out she was from Mexico City and had studied American History at her school there. This totally intimidated me.

On April 11th, I was sitting in U.S. History, totally stressing about a midterm we were having the next day. I didn't even notice the guidance counselor come in to talk to our teacher, Mr. Huston. When he called my name, I didn't hear him. Then I looked up, and both he and the counselor had strange expressions on their faces, and they were looking at me. Something was wrong. I figured I was in trouble, but I couldn't imagine for what.

I followed the guidance counselor down the hall and into her office. When we got there, the principal was there, too. They were both silent for a minute. Then the principal began to speak.

"Your father has had a heart attack. The paramedics and doctors did everything they could to save him, but I'm afraid he didn't make it."

"Okay," I said. "Well, I'd better be getting back to class. I don't want to miss the rest of the exam review."

They looked at me, stunned. I didn't really know what I was saying. I felt like they were telling me about someone else's dad. I just didn't get it.

The next few weeks were a blur as we had the funeral and began adjusting to life without my dad. I went back to school after I ran out of things to do at home. Everything felt a little different. I can't exactly explain how; it just did.

Back at school, everyone was super-nice to me. The teachers didn't call on me, and they kept asking me to stay after class to see if I was "okay." My friends were really weird. I felt like I couldn't talk to them about the same old things. It was all so strange. My dad was a great guy, and then all of a sudden he was dead. He didn't do anything wrong. He never hurt anyone. I started eating lunch alone. I just couldn't deal with listening to the same stupid jokes or talking about random stuff.

About three weeks after I went back to school, I was sitting in a corner of the quad, not really eating, just staring off into space. "Are you going to eat the rest of that sandwich?" I looked up and saw Leticia standing in front of me.

"Huh?" I responded. I looked down and realized I hadn't touched my sandwich. I handed it over.

As she gratefully accepted, she told me, "My mom packed me a meat and egg torta. Your tuna fish looks better." She sat down next to me and ate my sandwich. She didn't say a word to me, but seemed happy to just sit there.

After a few minutes, I grew too uncomfortable. "Why did you come over?" I asked.

"You looked like you could use a friend," she said. "I lost my father last year." I didn't know what to say to her, and she didn't know what to say to me. I didn't want to talk about my dad, but for the first time in a while, I felt okay just being with another person.

We started having lunch together on that bench every day. We never mentioned my dad or her dad, except she told me that was the reason they moved from Mexico. We talked about school, TV, movies and other meaningless stuff. I loved her mom's tortas, and she seemed to like my "American" sandwiches. I finally worked up the nerve to ask her to go to a movie with me.

"I'd like to," she said, "but I have to ask you a question first. Are you a Christian?"

"Huh?" I replied.

She told me her dad was a deeply spiritual man, and that it had been very important to him that she associate only with Christians. Basically, she was saying she couldn't go out with me unless I believed in the same stuff she did. I was confused. She had become my friend, and up till now she didn't care if I was a Christian or not.

I told her I wanted to go out with her, but I didn't think I was a Christian and I didn't think it should matter. Unfortunately, I then said something really stupid. I said, "It doesn't matter to me that you're Mexican." She looked at me, then got up and walked away.

A week went by. I came to the bench every day with a tuna fish sandwich, hoping Leticia would show up. No luck. But finally one day she was there.

"To love the Lord with all your heart, mind, soul and strength, and your neighbor as yourself, means to experience forgiveness and to forgive others as well as yourself. Matthew 6:12." That's all she said. Then she took my tuna sandwich and started eating it.

So we went back to our routine of daily lunch and sandwich exchange. I didn't bring up the dating thing again, and neither did she. The prom was coming up, and I really wanted to ask her.

"So what does it take to become a Christian, anyway? Do I have to shave my head or go spend the night in the woods or something?"

She ignored my sarcasm. "No, all you have to do is pray with me."

"All I have to do is pray?" That seemed pretty easy.

"Well, there is one catch," she said. "You have to mean it. I mean, really mean it. You have to give up your soul to God. You have to beg forgiveness for all your sins. Can you do that?"

Sure, I thought. A little prayer and I get to take Leticia to the prom. "Okay," I said. "Let's do it. Where do we go?"

"How about right here?" she responded.

"In front of everyone?"

"Why not?" She told me to close my eyes. Then she started to pray. She asked me to invite God's spirit into my heart. I started to say the words after her and stopped.

I saw this image in my mind of a closed door. I was about to open it and go through. I could see light streaming through the keyhole. We were silent for a long time as I had my hand on the doorknob. Then I turned it and opened the door.

I started to cry. I cried for my father. I cried for my mother and sister. I cried for Leticia's father. I cried for all the kids who lost their fathers and mothers. I couldn't stop crying. I felt God's grace.

Leticia and I went to the prom, and we had a great time. We're seniors now, and we're still together. I miss my dad a lot, and I think about him all the time. I still don't have all the answers. But I owe Leticia a lot because she gave me my faith. She rescued me.

~Matt Rivers
Chicken Soup for the Christian Teenage Soul

A Cross in the Sand

I wasn't abused as a child. I just felt lonely, neglected and unloved. I don't think it was my parents' fault necessarily. I just wasn't a happy kid.

My family did not attend church. I had never even set foot in one. We weren't rich, but we had enough money to take a beautiful trip to Florida every Christmas. Of course, my parents loved to tease me about Santa not doing address changes very well. But every year, packages marked "From Santa" made their way to our motel room.

One morning in Florida, I had decided to play in the warm, white sand with my shiny new pail and shovel. My parents weren't going to the beach, so I settled for digging in the motel courtyard. I looked at the sandy field, sparsely covered with tropical weeds. I set out to find the best spot to create my sandy masterpiece. I chose a place way out in the middle, sat down contentedly and began to dig.

About four inches down, my shovel clinked on something. I was always dreaming of finding lost pirate treasures or being the first one to find an unopened genie bottle. Therefore, it wasn't a stretch for me to think I had hit the jackpot. However, my little shovel had uncovered a treasure of a much different sort. It was a small, silver cross. I turned it over and over in my hands, looking at it as the sun made it glow brightly. Etched on the back of the cross were words I could just barely make out: "Jesus Christ is Lord." I wasn't sure what that meant. I never showed anyone the cross, but kept it hidden as one of my prized possessions, only taking it out when no one was around. To me, it wasn't just a cross; it was a sign.

During high school, I was a typical teen. I sought out fun and trouble, but rarely got caught for it. My life was going downhill fast, but I thought it was perfectly under control, except for the emptiness inside that I couldn't account for. Sometime during my sophomore year, I decided I wanted to know about God.

Most of the church services I attended with my friends were good, but one was life-changing. As the music began to play, I was consumed, and I felt Him. He was the One I had been searching for. He was the One who had been calling me. The pastor called for those who didn't know Him to come forward. I couldn't have stopped my feet if I had wanted to. He prayed, I prayed, and my life was never again the same. I went home and wept with joy. A seemingly lifelong void was finally filled. For some reason, I am quite sure my search began the day I hit metal with my little shovel and found a cross that said, "Jesus Christ is Lord." Now I no longer have to dig to find my treasures. All the treasures I'll ever need are just a prayer away.

~Lana L. Comstock
Chicken Soup for the Christian Teenage Soul

From Packin' to Preachin'

The more you are aware of God's unchanging love,
the safer you feel in the world.
~Susan L. Taylor

I started running away from home when I was eleven years old. Home was thirteen brothers and sisters, all of whom ran away from our crazy, abusive father by the time they were fourteen. Our mother had been murdered. I was desperate for attention, for a sense of who I was and what I was supposed to be, for a place where I felt safe. The gang found me. They took me in, taught me who I was to be, gave me protection, and filled me with pride and a sense of belonging. What do you have to give the gang in return? You have to give them all of yourself, and you never get it back completely.

The gang became my family for the next seventeen years. It was a family of drugs, guns and jailings, but I belonged, and that was my security. During those seventeen years, nearly fourteen of them were spent in foster homes, jail or prison. When I was twelve, I tried to kill my father. The charge was attempted murder. I was held, without remorse, in the juvenile justice system until I was eighteen. By this time, I was a drug addict.

The next ten years were filled with jailings, carrying guns, not having enough money for my drug habit and constant paranoia. The only women I knew were gang chicks. I knew I would just make more gang members with one of them. I had already gotten a fourteen-year-old girl pregnant when I was eighteen, married her (I didn't want to add statutory rape to my rap sheet), and then couldn't keep the relationship together. My life was going nowhere. I was tired. The gang offered me no way out. I wanted to get away, become a member of the "middle class." I figured I could accomplish this by pushing drugs in a bigger arena. I walked away from the neighborhood. I can never go back. There would be blood if I did. I know where I can go and where I'm not supposed to be.

Though leaving the neighborhood and the gang was not for honorable reasons, it was the first step that was to change my life forever. I was headed for redemption, although it was going to be a long journey. Too soon, I was serving five years in a federal prison for transporting drugs across the border. But when I got out, the first real sign of change happened.

I met some amazing people through a chance encounter. They took me in, and they loved me, unconditionally. I learned what love was about from these two people. They allowed me to call them "Grandma" and "Grandpa" and loved me, just as I was.

I quit the drugs except for Sundays. On Sunday mornings, I smoked a joint and then went to church with Grandma and Grandpa, relaxed and happy. I had no idea where this was all heading. How was I to know that God was not going to leave me alone?

The old ladies in the church knew that I had musical talents. One of them came to me and asked me to lead the morning worship service. I didn't want to, but I would do anything for those old ladies, so I did it. The next Sunday they asked me to lead the worship service again, and then the next Sunday, and the next. I gave up my Sunday joint. It's hard to lead a worship service when you're high!

I still carried a gun, but I was beginning to feel safe. One particular day, I just wasn't paying attention. I was enjoying a walk at the beach with my baby. I was pushing the stroller, head down, when I bumped into another stroller. I looked up into the face of the one man I had vowed to kill. The last time I had seen him, he had pistol-whipped me, hung me from a balcony and left me for dead. Now we stared into each other's eyes, instinctively reaching for our weapons. A bizarre coincidence. Two innocents, a moment away from the shattering blast that would make them fatherless. There was no movement, no sound; even the babies were quiet, as though waiting for a signal. And then a peace came over me. I dropped my hand from my weapon and extended it to the man I had hated. He reached out his hand to mine, and we shook hands. No words were spoken. I have never seen him again.

By this time, a landscaping business I had started was successful, I was still going to church with Grandpa and Grandma, I had put down my gun, and the Lord was still "bothering" me. The church had been without a pastor for months. One day I heard the Lord's voice saying, "I called you, Gilbert." I went to Grandma and Grandpa and said, "I think I'm supposed to be your pastor."

They just smiled at me and said, "What took you so long?"

I've been their pastor for twenty-five years now. Fifteen years ago, we established the Bittersweet Ministries for drug and alcohol rehabilitation. Over three thousand people have gone through the program to date. Our Bittersweet Gospel Band performs all over the country as ambassadors for our programs.

My life had really changed, but I didn't know how much until one night in Chicago. We were there with the band. My friend and I were standing outside the home of our host talking before we went inside. Two guys came up to us and asked what time it was. I looked at my watch and immediately felt a gun on my neck. The other guy was restraining my friend with a knife. I knew I could take the kid, but instead I started telling him that God loved him. His hand began to shake. I reached for his arm, saying, "Look, I'm not going to take the gun, but I'm afraid you're going to shoot someone if you don't stop shaking. I'm a pastor, and I want you to know the Lord loves you." I just kept telling him, "God loves you, son. God loves you." The boy looked into my eyes for a long moment, reached for the money I offered him, and then disappeared into the night with the other kid.

I don't know if his life was changed, but I sure realized at that moment how much mine had! I had been loved into a new life—a life of peace instead of paranoia, happiness instead of heroin, a life of preachin' love instead of packin' death.

~Gilbert Romero as told to Barbara Smythe
Chicken Soup for the Soul Stories for a Better World

5

How Sweet the Sound

Music was my refuge. I could crawl into the space between the notes
and curl my back to loneliness.
~Maya Angelou, Gather Together in My Name

The lead should have been mine. All my friends agreed with me. At least, it shouldn't have been Helen's, that strange new girl. She never had a word to say, always looking down at her feet as if her life was too heavy to bear. We thought she was just stuck-up. Things can't be all that bad for her, we reasoned, not with all the great clothes she wears. She hadn't worn the same thing more than twice in the two months she'd been at our school.

But the worst of it was when she showed up at our tryouts and sang for my part. Everyone knew the lead role was meant for me. After all, I had parts in all our high school musicals, and this was our senior year.

My friends were waiting for me, so I didn't hang around for Helen's audition. The shock came two days later when we hurried to check the bulletin board for the cast list.

We scanned the sheets looking for my name. When we found it, I stood there in shock. Helen was picked to play the lead! I was to be her mother and her understudy. Understudy? Nobody could believe it.

Rehearsals seemed to go on forever. Helen didn't seem to notice that we were going out of our way to ignore her. I'll admit it, Helen did have a beautiful voice. She was different on stage somehow. Not so much happy as settled and content.

Opening night brought its fair share of jitters. Everyone was quietly bustling around backstage, waiting for the curtain to go up. Everyone but Helen, of course. She seemed contained in her own world.

The performance was a hit. Our timing was perfect; our voices blended and soared. Helen and I flowed back and forth, weaving the story between us—I, the ailing mother praying for her wayward daughter, and Helen, the daughter who realizes as her mother dies that there is more to life than this life. The final scene reached its dramatic end. I was lying in the darkened bedroom. The prop bed I was on was uncomfortable, which made it hard to stay still. I was impatient, anxious for Helen's big finish to be over.

She was spotlighted on stage, the grieving daughter beginning to understand the true meaning of the hymn she had been singing as her mother passed away.

"Amazing grace, how sweet the sound...." Her voice lifted over the pain of her mother's death and the joy of God's promises.

"...That saved a wretch like me..." Something real was happening to me as Helen sang. My impatience was gone.

"...I once was lost, but now I'm found..." I started to cry.

"...Was blind but now I see." My spirit began to turn within me, and I turned to God. In that moment, I knew his love, his desire for me. Helen's voice lingered in the prayer on the last note. The curtain dropped.

Complete silence. Not a sound. Helen stood behind the closed curtain, head bowed, gently weeping.

Suddenly, applause and cheers erupted, and when the curtain parted the entire audience was standing.

We all made our final bows. My hugs were genuine. My heart had been opened wide.

Then it was over. The costumes were hung up, make-up tissued off and the lights dimmed. Everyone went off in their usual groupings, congratulating each other.

Everyone but Helen. I stayed because I needed to tell her something.

"Helen, your song... it was so real for me," I hesitated, my feelings intense. I suddenly felt shy. "You sang me into the heart of God."

Helen's eyes met mine.

"That's what my mother said to me the night she died." A tear slipped down her cheek. My heart leapt to hers. "My mother was in such pain. Singing 'Amazing Grace' always comforted her. She told me to remember God would always be good to me, and that his grace would lead her home."

Her face lit up from the inside out, her mother's love shining through. "Just before she died, she whispered, 'Sing me into the heart of God, Helen.' That night and tonight, I sang for my mother."

~Cynthia M. Hamond
Chicken Soup for the Christian Teenage Soul

6

Putting On the Boots

"**A** twelve-year-old girl is in desperate need of a home because both of her parents have been sentenced to prison."

As soon as this call came on the church prayer chain, my heart went out to her—within two days, Nikki came to live with us. She'd been knocked around from place to place, being rejected over and over. Some families had kept her for a few days, some for a few weeks. Nikki's self-confidence was zero.

But God began to do a miraculous work in her life, slowly convincing her He had great plans for her future. About a year later, she heard about an organization called Teen Missions, which offered short-term mission assignments to teenagers. She applied, got accepted and everything was in motion for her trip to Africa. She was so excited, I thought she'd burst!

The first thing she needed to do to prepare for this great mission assignment was to get a pair of big, high-top construction boots and wear them every day to break them in. She ordered the boots, then sent out her missionary support letters to raise the $5,000 to go.

The response was paltry.

She refused to put on the boots. They sat in her closet for three solid months with the tags still on them. Without clear signs of support from God and others, she wouldn't take a step.

As it happened, right around this time I was scheduled to speak at a women's conference, so Nikki decided to make bookmarks to sell at my book table. She designed one that involved cutting, ironing, gluing, hole punching, threading and tying a bow. She sat for hours cutting fabric until there was a purple indentation in her hand and tears streaming down her face.

"Why don't you stop now?" I urged.

"No," she declared. "I'm going to do this!"

I knew at that instant she had "put on the boots." Yet I could see she still felt discouraged and ill-equipped.

The next day, I reminded her that God had called Gideon to fight a tough battle, but Gideon didn't think he was good enough for the job. I told her, "Gideon said, 'God, I can't do what you're asking me to do! I'm just a kid. Besides, I'm from a lousy family. You better pick someone else.' None of that mattered to God," I reminded her. "In fact, God loves to pick the most unlikely people to do His work. The Lord eased Gideon's worry by posing a very simple question, 'Am I not sending you?'"

I explained to Nikki, "It's not about the one who's going, it's about the One who's sending. If God is sending you, you can go in complete confidence."

That day at the women's conference, she raised $742 — most of it in $1 donations. Some ladies donated $5, $10 or $20, shoving the money into her boots, which were set up on my book table.

When we returned from the conference, we filled our house with giant posters proclaiming "Who's Sending You?" Over the next several months, Nikki made almost four thousand bookmarks and raised $5,000 at my conferences around the country.

She demonstrated her faithfulness by "putting on the boots" for the One who was sending her.

~Donna Partow
Chicken Soup for the Christian Soul 2

Searching and Finding

I am a reader, and readers are dreamers and searchers. All readers, like me, know in their hearts that there is more to life than what they are living. Somewhere, there must be a handsome prince, a dashing rogue, a rugged mountain man to sweep me off my feet and bear me to a land bursting with myth and legend and beautiful scenery. And in that land I would uncover mysteries and secrets, things so simple and pure they can only be found in nature. I would breathe in the fresh, clean air and drink the sounds of birds and breezes and brooks, the soft sounds. There I would be fulfilled and happy. At peace, at last.

For me, this dreamland was Ireland. I was ushered to this place through my imagination and by the poetry of William Butler Yeats, especially his description of "The Lake Isle of Innisfree." He painted a picture of peace that he longed for and could only find on that island. He pined after it so, that no matter where he was he would "hear it in the deep heart's core." In my deep heart's core, I felt exactly that longing, that need for more; I was drawn to this place of peace.

Until recently, I thought that my vision of Ireland must remain simply a vision. But through the kindness of my grandparents, I was able to go. And, oh the excitement and joy that was mine! I journeyed there with all my hopes and dreams prepared to be fulfilled. And I saw the castles and the bogs, the mountains, the fairy forts, flowers and even the Isle of Innisfree. The beauty was indescribable. The hundreds of radiant flowers pleased my eyes. The sweet sounds of the birds and brooks and breezes soothed my ears. The fragrance of the pure air invigorated my nostrils. I could taste the rain and feel the serenity drop onto my skin and cleanse my soul. But the one sense that remained untouched was my heart. I was still searching, and for days I pulled at the land, needing that fulfillment I thought it offered. But I couldn't find it, and still I felt sad and empty.

One day, I was looking deep into a blossom, at its incredible beauty and worth, and I remembered how that flower first appeared. The source of its life, the source of mine, the very beginning, the light of life was where and only where I could find my fulfillment and peace of mind. And then my heart exploded, full of what was there all the time, what I could only find within myself, what so many people need and search for, but don't see because it is so simple and basic. And God is basic. God is the source of all things. God is our roots, and just as a tree looks to its roots for nourishment and a river looks to its source for replenishing waters, we must look to our roots and our source to fill the void in our hearts. God is our only nourishment; all else is transient.

So now I read, but I search no longer, because all the romance and adventure enticing me into the worlds between the pages is just a faint taste of the adventure of life, of my life. I am excited about each day as it comes; each one can be made to be fulfilling in its own right. And when my days run out, I will have lived just a blink of time and the rest will be eternal joy. And that is what I learned in Ireland.

~Abby Danielle Burlbaugh
Chicken Soup for the Christian Teenage Soul

8

A Father's Love

God loves each of us as if there were only one of us.
~St. Augustine

His name was Brian, and he was a student at the small high school I attended. Brian was a special education student who was constantly searching for attention, but usually got it for the wrong reasons. Students who wanted to have some "fun" would ask, "Brian, are you the Incredible Hulk?" He would then run down the halls roaring and flexing. He was the joke of the school and was "entertainment" for those who watched. Brian, who was looking for acceptance, didn't realize they were laughing at him and not with him.

One day I couldn't take it anymore. I told the other students I had had enough of their game and to knock it off. "Aw, come on, Mike! We're just having fun. Who do you think you are, anyway?" The teasing didn't stop for long, but Brian latched onto me that day. I had stuck up for him, and now he was my buddy. Thoughts of, "What will people think of you if you are friends with Brian?" swirled in my head, but I forced them out as I realized God wanted me to treat Brian as I would want to be treated.

Later that week, I invited Brian over to my house to play video games. We sat there playing video games and drinking Tang. Pretty soon, he started asking me questions like, "Hey, Mike. Where do you go to church?" I politely answered his questions, then turned my concentration back to the video games. He kept asking me questions about God, and why I was different from some of the kids at school. Finally, my girlfriend, Kristi, pulled me aside and said, "Michael, he needs to talk. How about you go down to your room where you can talk privately?" My perceptive girlfriend had picked up on the cues better than I had.

As soon as we got to my room, Brian asked again, "Hey, Mike. How come you're not like some of the other kids at school?" I wanted to tell him about the difference God had made in my life. I got out my Bible and shared John 3:16 and some verses in Romans with him. I explained that God loved him just the way he was, and that He had sent Jesus down to Earth to die on a cross, rise from the dead and make it possible for everyone, especially Brian, to spend eternity in heaven if they believed. I didn't know if he comprehended what I was telling him, but when I finished explaining, I asked him if he wanted to pray with me. He said he would like that.

We prayed together: "God, I know I'm a sinner, and that even if I were the only person on Earth, You still would have sent Your Son down to die on the cross for me and take my place. I accept the gift of salvation that you offer, and I ask that you come into my heart and take control. Thank you, Lord. Amen."

I looked at Brian and said, "Brian, if you meant those words you just prayed, where is Jesus right now?"

He pointed to his heart and said, "He's in here now."

Then he did something I will never forget as long as I live. Brian hugged the Bible to his chest, lay down on the bed and let the tears flow down the side of his cheeks. When I cry, my sobbing is very loud, but Brian's was unearthly silent as the emotions he'd held inside let loose. Finally, he said, "Mike, do you know that the love God has for me must be like the love a husband has for his wife?"

I was floored.

Here was someone who had trouble comprehending things in school, but had now understood one of eternity's great truths. He lay there for another five minutes or so as the tears continued to flow.

I still remember the incredible feeling I had at that moment: a high higher than anything a substance could ever give, the high of knowing that God works miracles in everyday life. John 10:10 immediately came to mind: "I have come that they may have life, and have it to the full."

About a week later, everything came into perspective for me. Brian really opened up to me. He explained that his dad had left him and his mom when he was five years old. As Brian stood on the porch that day, his dad told him he was leaving because he couldn't deal with having a son like him anymore. Then he walked out of Brian's life and was never seen again. Brian told me he had been looking for his dad ever since. Now I knew why the tears kept flowing that day in my bedroom. His search was over. He found what he had been looking for since he was five years old: a Father's love.

~Michael T. Powers
Chicken Soup for the Christian Teenage Soul

9

The Final Cut

No God, no peace. Know God, know peace.
~Author Unknown

One swift movement of the razor, and I am on my way. No more racing thoughts, no more screams of anger—just fresh cuts, vibrant blood and a familiar euphoria. The blood creeps from the thin slices I have created, and soon comfort will be restored and sanity found. Another cut means more blood, but less pain. I examine my arm carefully—the cuts are not deep enough and the pain not strong enough. I must be careful, though; the marks might be noticed. I choose a different spot—my stomach. I quickly untuck the blouse of my uniform and tighten my abdomen.

I am sitting in my car and have only thirty minutes before school starts. The fight with my mom this morning is now a distant memory as I quickly bandage my latest wounds. Arriving at school, I quickly check to make sure nothing is showing. I open the car door, and it is like a whole new world, a world where nobody, not even my close friends, knows me well enough to notice the quiver of my lip or the unsteadiness of my hands. It is a world I play like a game, leaving emotions for the poets and drama for the actors. The morning air is crisp enough that my shallow breath can be seen as I make my way toward the entrance. People shout to say hello from all the corners of the parking lot as I wave and smile effortlessly. I mumble quietly to myself, "Let the games begin."

I began hurting myself a long time ago. I can remember locking myself in the bathroom after a difficult day of elementary school or a fight with my parents and crying to God, asking Him for help, looking for someone or something to soothe my pain. When no relief came, I would scratch my face, my arms, my legs—anything.

Later, in middle school, my family went through the realization that country clubs and parochial schools cannot hide their children from the world of drugs. Watching from the sidelines as my oldest brother hit rock bottom and left for drug rehab, I made it my mission to hide every deep emotion I felt and started cutting each time these feelings crept into my conscience. I began using knives, razors and scissors—whatever would make me bleed. The blood made me stop hurting emotionally and start hurting physically. For me, dealing with the physical pain was nickels and dimes compared to some of the intense emotional pain I confronted in those first years of adolescence.

I could bandage my cuts and stop the bleeding, but I could never end my internal struggle with feeling valued by others unless I constantly appeared to be perfectly "normal." This meant hiding my problems, building those walls the therapists preach about and acting entirely unscathed by the turmoil I faced at home, in school, from my friends, from guys and from demanding athletic coaches. I became good at playing the part of the Patti Mason everyone wanted to be around, rather than the Patti Mason I really was.

I would never have broken out from my cutting routine if it hadn't been for my faith in Jesus Christ. Soon, the cuts became too deep and scars set in, which led to questions and, finally, my confession. And as I slowly let the walls crumble, revealing the true me to my friends and family, I opened myself up to God for healing and protection. Now tears were the way my sadness was expressed.

Each day, I got better. I discovered my faith again—my faith in life, in love, in myself and, above all, in Christ. It was through this faith that I realized the battle I was fighting would not end until I surrendered it to God and allowed myself to end the act. I had to feel the things inside, and I had to let people love the real me. I saw a therapist and was put on medication, and these two things definitely helped me to feel better. But getting myself back only happened when I surrendered to God. Resisting the urge to hurt myself is not something I could ever do by myself. God, and God alone, holds that power.

~Patricia H. Mason
Chicken Soup for the Christian Teenage Soul

10

Safe at Last

I'm so afraid.
Afraid that people might see
Who I really am.
I try to hide it:
Outside I'm calm, cool, collected.
But inside I'm crumbling
Into a million pieces.
I can't hide it forever;
Sometimes the mask slips off
And I'm exposed and vulnerable.
I feel so naked
And everyone is looking at me.
They can see right through me.
But I put my mask back on
And I'm safe behind it.
Nothing can happen to me there.
Safe.
But the fear comes back again
Just like it always does.
Then I'm crying out again,
Crying for help inside.
The mask comes off again.
That's when I feel him
Holding my hand.

The voice says,
"Do not fear, my child,
For I love you exactly as you are
And I will always be with you."
Suddenly a peace comes over me
And I'm not afraid anymore
Because I know he loves me
Just the way I am.

~Bethany Schwartz
Chicken Soup for the Christian Teenage Soul

CHRISTIAN Teen Talk

Real Friends

*The most beautiful discovery true friends make
is that they can grow separately without growing apart.*
~Elisabeth Foley

11

People Change but Friendships Remain

Challenge is a good thing. And in today's world, strength is an asset we have to have. Childhood, you have taught me many lessons.
~Patricia Reeder

Dear *Chicken Soup for the Teenage Soul*,

Most people don't really know what a typical teenager has to go through. I don't think that anyone fully understands the pressures of being a teen and all the obstacles we overcome every day. Sure, our parents and grandparents were once teens, but things are so different now. It has never been tougher to be a teenager.

It has never been more important to be in the "right group" or to have the "right brand" of shoes. And those are the easy things to deal with. We also face problems with family, friends, relationships and school pressures. Do you remember wondering when that guy you have admired for so long would finally glance in your direction and ask you your name? Or when your parents would stop pressuring you about your grades?

When it gets to be too much, I turn to my friends. One friend I could not live without is *Chicken Soup for the Teenage Soul*. Your books have been so inspiring to me and have helped me to deal with and understand the problems I go through. The stories have helped me grow as a person and truly made a big impact on my life.

I went through a confusing time with my friends when we got to junior high. I had known these friends since kindergarten, and when we began junior high it seemed like some of them began to change. We slowly drifted apart and started hanging out with different groups. When we were going through this "transition," I felt confused and hurt. It was as if we had never been friends in the first place, we had grown so far apart.

Sometime during this period I read the story "Friends Forever" in *Chicken Soup for the Teenage Soul II*. I felt so much better after reading it. It was like a weight was lifted from me when I realized that many friendships go through changes and that we weren't the only friends to experience them. Once I understood it as a normal part of being a teenager, I started to relax and let go.

People change, but that doesn't mean we have to lose the friendships we once shared. My friends and I still spend time together when we can and care about each other a lot. Just because things are different doesn't mean that I have to forget about all the good times we had. I will always keep the memories in a safe place in my heart. This story taught me that we will go through many different changes throughout our lives. The best thing to do is to move on and let go of the past—and leave the rest in God's hands.

Sincerely,

~Jiseon Choi
Chicken Soup for the Teenage Soul Letters

I Need You Now

Ah, how good it feels! The hand of a friend.
~Henry Wadsworth Longfellow

My friend, I need you now —
Please take me by the hand.
Stand by me in my hour of need,
Take time to understand.

Take my hand, dear friend,
And lead me from this place.
Chase away my doubts and fears,
Wipe the tears from off my face.

Friend, I cannot stand alone.
I need your hand to hold,
The warmth of your gentle touch
In my world that's grown so cold.

Please be a friend to me
And hold me day by day.
Because with your loving hand in mine,
I know we'll find the way.

~Becky Tucker
Chicken Soup for the Teenage Soul II

The Friendship Cake

I used to listen only halfheartedly when my parents told me I should be thankful for what I had. My friends were girls who had the same interests in soccer and school as me. We all tried to act like individuals, but let's face it... we wore the exact same style of jeans and sweatshirts. In fact, we were all pretty much alike. Things changed when I had the opportunity to go to Africa.

After a twenty-one-hour flight, we arrived at our destination—Bugala Island, Uganda, in the middle of Lake Victoria. The eight-mile-long island had only one rutted road. The people there lived in cow dung huts without running water or electricity. (I won't even describe what the toilets looked like.)

While on Bugala Island, I had a chance to meet the girl I sponsored through Childcare International, a Christian relief agency. Her name was Annette, and her parents and relatives had died of AIDS. Through the thirty-dollar donation my family made each month, Annette was able to live in a group home and go to school. Annette and I had been writing letters back and forth for some time. I made sure not to write about our house, my closet full of clothes or the big trips we took. Here was a girl my own age who owned only two dresses and one pair of flip-flops. Before we left for our trip, my mom and I thought about buying Annette a backpack. I'm glad that we didn't because I soon saw she had nothing to put in it—no stuffed animals, no boxes of markers... no books.

When I first met Annette, I had on my favorite khaki shorts, not knowing that most girls in Uganda seldom wear shorts or pants. She hugged me cautiously—after all, she had never seen a Caucasian girl before. Within five minutes, Annette disappeared into her group home. She returned moments later wearing a faded pair of shorts, trying to look like me. Annette spoke English fairly well, so we could talk, but I panicked. How could I be friends with someone who had never even seen water coming out of a faucet?

Surprisingly, it didn't take long for us to form a friendship. She showed me the room she shared with twenty other orphan girls, who by now were all wearing shorts, too. Annette taught me how to play their jump-rope games, and we played the drums together and did craft projects. I found myself having fun with Annette even though she had never seen a video or eaten at McDonald's. Our life experiences couldn't have been more different, yet there we were... hanging out like old friends.

On the last night of our trip, the kids there planned a celebration for me. Since they didn't have crepe-paper streamers, they twisted toilet paper along the walls to make decorations. Annette, still wearing her shorts, led the group in singing and dancing. The dancing consisted of shaking the hips back and forth so the grass skirts the girls wore swooshed in a blur of color. The children invited me to join in their dance. Three years of ballet lessons never could have prepared me for what was to come. Trying to mimic their dance, I fell short and resorted to my preschool years of twirling and waving my body wildly to the beating of the drums and chanting of the children. They laughed hysterically at my attempts at African dance.

After the dancing and singing, the director of the home announced a special treat—a frosted cake! He brought out a home-made, one-layer, eight-inch cake. Annette and I cut up the cake, and all 120 kids excitedly waited for the rare treat of sweet cake. I figured the Costco-size sheet cakes were on another table. After all, we had to serve over a hundred kids. Instead, Annette cut the eight-inch cake into smaller and smaller pieces... these were really small pieces! I then went around and passed them out, and each child picked up a tiny piece with his or her fingers. Everyone smiled at me as they ate their miniature piece of cake. No one asked for seconds, and no one tried to sneak two pieces. They were simply happy with what they had. Annette made sure I had a piece of cake, too.

The next day, while leaving the island, I thought back on that cake. In the United States, my friends would have complained about the tiny piece of cake. "We want a bigger piece! Where's the ice cream?" I found myself happily eating a few cake crumbs next to Annette. It wasn't about the sugar rush. It wasn't about the frosting. It was about the friendship.

~Sondra Clark
Chicken Soup for the Teenage Soul: The Real Deal Friends

Being There

A friend accepts us as we are, yet helps us to be what we should.
~Author Unknown

I wish that everyone could see friendship the way that I see it. Friendship is not just based on the type of music that someone listens to. Friendship is not just based on the type of clothing that you wear. Friendship is not even based on the sports teams that you prefer. It's not based on age, skin color, religious beliefs or gender.

Due to problems before my birth, I was born with cerebral palsy. I have been in an electronic wheelchair since I started school. I'm now in the ninth grade and have made friends all over the area near where I live. I have friends from all different age groups, young and old alike. There are friendly people everywhere I turn and so I gather friends very easily.

One of the ways that I experience friendship is through my own family. My cousin Chaz is a good example. Since I have limited use of my hands, I can't always do things myself. One time, while eating at McDonald's, we decided to eat at a table away from the adults. A Quarter Pounder is too big for me to pick up, so Chaz just picked it up and fed it to me. He didn't even think about doing it; he just picked it up and did it. That's friendship.

One time I went to a sleepover at my cousin Sky's house and he had about eight other guys there, too. In the middle of the night, after his parents were asleep, as you can guess, we were still awake. We were all lying on the floor talking our heads off when we decided to get up and go outside. Because I can't put myself in my wheelchair, all the boys grabbed my arms and legs and placed me in it. No adults were needed for the amazing feat. Sometimes, it's handy to have a lot of friends.

Then there's my grandpa. He's seventy-nine years old. Whenever I get time off from school, we take a day and go to the mall. First we go eat breakfast and he helps feed it to me. I play video games, and he helps to insert the coins. That's what I would call a really friendly grandpa.

I have another friend—a guy in his early thirties named Steve who went to summer camp with me for several years in a row. Without his help, I couldn't have participated in a lot of the activities. He totally didn't have to do that, but because he did, he showed me that's what friendship is all about.

My church youth group plays basketball at the church gym a lot. Whenever I go to these events, they allow me to play on one of the teams. Have you ever played against a team with a kid in a one hundred pound wheelchair? I'd say that's friendship.

Have you ever thought about where wheelchair ramps are located? They are sometimes in locations that are inconvenient to get to. Most people take the fastest route to the door, but when you're in a wheelchair, it's a little different. One of the coolest things that my friends do is walk the long way to the ramp with me. They could easily run up the stairs and leave me behind, but they don't.

If you've never really thought about the true meaning of friendship, I hope that reading this little piece of my life has given you something to think about. I have many friends who like the same sports teams that I do and even friends who wear the same style of clothes that I wear. I have friends who are part of my family and friends who are older and even younger than I am. My friends are as different as people can be from one another, but they all have something in common. Each of them recognizes that being a friend means being there for your friends. And, as you can see, they've all been there for me.

~Jared Garrett
Chicken Soup for the Preteen Soul 2

15

Change Comes to Maxwell Street

Though no one could take the place of Bloke as my best friend, Jack Caldwell was a welcome addition to my young life. We lived on the same floor of the same derelict tenement. We often sat out on the rickety back porch listening to baseball games on the radio after it had gotten too late to be traipsing around the neighborhood.

When Jack moved in with the O'Tooles across the landing from our door, I assumed his parents were dead, but I never did ask. I was more interested in gaining a new playmate and buddy, so where he came from was of minor importance.

"He's come to live with his aunt and uncle," Mama told us the afternoon we'd noticed the stocky, red-haired boy carrying a suitcase up the three flights of stairs to our floor. "Keep your noses to yourselves!"

When I realized Jack was my age and seemed to be a likable sort, I immediately invited him to join the tight-knit group that Bloke, Regan, Ritchie and I had formed. He fit in very easily, displaying a pleasant disposition and more than a bit of talent at stickball and other sports. In a very short time, it was as if he had always been a part of our Maxwell Street world.

The next spring, however, the friendship we had taken for granted seemed to crumble when I learned that Jack was leaving, most likely for good. I had just begun thinking of things to keep us busy during the lazy summer ahead.

"Goin' to live in Oregon," he said somberly, "with my Uncle Henry."

I was stunned.

"His uncle and aunt in Oregon have no children," Mama later explained, "and they felt it would be nice to have Jack there."

Though Mama had barely mentioned anything about the O'Tooles before then, I also learned that Jack had been summarily left at the O'Tooles with no further contact from his parents. Mr. and Mrs. O'Toole, up in years, were pleasant enough, but apparently they felt Jack would fare better with a younger set of substitute parents. Besides, everyone reasoned, Oregon was a beautiful place, a healthy and peaceful environment for raising a child.

Jack, though, seemed torn between his friends and the prospect of venturing farther west than any of us had dreamed. Looking after Jack's best interests, Mama solemnly declared it would help greatly for us to support him in the move rather than add to his troubles by moping about his leaving.

"But it isn't fair!" I moaned. "It just isn't fair!"

"Have you told him you'll miss him, Sean?" Mama asked seriously.

I shook my head. She, the mother of six sons, I thought, should realize that boys don't talk about things like that. Still, Mama had some reason for encouraging me. She knew that even my eleven-year-old heart had feelings and that I could cope better with missing my new friend if I talked about it.

A few days before Jack was to leave, after early Mass, I mouthed my displeasure about the situation to Father O'Toole, an assistant at St. Columbkille. I suppose I felt that a priest who bore the same last name as Jack's aunt and uncle might be sympathetic to my cause.

And while Father O'Toole did listen with polite attention and tell me that he understood my feelings, he also suggested that I prepare myself for the inevitable. In reply, I muttered a few choice comments about things not being "fair" and stalked off to be miserable by myself.

The day before Jack's scheduled departure, Mama added to her earlier suggestion. "I would think you might be helpin' your friend to pack," she said. "I imagine it's a chore for him to do it alone."

I nodded and walked down the hall to the O'Tooles'. Mrs. O'Toole let me in and told me that I was welcome to join Jack in his room.

I found my soon-to-be-lost friend sitting on his bed staring out the window at the sycamore tree that grew out of our tenement's cement backyard.

"I suppose Oregon is a nice place...." His voice trailed off. It was then I realized the parting must be even harder on him than on me. I was losing a friend. He was losing everything he knew.

We packed his clothes slowly and tucked small treasures between the folds of shirts or wrapped them in socks so they would survive the long train ride he was about to endure. What's more, I'd finally decided to tell Jack how much I would miss him. But just then, Danny appeared in the doorway and said that Mama wanted to see us in our apartment.

We hurried across the hall to find Father O'Toole sitting in the stuffed chair in our living room, talking to Mama.

He had dropped by to see how we were doing with Jack's impending departure.

Jack and I both frowned. In response, Father O'Toole handed each of us a paper bag and told us to look inside.

I opened the slim, flat bag to find a package of writing paper, twelve envelopes and twelve postage stamps. The priest had written the name of a month on the bottom of each envelope, and there were enough for one full year. Jack had an identical package.

We looked at Father O'Toole and smiled.

"It's only for one year," the priest grinned. "After that, you'll have to fend for yourself!"

Mama brought out her teapot, steeping with a rich Irish brew, for herself and Father O'Toole, while Danny mixed a pitcher of Kool-Aid for the boys. A plate of cookies had appeared, and we settled in for a small, unexpected treat.

The impromptu festivities, however, lasted only a short time. After

Father O'Toole departed, I took my bag with its paper, stamps and envelopes to my bedroom and walked Jack back to his apartment.

"I'm really hatin' to see you go, Jack," I said, struggling to find the right words. "I'll miss you a lot."

We stopped just outside the door and faced each other for the last time.

"We'll keep in touch, Sean-o!" Jack promised. I happily agreed.

Jack and I were faithful to our words. Writing was not difficult, especially considering Father O'Toole's wonderful gift. Eventually, too, I became certain that, just as night followed day, when I posted my letter to Jack for a certain month, I would receive one from my friend in a few short days.

Years after Father O'Toole's stationery had been used up, I remember Mama looking over my shoulder as I wrote to Jack about the happenings in our lives.

"You've kept up with your friend!" Mama smiled.

"It brings him closer... like he's just around the corner," I grinned, remembering how I'd moped and complained before he left. Though he'd been gone a long, long time, our friendship had grown instead of dying.

Mama put her hand on my shoulder, "Maybe," she said, "things did not change as much as you feared."

I leaned back. I was still a teenager, but some adult wisdom was perhaps setting in. "Place is all that changed, Mama," I replied a moment later. "Jack is still my friend, and that's what counts!"

Jack and I keep in touch even today. Not as often as when we were younger, but we still do write and sometimes even talk on the phone. Mama had been correct—we did not have to lose each other. In fact, if anything, our friendship had been cemented firmly by the move. With the loving help, of course, of a young priest who knew the true meaning of friendship—as well as the value of a few postage stamps, some envelopes and a stack of paper.

~Sean Patrick
Chicken Soup for the Christian Family Soul

16

No, Really... Barney Ate My Report Card!

With lies you may get ahead in the world—but you can never go back.
~Russian proverb

As a preteen, I felt hopelessly ordinary. When I had to go to a new school where I didn't know anyone, I decided that I was going to make a lot of friends quickly and be really popular. I decided that the only way I could be popular was to make myself interesting, intriguing and therefore, worth knowing. So... I decided to tell fibs to get people to like me.

Most of the fibs I told were what my grandmother called "white lies," which are lies you tell people that "won't hurt them." I made up tall tales about celebrities I knew, how rich my family was and exotic places I had visited. I figured that since these lies didn't hurt anyone, that made them only "white lies."

My strategy began to work, and I suddenly became very popular. All my new friends thought I was cool. Of course, none of the stuff I told them was true and eventually, I started to feel a little guilty about it. My newfound popularity was also causing my grades to suffer terribly because being very social was my main focus. I simply didn't have time for homework.

The day our third semester report cards came out, my heart dropped into my stomach. My grade point average went from a 92 percent to a 79 percent. And... I had actually flunked English! How crazy was that?

I visualized what kind of torturous punishment my parents would have in store for me because of my bad grades. I figured it would be something like losing my phone privileges, or being grounded until the following semester.

Before I went home that day, my new best friend invited me to her birthday sleepover party. Everyone who was anyone in the school was going to be there. There was no doubt in my mind that my parents wouldn't allow me to go after they saw my report card. There was only one thing for me to do. I would hide my report card until after the party was over.

Weeks went by and my parents asked me every day where my report card was. I kept telling them that I hadn't gotten it yet. They had no reason not to believe me, as I had never lied to them before.

The party came and went and I decided that I was ready to face the music about my report card. There was just one little problem. I forgot where I had put it!

One morning at breakfast, Mom finally threatened to call the school. I panicked. I needed more time to try and find where I'd hidden it. If she called the school, she'd find out that I'd gotten the report card almost a month before. Somehow, I talked her out of it.

When I came home from school that day, I glanced at my dog Barney, who was lying on the floor. I noticed a little piece of blue paper sticking out of her mouth and I froze in my tracks. There was my dog, sitting in the middle of the kitchen floor, chewing on my report card! My mind reeled. Then, I remembered. I had hidden it in the downstairs closet on the shelf below the dog food. I thought that no one would find it there. Okay—no one with two legs, anyway. With perfect timing, my mom walked into the room, and asked the million dollar question:

"What's Barney chewing on?"

I felt like I was wearing cement shoes as my mother walked over to the dog and pulled the report card out of her mouth. Unfortunately for me, the paper apparently wasn't too appetizing to a dog's taste buds. All of my substandard grades were still as clear as day. So was the date on the top of the report card, which was dated four weeks before.

Needless to say, for lying to them (more so than for the bad grades) my parents grounded me from the phone and from going anywhere with my friends until the end of the school year. That really screwed up my social life. Plus, I had bragged to my friends about how cool my parents were because they never grounded me.

When my friends called, not only did they find out that the "no grounding" policy was not exactly accurate, but through conversations with my parents, they found out that I had been lying about almost everything else as well.

It took a long time for me to get my friends' trust back, and even longer for me to regain my parents' belief in me. But I learned the most valuable lesson in my life—there is no such thing as a white lie. Every lie, no matter how small it may seem, is still a lie. Eventually, it will end up biting you in the rear.

~Jenn Dlugos
Chicken Soup for the Preteen Soul 2

CHRISTIAN Teen Talk

Having Values

Open your arms to change, but don't let go of your values.
~Dalai Lama

17

Making Dad Proud

I t was about 7:30 as I pulled into the driveway on that hot July evening. I shut the door of my Jeep and packed my stuff into the house. I passed the ancient, brick-red Chevrolet with the cancerous case of rust. That meant Dad was home.

I opened the front door, dropped my bag on the floor and started to fix myself something to drink. As I thumbed through the mail on the kitchen counter, a faint rumbling from the backyard grew louder, then dissipated into near obscurity again. Dad was mowing the lawn.

From the paperwork on the couch, it was evident that he had not been home from work long. Sometimes I just don't understand how he does it. As if being a father and husband weren't enough, he manages a full-time job, church activities and carpentry jobs for friends and family. On most nights, he stays up later than I do and wakes up at the crack of dawn to leave for work. Nevertheless, he can tap his energy reserve when challenged to a game of Nintendo or the rare pickup basketball contest. Gray temples and a slight paunch season his thirty-five-year-old frame with traces of sagacity. If he is old before his time, it is because he has had so little time to be young.

Dad's premature journey into the adult world was, in a way, my fault. There's not much a high school senior with a pregnant wife can do but grow up. Sacrificing the things and life to which he was accustomed, he took on a full-time job bagging groceries and stocking shelves at Sureway during the night. School took up his days.

This might explain his tendency toward late-night television viewing. I mention all this so that you may better understand, or at least attempt to understand, a special day in May.

On that Sunday evening, I sat between my parents in a pew at First Assembly of God. We patiently waited as my youth pastor explained to the congregation the meaning of True Love Waits, a nationwide and nondenominational campaign for sexual abstinence until marriage. I had gone through about six weeks of sermons, videos and presentations about love, sex, dating and marriage. I was here to make a commitment to God, myself and my future spouse. The participants of the program were brought forward and presented with rings, symbols of our commitment that were to be presented to our husbands/wives on our wedding nights.

As I returned to my pew, hands folded and head bowed in prayer, I felt a weathered and callused hand close over mine. I looked at my father. This man, who had always remained stoic during emotional moments, had eyes that were glazed over with tears. A single tear fell, and then another, as he wrapped his arms around me. Without a single word, he communicated volumes. That moment told me that he was proud. I think it told him that he had not sacrificed all those things for nothing. That maybe it was a chance for him to start over. A chance, for awhile, to be young.

~Josh Nally
Chicken Soup for the Teenage Soul II

18

Truth at a Tender Age

Truth only reveals itself when one gives up all preconceived ideas.
~Shoseki

I t happened more than forty years ago, but I clearly remember each moment of the entire frightening episode. I was a small, physically underdeveloped, freckled, blond seventh grade girl in an ethnically mixed, inner-city junior high school. A verbally prolific little kid, I had the unfortunate habit of getting into trouble for saying things without thinking. Yolanda, a Latina classmate, was exotically beautiful and well-developed. She had jet-black hair and olive skin, and wore dark red lipstick, crucifix earrings and lots of make-up. Everywhere she went, she was accompanied by four girls of similar appearance with whom she engaged in a clever mix of Spanish and English. Their partially understandable conversation was punctuated with occasional bursts of sarcastic laughter. Tantalized, I yearned to be Yolanda's friend, but her attitude toward my overtures was disdainful. She scowled at me and my friends, if she looked at us at all.

One day toward the end of the second semester, I confided to a friend that I didn't like Yolanda, unaware of being overheard by one of Yolanda's allies. To my horror, Yolanda approached me shortly afterward and scathingly announced that she and I would "have it out" after school. "Meet me by the tunnel," she sneered. "Be alone, and don't even think about not showing up!" Her friends were beside her, snickering and adding insults.

I was practically paralyzed with terror for the next two hours.

Word spread among the students about the upcoming event, and I heard bits and pieces of conversations about bets of how bad I would "get it." My friends felt sorry for me, but were visibly relieved that Yolanda demanded I show up at the tunnel alone.

When the dismissal bell rang, I walked out of the building into a throng of kids jeering in English and Spanish. They followed me as I walked toward the tunnel like a prisoner to her execution. Suddenly, Yolanda appeared with her friends and stopped me on the sidewalk when I was about halfway there. Apparently, she wanted to begin the confrontation where the widest possible audience could look on. There wouldn't be much room for a crowd in the tunnel.

Yolanda began by calling me a very bad name. Looking at the ground and humiliated to the core, I nodded, and everyone laughed. Next, she grabbed my collar and made me look at her. "You don't like me because I'm Mexican," she announced loudly. An ominous rumbling growl issued from the crowd.

Instantly, I protested in a stronger voice than I expected myself to generate, "No! No, that's not true." And then I shocked everyone, especially myself, by blurting, "That is not why I don't like you!"

Seconds of silence that seemed to last forever followed; then Yolanda shrieked, "What? You admit it? You don't like me?" Then she shoved me toward the tunnel and hissed, "Okay, you asked for it. Get going."

Suddenly, hooting and laughter erupted. I heard a boy's voice say, "Hey, Yolanda! You hear that? Who can blame her?"

Another said, "Oh, man, she tells the truth!"

Another taunted, "Ay, Yolanda, possible tiene razon!" (Maybe she has a reason.)

Others were out for blood: "Give it to her, Yoli!" and "Que pega la pendeja." (Just hit the idiot.)

Yolanda gripped my arm as she forced me down the stairs into the narrow pit, reeking of urine, that ran from one side of the boulevard to the other. Every kid who could find a toehold around us crowded in. Yolanda screamed at them to back off to give her some room, and she began to circle me like a hungry wolf. To my surprise, she repeated, "You don't like me because I'm Mexican. That's why you don't like any of us."

Once again, the crowd reacted with a hateful growl.

A deep sadness overcame me. I was quivering inside, but looking her straight in the eye, I said, "I was stupid to say what I said so loudly that your friend heard me. I never wanted you to hear it. But your being Mexican isn't why I said it."

Yolanda objected again. "Tell the truth. You don't like Mexicans!"

Again, I denied it by shaking my head firmly.

"Okay, then, tell her why you don't like her," someone shouted to me.

"Yeah, gringita, tell her the truth," came another voice.

"Shut up!" Yolanda screamed, and her friends gave the crowd menacing looks. But they persisted: "Yeah. Tell her. Do it! Do it!"

I was not relieved by any of this. All I wanted to do was either die on the spot or be magically transported out of there. What to do? Being outnumbered, I would be a fool to fight back. I looked at Yolanda and realized that in a far more serious way she, too, was miserable. I took a deep breath, held her gaze and quietly said, "I don't like you because you aren't friendly. At the beginning of the year, I tried to make friends with you, but you never said hi when I said hi, and when I smiled at you, you never smiled back. I liked you a lot at first, but then I gave up."

Yolanda was frozen in space, staring at me.

After a few moments, I continued, "You think I don't like Mexicans, but you're wrong. You want the truth? I would love to have your hair and your skin. And I wish I could speak two languages like you, and I'm sorry that I hurt your feelings."

Yolanda listened, and her eyes grew larger. She seemed to be amazed, then suddenly swallowed, shook herself and sneered, "Well, look who's kissing up!"

At this point my humiliation was overwhelming, and I looked at the floor of the tunnel waiting for whatever would happen next.

"Get away from me!" she screamed. "Just get out of here!" Without looking at anyone, Yolanda gestured at the crowd to part and let me climb the steps. Surprised, but eager to get away as fast as I could, I rushed up the stairs and ran across the boulevard. Thank God, a bus going my way was taking on passengers on the other side. I hurriedly climbed aboard, showed the driver my pass and found a seat. Instantly, I was overcome with racking sobs. Without looking at anyone, I used my dress to sop up torrents of tears.

The end of the term came soon thereafter, and, terrified of Yolanda, I carefully avoided her. There were no confrontations, not even eye contact. Summer came and went. When school started again in September, something happened that still mystifies me: I was seated in a classroom as Yolanda entered. We spied each other, but before I could avert my gaze, she smiled and cheerily said, "Hi, girl, how've you been?" I literally looked behind me and, seeing no one, looked back, supposing that she was baiting me for another confrontation. But Yolanda, keeping her distance, kept smiling an apparently sincere smile. "Did you have a good summer?" she asked. But I was too shocked to respond.

During the rest of our eighth grade year, Yolanda, who no longer hung out with her former friends, went out of her way to greet me with a warm smile. I was still so freaked out that I rarely responded with a fraction of her friendly energy, but it didn't seem to matter to her. We never became close friends, but I lost my fear and actually grew to like her.

Through the years, as I've pondered what happened that day in the tunnel, I've come to an important understanding: Finding the courage to tell the truth opens the heart to the possibilities of peace and reconciliation.

~Gerry Dunne, Ph.D.
Chicken Soup for the Soul Stories for a Better World

Friends to the End

You can always tell a real friend: when you've made a fool of yourself he doesn't feel you've done a permanent job.
~Laurence J. Peter

"Friends to the end!" Breana had signed the picture of us that hung on my bedroom wall. We were so happy the night it was taken, all confidence and smiles.

Breana's handwritten promise looped and curled with the joy we had shared. "Friends to the end"—and I was the one who ended it.

We had been friends for ten years, since the day I'd moved next door the summer before second grade. I was standing on the sidewalk watching the moving van being unloaded and there was Breana, straddling her bike beside me.

"That your bike?" She pointed at the pink bike my father was wheeling into the garage.

"Yes."

"Wanna ride to the park?"

"Sure."

Just like that, we became friends. We were next-door sisters.

Maybe if I could look back and say, "This is the moment our friendship ended," I could repair it. But there wasn't a dramatic split. I made one choice, one step, one rip at a time, until I had walked away from Breana and into my new life with my new friends.

I guess I could say that Breana started it. It was her idea that I try out for cheerleading. "You're the best dancer in our class and the best gymnast at the club. You'd be a natural."

"You're crazy," I protested, though I really did believe her and I did want to try out. I knew that Breana knew that. It was her job to talk me into it, though. That way, if I failed I could shrug it off with a "What did I tell you?"

I agreed to go for it when Breana promised to try out with me. She went to all the practices, learned the routines and spent two weeks in the backyard coaching me.

Breana was as excited as I was when I made the squad and more surprised than I was when she did, too.

The night of our first football game, Breana gave me a cross necklace that matched the one she had on. It was a great reminder that we were in this together, and we both shared our gratitude to God.

Our halftime performance was flawless, even the grand finale big lift. I jumped into my stance with Breana beneath me as my secure base. I posed on her shoulders and smiled for the flash of my father's camera.

It was this picture of us that Breana signed.

One afternoon after football practice, Drew Peterson caught up with us and asked me to the Homecoming Dance. My brain didn't know how to talk to a Drew Peterson. I could only nod. His blue eyes alone were enough to leave me speechless.

Breana was the one who finally spoke: "She'd love to!"

The night of the dance, Breana helped me do my hair and make-up and then left me with a hug. "Look for the heart. I'll be waiting up."

The heart. We had made those hearts for each other so many Valentine's Days ago that I don't remember when we started hanging them in our bedroom windows as a signal to meet at the back porch swing.

I shared everything with Breana after the first, second and even the third date. After that, I began to make up excuses. It was too late, or I was too tired. It wasn't like I was doing anything really wrong. It was just that I knew Breana wouldn't understand the kind of parties I was going to and the people I was with. Why did I have to explain myself to her anyway?

That stupid heart began to anger me. "Just grow up, Breana," I'd spit under my breath when I passed by her window after a night out with Drew.

Last night I didn't just pass by her window, I nearly passed out under it. I was losing my balance, and the next thing I knew, Breana was cradling my head in her lap.

She brushed my hair back out of my eyes.

"You are the real Miss Goody Two Shoes," I said, and burst into tears.

That's what Drew had called me at the party. "A toast to Miss Goody Two Shoes. She's too good to drink with the rest of us sinners," he had said, loud enough for everyone to hear.

My new friends lifted their drinks in a mock salute. "To Saint Jenny."

I laughed the hollow laugh that I had heard myself use so often during the last four weeks. Then I grabbed Drew's drink from his hand and gulped it down. They all hooted their approval.

The alcohol's harshness shocked me. I couldn't breathe and when I finally gasped in air, I went into a coughing spasm. My stomach rolled. I needed help. I grabbed for Drew, but he dodged my reach.

"I guess some people just can't handle their liquor." He pointed at me, and they all snickered. Standing in the center of their ridicule, I suddenly wanted nothing more than to be the person they were accusing me of being.

These were my new friends? They laughed with me if I did what they did but at me if I didn't?

"Please, Drew, I want to go home."

"Sure thing," he said, much to my relief. He wasn't such a bad guy. Tomorrow I would talk to him. I knew I could make him understand about his friends and these parties. After all, he had said that he loved me.

Drew took my hand and led me out the door to the sidewalk. He turned me towards home. "Go play with your dolls. Call me when you grow up."

I stumbled the six blocks to home. It wasn't until I saw the heart in Breana's window that I knew I had made it, but not without taking a spill on the porch and making the rude comment to Breana.

The next morning came fresh and new, but just a little too early for me. I struggled out of bed and cleaned up for the day. I put on my cross that Breana had given to me. Faith renewed, I fastened the chain with a sense of joy. I was starting over.

I flung open my curtains and hung my old Valentine's heart in the window. I wanted it to be the first thing Breana saw. I could hardly wait for our reunion on the back porch swing, to be together again.

Looking across at her bedroom, I almost expected to see Breana smiling over at me. The last thing I expected to see is what I saw. The heart was gone. Her window was empty.

I walked through the house and out to our swing in a fog of shock. There the shock turned to pain. On the swing cushion was half of the heart from her window. Breana had written just two words: The End.

I sank into the swing as torn apart as the heart I held on my lap. The faded heart turned deep red where my tears dropped on it. It had taken me too long to see the truth. I was too late.

I was crying and gasping so I didn't hear her approaching. But I looked up and saw Breana standing over me. I wiped my tears and nodded.

Breana sat down. She placed the other half of the heart beside the one in my lap. On it were the words: Friends to.

I studied the pieced-together heart for a moment before grasping what it meant. Hope started to fill me, and I began to cry.

"Friends to the end?" I finally managed to ask.

"Yes." Breana smiled and gave the swing a little push start with her foot. "Friends to the end."

~Jenny Michaels as told to Cynthia Hamond
Chicken Soup for the Teenage Soul on Tough Stuff

20

Staying True to Myself

Let God's promises shine on your problems.
~Corrie Ten Boom

I don't know why I believed them after all the teasing and bullying they had put me through.

When the bell rang for our lunch period, once again, the four of them tricked me. "Oh, y'all, we're just gonna go out and play," they said as two of them grabbed my hands.

It was cold outside and there was a lot of snow on the ground. They led me far away from where all the other kids were playing and then, before I knew it, they pushed me down and began hitting me. They said all kinds of mean things to me, like I was the teacher's pet and that I thought I was better than them. Then they dug my head into the snow until I thought I was about to suffocate.

"Stop it. I can't breathe! I can't breathe!" I pleaded. That kind of scared them, and they finally got off me, pulled me up out of the slush and helped me into the nurse's office. Scratched, bruised and cold, I listened to them tell the nurse, "We was just playin' and all of a sudden she say she can't breathe." I couldn't wait for those girls to get out of the nurse's office, so that I could tell the truth.

After that, my mother came up to the school and had meetings with everybody she could, but nothing changed. The girls continued to bully me every chance they got.

As a fourth-grader growing up in a small town in Illinois, I didn't have the best of everything, like designer clothes, but Mom made sure my clothes were clean. I was light skinned with long hair, and it could be that those girls thought that I was stuck up because of it. But I was just a kid who enjoyed doing my schoolwork and getting good grades. I always tried to make friends with everybody. As far as I knew, I never did anything wrong to any of those four girls.

After that day on the playground, I was scared every single day. Being at school was a living nightmare. Even after school I was terrified that once I left the classroom to go to my grandmother's car, the girls would jump me. So, I had to have a security officer escort me out every day. My mother had to take me to the doctor's office all the time because there would be something wrong with my stomach, but they could never figure out what it was. Finally, in the fifth grade, I switched elementary schools. School is supposed to be where you learn and make friends—it shouldn't be about having your grades suffer because you have to watch your back instead of pay attention and do the work.

For the next two years, my school life was wonderful. I made good grades and good friends. Then in seventh grade, I had to face the bully girls again. We hadn't seen each other in several years, so I was thinking that maybe they had grown up some. You know, I actually almost befriended them because I was so scared that if I didn't, they would mess with me again. But I asked myself, "Do I change or stay myself and succeed?" I chose to stay true to myself.

As the year went on, the girls would get into fights all the time and mess with other girls. At one point, some friends of mine that I had grown up with got into it with them. It was one group of girls against the other group of girls. The bully girls were pressuring me to fight on their side. I figured that if I didn't, I would probably become the target of their abuse again.

I knew it was about to be blood, sweat and tears in the hallway, and I felt trapped. Then, just as the fight was about to go down, I heard one of the girls say, "Don't mess with her." I was like, "Thank you, 'cause I didn't do anything." I strongly believe that this was God's protection for me.

I quickly ran into a nearby classroom, and I told the teacher what was about to happen. But before anyone could stop them, the fight began. Girls were screaming, punching, pulling hair and just going crazy. Thankfully, the teachers and principal stopped them before anyone got seriously hurt.

From then on, I knew that God really was looking out for me. I was able to trust him with my life and move forward with less fear of the bully girls. Amazingly, they finally lost interest in me and picked on other girls instead. When high school came, we were zoned to go to different schools. Finally, I had the peace of knowing that I never had to deal with them again.

As I matured and was able to look at those girls' situations, I realized that most of them did not have the love and support of a stable family. I had both parents at home and a very close family. Plus, I was raised in church, and there is something different about people who really are committed to having a Christian life. I had a strong knowledge that I was unique and that the people who really mattered to me loved me. Those girls could never persuade me that being part of a gang could offer me more than that truth. But since they didn't have a strong family or spiritual life, I guess being part of that girl gang gave them a sense of belonging and some security.

My small town hasn't changed much. Over the years, when I go home, I sometimes hear about what has become of the girls who bullied me. One was always back and forth into juvenile hall. I'm not sure what became of her in the long run. All I know is, I wouldn't trade places with any of them.

I'm just so thankful that I stayed on track with my studies and stayed true to expressing my talents and interests. It has taken me to the most amazing places: bestselling records, Grammys, a leading role on Broadway....

From here, my destiny is in God's hands, just as it always has been.

~Michelle Williams
Chicken Soup for the Preteen Soul 2

21

Feeding the Soul

Exercise daily. Walk with the Lord!
~Author Unknown

My parents are not educated. On my mother's side of the family, we are third-generation Texans. My father's parents were from Spain, and he was born in Mexico. Both my parents were very religious and active in the Catholic Church. We couldn't afford to go to Catholic school, but we went to daily Mass in the same way we brushed our teeth. In the evening, we would pray the rosary together as a family, and if our friends came around, Catholic or not, they too were included in our family rituals.

I recall one morning when I overslept and was the only one in the family who missed Mass. It was a weekday, so I didn't think much of it. However, I knew my father would be waiting in his pickup that evening (as he was known to do for those of us who overslept in the morning). Since I knew I was the only one who hadn't gone, I didn't think my father would "bother;" but a few minutes before the evening Mass at our local church, I heard my father's knock on my door.

"Chela, didn't you oversleep this morning?" he asked.

"Yes," I replied, "but, Dad, I have a lot of homework, and I don't think I'll be going to Mass today."

I thought the issue was resolved (and way too easily) when my father responded compassionately, "Oh, I see. You have homework. Okay."

He started to walk away, and I thought, "Wow! That was easy." I actually didn't think his response was too out-of-place. Since none of my siblings had ever challenged going to Mass on a daily basis, we really didn't know how he would react. "Hey," I thought, "we really don't have to go." I felt somewhat of a heroine, one who had rescued my other siblings from having to attend daily Mass.

But my father hadn't really left.

"So, you have a lot of homework?" he continued to ask.

"Yes," I justified, as I showed him my assignments.

"Okay," he replied, maintaining his interest. "I know now what you studied in school today, so I know you learned something, thus you've fed your mind. What did you have for lunch?"

I replied, telling him as much of the school menu as I recalled.

"That's wonderful!" he said. "I know you fed your mind because you have told me what you learned today at school. I know you fed your body, for you have given me the day's menu. Have you fed your soul today?"

That's all he had to say. I followed him to his pickup and attended Mass. But even more than that, I began to take seriously my father's lesson that I should spend as much time feeding my soul as the rest of me.

My father's lesson that day made me who I am. I went on to combine feeding my mind, body and soul by pursuing graduate degrees in theology, and to this day, I have always worked in ministry positions.

Thanks to my father, when I wake up in the morning, the first question I ask myself is: "How will you feed your soul today?"

~Chela González
Chicken Soup for the Latino Soul

Meeting God at 30,000 Feet

Humanity is never so beautiful as when praying for forgiveness,
or else forgiving another.
~Jean Paul Richter

I did some dumb things in junior high school. I think it just comes with the territory. But one particularly dumb thing involved a theft. I didn't steal money or shoplift, and I didn't take anyone's boyfriend. I simply stole a few votes.

The scene of the crime was journalism class, where those of us on the yearbook staff sat counting ballots for the school superlatives contest. Suddenly someone yelled out, "Caron! It looks like you may get enough votes to win Most Talented."

Until that moment, I had been the epitome of average. Winning a category in the superlatives contest would skyrocket my approval rating at Glenridge Junior High. I was eking out a social existence because my friends had friends who were cool. Like a mere feeder fish, I hovered close to the big fish in hopes of sucking some algae off them.

I soon found out, however, that I was not the only one up for Most Talented. Trailing close behind me was Cindy, our school's guitar-playing singer. Cindy had real talent. She was even asked to sing her original song, "Beauty," at a school assembly. My only claim to fame was the pen and ink drawings I did on notebooks and book covers. Hardly a class went by that I didn't get at least one request for "Judy & Johnny 4-Ever," or "S. M. loves T. P."

Clearly, my talent was no match for Cindy's. Someone important once said, "The pen is mightier than the sword." But no one ever mentioned how the pen would do against the guitar. Guitars were big deals. I knew if I didn't do something fast, I would live my whole life in obscurity.

So, while votes were being tallied for other categories, I secretly grabbed a handful of uncounted ballots and tossed them in the trash. I was pretty sure no one saw me. I should have felt guilty, but I didn't. At the end of the day, I had won. And suddenly the demand for notebook art increased a good 40 percent.

Why it took God fifteen years to confront me on this, I'll never know. But it was He who brought it up one morning in my prayer time. By then we were on a first name basis, and He had full permission to speak to me about anything that bothered Him. Here is an abbreviated version of our conversation:

Me: God, I want to be all I can be for You. I've searched my heart for anything that might be standing in the way of this, and I've come up empty. I think I've dealt with all the sins I've ever committed. But I'll just sit here and wait for You to go through your files and see if You have something there I may have left out.

God: *Well, there was that time in junior high school.*

Me: Which time?

God: *Most Talented?*

Me: You saw that? It was such a long time ago. Surely You have a statute of limitations or some kind of cutoff date for people who do dumb things prior to high school.

God: *Not really.*

Me: But, I'm 1,200 miles away. No telling where Cindy is. Do You realize the difficulty I would have in finding her? Okay, here's what I'll do. If one day I'm walking down the street and I happen to see her, I'll know You sent her and I'll make things right with her. Fair enough?

God: Fair enough.

I felt pretty safe. I hadn't seen Cindy in years. The odds of running into her in another state were microscopic.

Six months later, my husband and I were racing through the airport trying to catch a plane. When we reached the door of the 747, it had just been shut. My husband, forever the determined optimist, banged on the door as the noise of the engines accelerated. Suddenly, a nice flight attendant with exceptional hearing came to our rescue and opened the door.

We made our way to the back of the plane, comparing our tickets to the numbers overhead until we found a match. I plopped down in the middle seat assigned to me. Using my polite voice I said "Hello" to a woman next to me who was looking out the window. When she returned my greeting, adrenaline shot through me. In unison we both exclaimed, "Oh, my gosh! I can't believe it!"

There was Cindy, the guitar-playing singer.

A boxing match began inside me. From one corner came the feeling of someone who had just been given a million dollars. And from the other came the emotions of a hunted felon. Immediately I began carrying on two conversations, one on the surface with Cindy, the other internally with God.

Me: You actually found her! This is an outright miracle! I can't believe You are forcing me to do this. You really are into the details, aren't You?

God: Yes.

From takeoff to landing, Cindy and I chattered away, but all I could think of was how, out of the hundreds of thousands of people on airplanes that day, God looked for a needle in a haystack, found it, threaded it and placed it in my hand.

My palms started to sweat. I swallowed hard. No use stalling any longer. It was time to let Cindy in on the whole story. "Cindy," I said. "You're not going to believe this, but it's no accident we met today.

Several months ago, I promised God I would make things right if our paths should ever cross again."

As I explained, Cindy laughed. She easily forgave me. It barely fazed her. I felt like scolding God for orchestrating such an ordeal. Then a familiar quote popped into my mind, "To whom much is given, much is required." God knew that if I'd confess a small matter from the past, He could trust me with greater responsibilities in the future.

I felt far from the epitome of average.

~Caron Loveless
Chicken Soup for the Christian Woman's Soul

23

The Soft Voice of Forgiveness

The weak can never forgive. Forgiveness is the attribute of the strong.
~Mahatma Gandhi

Dear Chicken Soup for the Teenage Soul,

We hear so many negative things about teenagers and certainly some episodes concern us all. But we need to be sure to spread the good news, too, and I feel the following is indeed good news.

As a vice principal of a high school for many years, I was a pretty good judge of character and nothing surprised me. That was until I got to know a soft-spoken teenager named Stephanie. She entered my office in tears one day when her wallet had been stolen from her backpack during chemistry class. Her classmates had seen another student, Dustin, take her wallet and escape to a nearby restroom. By the time her friends could alert campus security, twenty-three dollars had been taken from her wallet.

When I summoned Dustin to my office, he admitted taking the wallet to the restroom and looking in it. He would not, however, confess to taking the money even though the empty wallet was found in the restroom. I told him that since he took the wallet, he was now responsible for replacing its contents. He had one week to bring the money, or I would suspend him for stealing, which as a violation of the school athletic code would also mean he would be off the track team.

I tried to call Dustin's father all that afternoon, but the phone was always busy. Finally at 7:00 P.M., I managed to contact him and told him of the incident. He assured me that Dustin would return the money.

A week flew by, and Stephanie stood meekly in my doorway once more. With downcast eyes and a sad smile on her face, she said that Dustin had not yet returned the money. I tried Dustin's father's work number again and this time was able to get through right away. What a shock it was for me to hear a different voice. He was clearly not the person I had talked to the week before. I quickly explained the theft of the wallet, telling him that I had given Dustin a chance to save face by returning the money. Dustin had not only ignored the opportunity, but had compounded his error by impersonating his father on the phone and withholding the truth from him. Dustin's father said that he didn't take this lightly and insisted on bringing Dustin in personally, after his suspension was over, to meet with Stephanie and me.

During the conference, while we waited for Stephanie to come to my office, Dustin's father filled me in on some background. Up until two years before, Dustin had lived with his mother in Los Angeles until she could no longer deal with his rebellious nature. He had come to Sacramento to live with his father, who was much more of a disciplinarian. Dustin was having a difficult time making the adjustment, as was his father, a single, working parent. His father appreciated my willingness to work with Dustin, rather than merely dole out punishment, as was done in the Washington, D.C., high school he himself had attended as a teenager. He confided that if he had done what Dustin had, he would have been sent to juvenile hall and immediately locked up.

When Stephanie arrived, Dustin squirmed in his chair and crossed his arms. His father introduced himself to Stephanie and apologized to her on Dustin's behalf. Dustin kept his face blank, staring at a picture on my wall. After a long pause, his father prompted him to speak to her. "Dustin, don't you have something to say?" Dustin shrugged his shoulders but stayed put, glaring at his father whose eyes had suddenly narrowed. Through clenched teeth, he said, "Say it, Dustin. Now!" Walking over to Stephanie, Dustin reluctantly handed her a closed envelope and begrudgingly muttered, "I'm sorry I took your wallet. Here's your money." Stephanie looked at him with wide brown eyes and gently said, "I forgive you."

Stunned, Dustin stared at her in disbelief. He blinked his eyes and grimaced, as if the spotlight had suddenly been turned on him.

After both students had returned to class, Dustin's father stayed to talk to me. He shared with me that he had recently taken Dustin to a therapist to begin working on the root of his behavioral problems. Some trauma had happened to Dustin around the age of eight, and, now that it had been uncovered, counseling might help him get rid of his self-destructive tendencies and improve his self-esteem. I told him that I was glad to hear he was seeking professional help for his son and promised to keep in touch with him if any more problems arose. They never did.

Dustin stayed on the track team, went on to excel academically and was never referred to this office again. Through ongoing counseling, he was eventually able to accept and even like himself. Stephanie had shown him the way. By forgiving him, she taught him how to forgive himself. I often think of Stephanie because, on the surface, she looked like a fragile flower that might drop its petals at the slightest breeze. But she had me fooled. Inside, where it really counts, she was invincible, using her wisdom, power and courage to help a classmate who needed to turn his life around. Laurence Sterne once wrote: "Only the brave know how to forgive." Meek and soft-spoken Stephanie turned out to be the bravest one of all.

Thanks so much,

~Jennifer Martin
Chicken Soup for the Teenage Soul Letters

CHRISTIAN Teen Talk

The Power of Prayer

Don't pray when it rains if you don't pray when the sun shines.
~Satchel Paige

24

Building Bridges

I wear a coat of angels' breath and warm myself with His love.
~Emme Woodhull-Bäche

The day started out just like most other Tuesdays. I'm in a show choir called "Unclaimed Freight" at Columbine High School; we rehearse in the mornings before school. I got to school at 6:50 A.M., saw friends and said hello on my way in.

We went through the day normally until fifth period, which for me is Concert Choir. We were starting our warm-ups when a student in the choir came into the room and said there was a guy downstairs with a gun.

This student was known to be a jokester. But he had a pretty serious look on his face, and I saw kids running by when I looked out the window. The choir director told us all to chill out. He didn't want us to panic—there were 114 choir members. He was walking toward the door near the stairwell when two girls opened the door, and we heard two shotgun bursts. Half the choir hit the ground.

My first instinct was to run. I went out the opposite door, into a corridor that leads to the auditorium.

I saw a stampede of people running down the hallways. I heard screams. I decided I wasn't going to try and join the mob, so I ran into the auditorium. I stood at the back of the auditorium, wondering what refuge kids were finding behind plastic chairs. Then I heard the semi-automatic fire. At some point, somebody pulled the fire alarm down, so lots of kids in the east end of the school got out without a notion of what was happening.

I headed out the north door. I saw the fire doors at the north hallway—the main hallway—were closed, so I turned and ran for the front door. As I got closer I saw there were already bullet holes in the glass.

Seeing the bullet holes made me run even faster. I reached the front door and pushed it open. The bullets had weakened the glass, and shattered glass came showering off the door all over me. I just kept running. I didn't even notice the blood all over me until much later. I later went to the hospital for stitches.

About fifteen kids followed me and got out the front door. I learned later that we barely made it out. Seconds later, one of the shooters, Dylan, came into the main office and started spraying bullets.

I saw a friend, and we ran to her house. From her house we could see the front of the school. We watched the police, firefighters, paramedics, SWAT teams from Denver and other areas, and the National Guard as they showed up. State patrolmen and sheriffs pulled up and got out of their cars with their guns. They stood behind trees and told kids to run.

The next few hours seemed to last forever. At first I thought that if a kid was in the school with a gun, that he might have shot a few kids, maybe injured somebody, but I hoped he hadn't caused much harm. As I watched the different teams of police show up and heard on the radio there were two gunmen, possibly three, I started to realize how big this really was.

A group of police drove a fire truck close to the building. They jumped out and ran inside. I found out later that lots of those guys weren't trained to be in the positions they were leading. They went in and risked their lives—they didn't even think about it, they just did it to save lives.

It scared me to death when later reports on the radio said that twenty-five kids were killed. I hadn't seen my best friend Dustin come out. I prayed he was all right. I didn't find out he was safe until much later. He had hidden in a bathroom in the kitchen and was evacuated with other kids who hid nearby.

It was a living nightmare, a bad day multiplied by the biggest number you can think of. The day seemed to go on for years — hours seemed like days; everything was wrong.

The night of the shootings, a lot of us went to a service at St. Francis Cabrini Catholic Church. It was really emotional for all of us because we knew that our friends who should be there were gone forever. I couldn't even imagine that friends of mine — Cory, Rachel, Isaiah, Cassie — wouldn't be back at school. How could their lives end so violently? How could Eric's and Dylan's minds get so messed up?

For the longest time I didn't know what day it was. The day of the week, the date — it all just kind of ran together. I didn't eat anything for three days — I had a sick feeling inside. I kept crying. Every emotion ran through my head. I was sad, mad, confused, helpless and lost.

I spent a little time with my parents. I hugged them a lot and told them I loved them. But I needed to be with my friends, the people who had experienced this with me. People can say, "I know how you feel," but it's not true if you weren't there.

There were lots of counselors around. The media were everywhere. People showed up trying to get kids to come to their church. What touched me most were the people who came just to be available for us. They were there if we needed someone to talk to. They didn't force themselves on us at all.

We had lots of get-togethers on private property where the media couldn't get to us. We would just go and be together — the first week that's all we did. We didn't have to speak to each other — it was enough to share the silence.

The first place that the faculty and students got back together was at a community church. The student body was sitting together waiting for the faculty. The choir decided we wanted to sing, because before the tragedy we were practicing some very spiritual, very touching songs that had a high level of difficulty. We got up together and went up on the stage. The faculty still hadn't made it in, so I was "volunteered" to conduct.

We started singing "Ave Maria." I had chills and the hair on the back of my neck was standing up. We hadn't warmed up and the song has some very high notes for females. But they were just ripping them out—the sound was unbelievable.

As we sang "The Lord's Prayer," the faculty came into the sanctuary and started singing with us. Then the whole student body joined in. Here we were, together for the first time after a living nightmare, singing "The Lord's Prayer." As I conducted and heard the most beautiful sounds ever, I felt the love in that room. At that moment I knew we would be all right.

~Charlie Simmons
Chicken Soup for the Teenage Soul on Tough Stuff

25

Our Day to Give Thanks

I know God will not give me anything I can't handle.
I just wish that He didn't trust me so much.
~Mother Theresa

I remember when I was a boy growing up in Texas, my dad would always say that each Sunday was our day to give thanks. I never understood what he meant by this, but each Sunday we would go to church and pray to God and Jesus Christ. As I recall, I didn't like going because my friends would be playing football or baseball while I would be inside studying the Bible.

My dad worked construction and was a very private man who never said much. For as long as I can remember, it was always just him and me. I never really knew my mom, but my dad said that after I was born she had fallen in love with another man. He never liked to talk about her, and I never really liked to talk about how much I missed her. I would think of her mostly on Sundays when he and I were at church. I would always ask God why he took my mom away, but no matter how much I prayed, he never answered. Sometimes I could tell my dad was asking God the same thing.

As I got older, we would still keep the same routine: church every Sunday and the occasional baseball game afterwards. I liked the game, and although my dad never really cared for it, he would still take me after services. I think it was his way of staying even, since he knew I didn't like going to church that much. When I was a freshman in high school, he even agreed to let me try out for the baseball team at school. When I told him I had made it, I could tell he was really proud, even though he didn't say much. Although he was always strict with his rules, my dad and I couldn't have gotten along without one another. All in all, my dad and I were happy.

I think it was October when the principal at my school interrupted class and asked me to come to her office. I was afraid of what she was going to say, and when I got there she said my dad had been in a bad accident at work. My eyes began to fill with tears, but I held them back, knowing he would want me to be strong.

When I got to the hospital, the doctors said he was in intensive care and that I couldn't see him. Never in my life had I been so scared, and never in my life did I need God more than at that moment. I sat in that waiting room for what seemed like forever until finally my dad's friend came and picked me up. He told me that a truck's gates holding steel beams had come unlocked and pinned my dad underneath them. When I heard this, I instantly thought of God—not in prayer but in anger—an anger I had never felt in my life. I had always deep down blamed God for taking away my mom, and all of a sudden it seemed he was going take my dad, too.

The next day they said I could visit him, but only for a short time. He looked so bad I wanted to cry, but I saw his face brighten when I entered the room, so I couldn't.

His voice was raspy, and all he told me was to pray for him. That Sunday I went to church alone. Once there, all I could do was look at the empty seat my dad usually filled. I cried as I did what he had asked me to do—pray.

As I prayed, I told Jesus how much I loved him and my dad. Later that day, I got a call saying that my dad's situation had improved, and within a month he would be back home with me again.

After he returned, we decided to move to Colorado where his brother and his wife lived, so they could take care of him for a while. Although he still wasn't 100 percent well, he was alive, and I was very happy about that. I told him that I prayed for him just like he asked me to, and he said, "I know you did, son."

Now when Dad says that Sundays are our days to give thanks,

I know what he means. I think of God and Jesus Christ, and I give thanks for all they have given us.

~Michael Manzi
Chicken Soup for the Christian Teenage Soul

26

One Miracle After Another

S he was only nineteen when she asked to work with us. We always welcomed good, energetic people to help in the afternoons at our childcare center. Alicia, a pretty, smiling blond who loved children, was a sophomore at the local college.

The entire three-year-old class received lots of loving care from Alicia, but she took a special interest in those with special needs. When Ken, our little ADHD boy, had trouble focusing on a task for any length of time, Alicia brought in activity books and devised games to challenge him. When Hannah, our Down syndrome child, came, Alicia learned simple sign language so she could communicate with her in the same way her special education teacher did.

Alicia was a special young lady who wanted to please everyone. Despite going to school in the mornings and working in the afternoons, it was hard for her to say no when anyone asked her to do something else. One staff member asked her to babysit long hours, sometimes "forgetting" to pay her. Another wanted her to sell Mary Kay products in her "spare" time.

One afternoon in April, Alicia came to work even though she had been sick all day and hadn't had anything to eat or drink. As she went to her classroom, she passed out in the doorway, flat on the floor.

Devon's dad was there and helped us move Alicia to a quiet corner. He stayed with her while I rushed frantically to call her mother. Mrs. C. wasn't aware that Alicia was sick and had missed her morning classes. She rushed to the center and took her home. We all assumed she had some sort of virus and would be fine.

I was in total shock and disbelief when the phone call came the next day: Alicia was in the intensive care unit of our trauma hospital. She had shot herself that morning while her parents were out for breakfast. Doctors were not optimistic about her survival. Why? I wondered, heartbroken. Why would our sweet Alicia, who was so kind and loving and giving, attempt to take her life?

When I went to the hospital, Alicia was in a coma and on life support. Her parents felt there was no hope. If she lived, there would be no quality of life. She would not be able to walk or talk; she might never be aware of her surroundings. I prayed with them, asking God to heal her, asking Him to comfort them and give them hope. Alicia was too precious; she had too much to give to die so early.

On Monday, a couple of teachers asked if we could get together and pray for Alicia. We agreed to meet at six o'clock, after working hours, when there would be no interruptions. I expected no more than three or four to come, just those who worked directly with her. Before our meeting, I called Mrs. C. to ask about Alicia. She said the situation was very grim. The doctors thought they should take her off life support the next day—there was no hope for her survival. I cried, "Oh, please don't do it. We're getting together to pray for her tonight. Please don't do it yet!"

How amazed I was when at six o'clock not three or four, but every one of our staff members came to pray. As a "family," our hearts were broken. Rick, our administrative director, asked a parent who was a pastor to tell us about suicide and grief. He talked as though Alicia were already dead. As he spoke, everything in me cried out, "She's not dead! She's not going to die!" I said to the group, "Let's stop talking about death. Let's pray now that she will live."

Several staff members prayed aloud. Miss Connie prayed the most beautiful prayer imploring God to reach down and touch every part of the brain the bullet creased, every cell that was damaged, and to heal Alicia from the inside out—body, mind, soul and spirit. Miss Amy started singing "Amazing Grace." We all joined in and sang songs of praise, knowing that nothing is impossible for God.

The next day Mrs. C. called. "The most amazing thing happened last night! Alicia opened her eyes! The doctors want to keep her on life support for a while now."

Rejoicing, I asked, "What time did Alicia open her eyes?"

"Six o'clock."

Every day, each of us prayed for Alicia, our parents prayed, people all over the city prayed with faith that she would be healed.

Miraculously, Alicia came out of the coma, but progress was slow. Doctors still had no hope that she would have any quality of life. Several weeks later, Mrs. C. called me at work. "Miss Frances, somebody wants to talk to you."

I heard a soft, small voice on the phone. "Miss Frances, this is Alicia." I wanted to laugh. I wanted to cry. I wanted to raise my hands in praise and fall on the floor in awe!

Day by day, Alicia got a little better. She was transferred to Shepherd's Spinal Clinic, where she learned to talk and walk again. While she had no memory of any events surrounding her "accident," she remembered the children in her class and asked about them when I went to visit.

One miracle followed another. Three months after the accident, Alicia went home for her twentieth birthday. Only weeks later, she drove alone to downtown Atlanta for therapy each week. Then miracle of all miracles—she, who would never be able to walk or talk, came back to work with us the following summer.

Yet the greatest miracle is still in process. Only four years after the accident, Alicia went back to college, earned a bachelor's degree in special education and is now enrolled in graduate school to work with deaf children. Although a slight speech defect remains, Alicia has the most radiant smile! She still has no memory of the accident or why she pulled the trigger that day, but she knows that God has healed her from the inside out. She knows He has a special plan for her life, that He saved her so that she can help others with the same kind of help she received from Him.

~Frances Griffin
Chicken Soup for the Christian Soul 2

27

When Daddy Died

Filled with the frenetic restlessness of my fourteen years, I impatiently stood in my parents' kitchen listening to the drone of their conversation. Hurry up, hurry up, was my sole thought as I beat an accompanying tap with my foot. The bus would be arriving at the corner stop any minute, and I was tired of listening to chatter about doctors' appointments and chest pain and shortness of breath. My main goal was to get to school on time and avoid a detention slip.

I couldn't wait any longer. "Bye, Pop," I called out. Totally out of character, my father was lying in bed while I tore through the house grabbing my jacket, lunch and bus fare. Mother was making Daddy a cup of tea when I hesitated at the door. It was the first time in my life that I could remember not kissing him goodbye. Oh, well. No time for a kiss today. Gotta go. My friends were waiting. He'll be here this afternoon. I'll kiss him then.

Besides, Daddy, at age fifty-four, was a strapping five feet, eleven inches. He was a railroad engineer, working long, unorthodox hours on his daily train routes. He led the life of the rails, playing cards at the station house with the rest of the crew until his next "run." Sure, he smoked unfiltered Camel cigarettes, but so did most of his friends and coworkers. He was usually the first one on the dance floor, whirling my mother around in a dizzying polka, stopping long enough to quench his thirst with a beer.

In between his extended train trips, Pop tilled and weeded his garden, coaxing abundant crops from the earth. The back porches of the neighborhood were filled with the fruits of his labor, and if the neighbor lady were home, he'd stop by for a cup of coffee and a good joke. Everyone loved to see his big smile.

So, on that cold February morning, I didn't give it much of a thought when I naively decided to exit without my usual hug and kiss. There was nothing to worry about. Besides, my father had promised to refinish a piece of battered furniture he'd picked up at the salvage yard. His workshop in the cellar was outfitted with the lifetime collection of a man who saw beauty in wood and castoffs. A favorite comment of his after a trip to the dump was, "Look at this beauty. Why, just a little sanding and it will be as good as new." Our home was filled with little beauties.

His lesson to look beyond the outer shell of a piece of furniture also included the people we met. A particularly grouchy salesclerk was excused with, "Well, her husband is sick. She has a lot on her mind." He didn't let other people's bad moods ruin his day.

As I ran into the brisk air I called over my shoulder, "See ya later!" But the guilty nagging of unfinished business bore into my conscience. I tried to relieve the ache by calling home at the end of the school day. Daddy was about to drive to the doctor's office for his appointment, and he'd see me when I got home. Absolved, I went about the business of a high school freshman.

Something was very wrong when I got off the bus at the end of my road. I could see a black stretch limousine parked in front of my house — the kind of car only the funeral director in town drove. I tried to run on rubbery legs, but no matter how hard I pushed myself, it felt like I was going in slow motion. Breathlessly, I flung open the kitchen door and stopped in my tracks. My mother's face told the story. Next to her, the mortician began his technical explanation of what had happened. I couldn't hear for the blood rushing into my ears. The only sound was an empty roar.

The next few days were tearless and raw. I sat in the back of the funeral parlor looking at the body of my father in the casket. I'm only a kid! He's not supposed to die yet! My friends all have their fathers.

He's too good and too young. It isn't fair. I spiraled into my empty core and knew that life as I knew it was over.

There was no rushing out the door now. I didn't care about school or my friends. Burning into my brain was the memory of the lost moment, words never spoken and the hug never felt. Time was the enemy, and it overwhelmed me as the clock tick-tocked through the night. Hour after hour I heard the chime until dawn viciously invaded my room. I was in no hurry for the day's events.

I wouldn't allow the tears that were pushing against my eyes to fall for fear that I'd be unable to stop the torrent. The pain that saturated every pore of my body prevented me from hearing or seeing anything but my father. I wanted to be invisible, to be with Daddy. Who would come to my concerts? My graduation? My whole being screamed, I need you! How could God do this?

The hours, the days, the years after my father's death were blurry and turbulent as I foolishly tried to escape reality. Attempting to fill the aching void in my heart with the empty promises of a fast life delivered only trouble, and time did not heal my wounds. I was too busy being angry about my loss, but the day came when my grades couldn't fall any lower, when there were no more parties, when my dearest and oldest friends stopped calling, when I couldn't look at myself in the mirror without shame, and the dam of tears broke.

For the first time, I mourned the death of my father, allowing emotion to wash over me. I cried for the loss of my childhood, for the way things used to be when my father was in our home, for the good times never to be realized, but most of all, for the person I had become. I felt like I could never be normal again.

Powerless, I called on the God of my childhood, and the healing began. The simple act of asking for help was the first step of a long and difficult journey. Daddy's death lost its sting as my rebellious, destructive existence became a new life filled with self-discipline and responsibility. There were many times when I felt like a jigsaw piece that didn't fit into a puzzle, but eventually that feeling left. Gratitude stepped in and took its place.

I had known pain. I learned to know joy. Finally, I had become my father's daughter.

~Irene Budzynski
Chicken Soup for the Teenage Soul IV

28

Praying for Your Enemies

Prayer is less about changing the world than it is about changing ourselves.
~David J. Wolpe

Last year I was put into a lower-level math class at school. The reason I was in the class had nothing to do with my intellect or math skills. I am blind. The school decided that it would be better for me to learn at a lower level because it takes me a great deal longer to complete assignments and grasp visual concepts.

The only problem with being in this class was that I was surrounded by "at-risk" students. These were kids who did not do well in school and didn't want to be there most of the time. Their home lives were obviously much different from mine, and they were constantly in trouble with the school and the law.

I remember sitting at my desk one morning, wondering what I had gotten myself into. We had already finished our lesson for the day, and the rest of the kids had begun to talk about what they had done the past weekend. I tried not to listen, but it was virtually impossible not to. I heard things in that classroom that shocked me. Even though the teacher was in the room, that didn't stop my classmates from discussing the parties they had been to, how drunk they had been and who they had slept with.

I began to dread going to math. I was tired of their swear words, their stories of drugs and violence, and their negative attitudes. Some days they would come into the room in such a bad mood that everyone could feel it. I began to resent the fact that I had to be there. One girl in particular began to eat away at my nerves. Some days I wanted to hide under my desk.

One Tuesday morning, I went to a Christian Student Union meeting before school. There was a guest speaker there that day talking to us about praying for our enemies.

I began to think about this. As I pondered the idea, I prayed and asked God how I could pray for the kids in my class. I had forgotten that they weren't bad kids; they were just lost.

At first, the prayers were mechanical. When I would hear their voices in class, I would pray, "Dear God, please bless so-and-so..." But as I continued, I began to think of the kids more often. I especially thought of the girl who got on my nerves the most. I began to think of her more and more, and in my quiet time at home I would ask God to bless her and the rest of my classmates.

As time went on, my classmates became more than just annoying kids to me. There was something growing inside my heart for them, something that wasn't there before. They began to feel like family, and I was learning to love them in a way I never thought possible.

I now see that praying is such a powerful act. Prayer is the most powerful tool a Christian has. When I pray for those around me, it also blesses my life, and it changes my perception of others. I realized I needed God's blessings to see the world through loving eyes. The prayers I said for others turned out to help me the most.

~Julie Johnston
Chicken Soup for the Christian Teenage Soul

God Listens to Even the Smallest Prayers

Weave in faith and God will find the thread.
~Author Unknown

My daughter was fourteen. She had accepted Christ into her life when she was seven. Seven years later, she was questioning her faith.

"Mom, I don't think God is with me anymore," she said one day.

I asked her why she felt that way, and she said she couldn't hear God talking to her, almost as if He didn't notice her at all anymore.

My heart ached as I listened to this young child—my child—share her feelings of being abandoned by God. I gave her a hug and searched my mind for the right words to reassure her.

It just so happened that she was planning and saving for the annual youth camping trip. The camp coordinators made camping fun; they had energetic speakers, lots of food, late night expeditions and great crafts. Kids from all over the country met every year, renewing friendships and making new ones. And each year the camp coordinators added extras like a gift shop, special crafts and extracurricular activities, for which there was a small fee. Knowing this, all the kids brought extra spending money.

I thought the camping trip would be a great time to renew her friendship with God and I told her to ask God to speak to her while she was at camp.

"How will I know it's Him and not just my own thoughts?"

"God has a way of speaking to us that we just know it is Him and not just our own thinking," I explained. She looked skeptical, but agreed to give it a try.

Over the next few days, my heart was heavy for her. I knew it was very important for her to hear from Him now. I pleaded with Him to speak to her.

"Mom!" she called when she arrived home from camp. "You won't believe what happened! You remember I only had fifteen dollars to spend for crafts and things, right?"

"Yes, I remember."

She continued excitedly, "Well, I bought some friendship bracelets for myself and my friends, and I made a craft. I decided to save the last four dollars so I could do another craft. The first morning of camp, I asked God to speak to me just like you said, and during the second session the speaker talked about giving to missionaries. He said they had a hard time out there in the field and they needed all of us to help out. And even though we couldn't be there, we could help by sending money.

"Right then I felt God wanted me to give to missions. Mom, I really wanted to do the craft. It was all the money I had left, but I didn't care. I knew it was the right thing to do, so when the time came I put the four dollars I was saving in the basket. I felt good inside.

"And then, that afternoon, during mail call, the leader called my name. Mom, I was surprised because we only have four days at camp and I've never gotten mail before. And guess what? It was a letter from you with four dollars in it! Mom, how did you know?"

"I didn't know! A few days before you left for camp, I prayed for God to speak to you in a special way, where you would know for sure it was Him. After I prayed, I felt a strong urge to take all the money from my pocket and mail it to you. At first I thought it strange, but I knew God wanted me to do it and it had to be mailed that day."

"Mom, God is so awesome! He asked me to give all the money I had to help someone else, and then He sent me money to do my favorite craft! He listens even to the smallest prayer, doesn't He?"

"Yes, my love, indeed He does!" My heart raced with gratitude that not only had God listened to her smallest prayers but that I had been obedient to His smallest messages as well.

~Ray Driver
Chicken Soup for the African American Soul

30

The Days We Prayed

It must be recess in heaven if St. Peter is letting his angels out.
~Zora Neale Hurston

I was thirty-five years old and an hour and a half into my new teaching career when I saw Jason at the opposite end of the hall-way. He was the reason I almost didn't take the job. Then later, when I wanted to quit a hundred times, he was the reason I didn't.

Jason was a special needs student, thirteen years old and pretty much confined to a wheelchair since birth. As the school's newest special education teacher, it would be my job to teach Jason and attend to his personal needs. He had medicines that would have to be administered and diapers that would need to be changed twice a day—odd tasks for a man who had made a habit of fleeing his own kids at medicine and diaper-changing time.

My educational background was in business, but there had been no positions available in that area. To take the job meant I would have to return to school during summers and evenings in order to obtain the necessary certification. Because my own kids attended this school system, I wanted very much to be a part of it, and special education was the only position available.

I expected an angry child, resentful of what life had delivered, and as I watched him approach, I had to admit that Jason had every right to be. His condition was called spina bifida, a congenital defect of the vertebrae. He had already undergone a dozen surgeries, and his family anticipated more. He was being cared for full-time by elderly grandparents.

His prognosis, too, was poor. Only a season before, I had attended the school's sixth grade graduation. At that ceremony, his grandmother had invited the entire family and had ordered balloons and flowers for the event. She wanted the celebration to be special for Jason because, as she later explained, it might be the only graduation he would ever see.

Yet if Jason was embittered, I saw no sign of it that day. As he approached slowly and steadily, he must have realized who I was and held out both arms in greeting. "Welcome, friend. It's good to see you!"

Though it took us awhile to adjust—Jason as a new junior high student and I as a new teacher—we eventually came to terms. More than a student, Jason became a friend. Later, Jason became like a son.

During our times together, Jason shared his heart. He told me he had attended church for as long as he could remember. A couple of years before, he had turned his life over to Jesus, and someday he hoped to become a preacher. Though Jason never made it into the ministry, I believe he helped me grow as a Christian and as a teacher.

I remember one time in particular, when his eighty-year-old grandfather had become ill, Jason asked me to pray with him. As a first-year teacher and not tremendously secure with my own future, I was reluctant. Tactfully, I brushed away the suggestion, explaining that the government had guidelines and regulations about teachers and students praying together on school grounds.

Jason, as always, seemed to understand.

Two hours later, though, when Jason was in his band class, God spoke to me—not in an audible voice, but rather with a feeling of deep remorse that weighed heavily on my heart. It is a sad world indeed, I came to realize, when a public school teacher is so wrapped up in the system that he is afraid to pray with a frightened child. I dropped what I was doing and went among the tubas and clarinets to find my friend. I wheeled him back to the nurse's station, and there in the quiet of the room, Jason and I prayed for his grandfather.

Shortly thereafter, Jason's grandfather began his recovery. Many times after that, Jason and I prayed together. I shared with Jason that I often prayed silently in my classroom, and Jason suggested a way that he and I could pray silently together. He would lay his pencils (he always had at least two) on his desk in the form of a cross as a signal to me that he was praying. Silently then, from wherever I was in the room, I would join him.

Once, when I was having a bad day, Jason's friend Delbert came to class without a pencil. Jason and Delbert knew what a stickler I was for bringing necessary materials to class, and Jason would often secretly loan things to Delbert. I noticed (and though I was annoyed, said nothing) as Jason slipped a pencil to his friend.

Later, I gave a written assignment and was surprised when Jason wheeled up to my desk with tears welling in his eyes. "I don't have my pencil," he said, and immediately I remembered Delbert.

"Jason," I said, almost in a shout. "If you didn't keep giving your things to Delbert, you'd have a pencil, wouldn't you?" Then as I looked up, I noticed a pencil in his shirt pocket. All the more annoyed that the disruption had been entirely unnecessary, I pulled out the pencil and held it in front of him. "Jason, here's your pencil."

A tear rolled down his cheek. "That's the pencil I write with," he explained. "It's the pencil I pray with that I don't have."

From that moment forward, I made a point to have lots of spare materials on hand. Sometimes my students come to school in the winter with no socks on their feet or coats on their backs. A pencil, at times, seems like a small thing.

It was late last year, on the Thursday before he went in for a scheduled heart surgery, that Jason (now an eleventh-grader) and I prayed for what would be the last time. He hugged me as he left that day and, as I returned to the classroom to gather my belongings for the trip home, I saw the desk where he sat and the two pencils he had left behind.

When I think of Jason now, I remember perhaps the most remarkable young man I have ever known, yet I have a hard time becoming sad for him, because I know he was not afraid.

And I know that I will see him again one day, only this time without the chair that bound him as a child. In my mind, I see him there in the distance, standing with a friend, the same friend who once answered his prayers and who, from heaven, watched over Jason as he toiled and struggled with life's situations below. The struggles now are gone, but the happy smiles remain, and with laughing eyes and open arms he makes his way toward me.

"Welcome, friend. It's good to see you!"

~Hugh T. Chapman
Chicken Soup for the Christian Teenage Soul

31

Roadside Rescue

Anyone can be an angel.
~Author Unknown

It's a good thing the summer wedding was beautiful, because the rest of the day was nothing but problems. My friend John and I had borrowed Dad's car to attend the wedding of our college friend 150 miles away. Shortly after our venture began, John discovered he had forgotten his wallet at home. Later, at the restaurant, I realized I had left my driver's license in the jeans I'd worn the night before. Then, on the way home, John got really sick. He took out his contacts and slumped in the seat next to me, holding his stomach and looking pale.

That's when the car died at the side of the interstate. Over and over again, I turned the key, pumped the accelerator and rocked with the sound of the groaning engine.

"Where's my guardian angel when I need her?" I moaned. Dad had recently shared with Mom and me two books he had received on angels working in our lives. Each of the stories was fascinating and believable. I always knew I had a guardian angel, yet questioned if I had ever personally experienced it.

"It's seven o'clock," John said, squinting at his watch. "We'd better walk back to that gas station before it closes."

So I led my visually impaired, nauseated friend down the shoulder of the highway. It was hard to tell if he was sweating from the ninety-six-degree heat or from his fever. My white high heels clicked on the pavement, and the strand of imitation pearls clung to my neck as we trudged along the roadside.

I called Dad from the gas station and listened to his mechanic's advice. If his suggestions didn't work, I'd have to call a tow truck.

"It's 7:15," Mom said into the speaker phone. "If you aren't back on the road in one hour, call again so we know how you're doing." She tried not to worry about me now that I was in college, but at times like these, I knew she couldn't help it.

John and I plodded back down the scorching pavement to the car and tried Dad's long-distance advice. The car coughed and choked, but refused to start.

I draped myself over the steering wheel. "What if no one stops to help us?"

"What if someone does?" John worried out loud. He propped his aching head on the dashboard while we swapped tales of horrible crimes along the highway.

At 7:50, we admitted our defeat and traipsed across the highway to walk back to the gas station. Just then, a white, dilapidated station wagon sputtered to a stop in front of our car. I could see the two male occupants through the missing rear window. The driver's long, stringy hair touched the shoulders of his ragged shirt. As we stood across the road from them, John and I agreed they looked pretty rough.

"And we look pretty rich," John said, motioning to our wedding attire. "Think they'll believe we're poor college students?"

"Need some help?" the driver hollered. His smile leered through his scraggly beard. "I know some 'bout cars." As we headed back across the interstate, we could see the sleeves had been torn from the denim jacket he was wearing. His tall, leather moccasins had fringe hanging just beneath the knees of his holey blue jeans.

"I always knew my guardian angel would be unique," I teased in a whisper. "Maybe he will help us."

"Or rob us," John cautioned as we crossed the highway.

A second unshaven man silently exited the car. I thanked them both for stopping and, with trembling hands, released the hood, hoping I wasn't making a big mistake in letting them help us.

The driver bent over the car engine. I read the back of his worn jacket: Christian Motorcycle Association. John and I beamed at each other. I nodded and winked—and breathed a sigh of relief.

Within minutes, the car was running, and the four of us stood together smiling and shaking hands. John and I each offered them the only money we had with us—five dollars each, some of it in change. They accepted it gratefully saying it was more than they'd had in a long time.

I drove home, collapsed in the chair and recounted my "guardian angel" story to my parents.

Mom's face was serious. "What time did they stop?"

I thought for a minute. "About ten 'til eight."

She smiled at Dad. "I looked at my watch at 7:50 and said to Dad, 'Let's pray an angel stops to help her.'"

Dad said, "That's when I sent you mine."

~Christie Rogers
Chicken Soup for the Father & Daughter Soul

32

Childish Faith

Faith is believing in things when common sense tells you not to.
~George Seaton

"Chrissy! Chrissy! Abby's gone!" My seven-year-old brother Matthew pounded on my bedroom door. Flinging it open, I found myself gazing into his frantic eyes. "We looked everywhere," Matthew cried. "What if she got outside? Abby's never been outside alone!"

Fear ran down my spine as I thought of the little black-and-white kitten we'd brought home only three days before. Abby was supposedly a family pet, but Matthew had formed a special bond with her. Now, as I stared at my brother's tear-streaked face, I felt my heart break. He had lost his new best friend.

"Don't worry. We'll find her," I said, trying to sound like a reassuring big sister. A tiny creature like Abby could be lost almost anywhere.

I led Matthew downstairs where we joined the rest of the family in turning the house upside down. We searched through closets, under couches, inside potted plants and anywhere else a kitten might hide. I kept praying that Abby would suddenly leap out and pounce on our ankles, but she never showed up.

"She must be outside," I told Matthew. "Let's go look."

"You'll never find her out there," our older brother, Anthony, informed us. "She's probably been eaten by a hawk or squashed in the road by now." Sometimes he could be negative.

"Hush up!" I snapped, throwing him a sharp look. "Don't listen to him," I told Matthew. "Abby's fine."

"Okay," Matthew replied. But I could tell he didn't believe me.

Together, Matthew and I searched the soybean fields that surrounded our house. We slithered under the porch. We checked every tree in the yard. The sun set, and there was still no sign of our kitten.

"Will she be okay?" Matthew asked me, as I tucked him into bed that night.

"I don't know," I sighed. I had spent the entire evening trying to convince my brother that everything would be fine, yet I could no longer hide my disappointment. I was sure we'd never see Abby again.

Now Matthew tried to cheer me up. "We'll find her," he said, suddenly confident. "I'm gonna pray that Jesus lets her be here in the morning. How's that?"

That's crazy, I wanted to say, but I didn't. Instead, I tucked the covers under Matthew's chin. "Go ahead and pray," I said, "but don't get your hopes up."

I tried not to show how doubtful I was, but Matthew saw right through me. "Jesus cares about kittens, too," he insisted.

To make Matthew feel better, I knelt and listened to his simple, childish prayer. It was sweet, but it was obvious we'd been reading my brother way too many of those Christian bedtime stories in which children were constantly praying for and getting miracles. He had a lot to learn about the real world.

"Is Matthew asleep?" Mom asked when I came downstairs.

"Yeah," I replied, staring at my feet. I missed having Abby chew on my socks.

"Oh, by the way," I added, "don't be surprised if your son doesn't believe in God in the morning."

"What do you mean?" Mom asked, surprised.

"Well, Matthew just prayed that God would send Abby back by tomorrow, and he really thinks it's going to happen."

"And you don't?"

"Oh, please!" I exclaimed. "I'm not seven years old, Mom. I know God's not a genie in some lamp you just rub and make a wish to."

"No," Mom agreed, "but He still cares about everything that concerns His children, no matter how small."

"Sure, Mom," I replied. "I'll remember to tell Matthew that when he wakes up tomorrow and his kitten isn't waiting to play with him."

As I stalked out of the room, I heard my mother sigh. "Oh, Chrissy," she whispered softly. "What's happened to your faith?"

I tossed and turned trying to fall asleep. Visions of Abby's whiskered face and Matthew's trusting eyes swam through my head, along with my mother's lingering words: What's happened to your faith?

I rolled onto my stomach. I remembered when I was a child, how I used to pray about every little thing, from a broken toy to a rained-out picnic. What was it that I had back then that made me so quick to turn to God and so certain that He cared? Was it really ignorance, or was it faith?

I yanked the blanket over my head, trying to block the questions from my mind. After all, these were questions I had worked hard at erasing from my mind a long time ago. I wasn't going to allow a kitten to bring them back.

I woke up early the next morning and rolled out of bed. I needed to be up in time to run damage control when Matthew realized his kitten was gone for good.

Suddenly, I felt something pounce on my foot. There was Abby, staring at me with her shining, green eyes. She let out a playful "meow" and tugged at my sock.

I lifted the tiny kitten in wonder, rubbing her furry face against my cheek. As happy as I was to find Abby safe, I was a bit overwhelmed. I felt guilty that I had spent half the night refusing to have faith that God would bring our kitten home.

Matthew!

Cradling Abby in my arms, I ran out of my bedroom and across the hall, where my brother was still asleep. Setting Abby on Matthew's stomach, I watched her crawl across his chest and place a tiny paw on his cheek. Finally, he opened his eyes.

"Abby!" he yelled, throwing his arms around his precious pet.

"Oh, Abby, I knew God would find you! Didn't I tell you, Chrissy? Didn't I?"

"You sure did," I said, smiling.

"Now we need to thank Him," Matthew reminded me. "We have to thank Jesus for taking care of our Abby."

Matthew bowed his head and folded his hands, one finger resting on Abby's tail. Now humbled, I followed his lead. I realized that although I was much older than my little brother, there was a lot I could learn from his innocent faith.

~Christina Marie Dotson
Chicken Soup for the Christian Teenage Soul

CHRISTIAN *Teen Talk*

Family

*This is my commandment,
that you love one another as I have loved you.
~John 15:12*

33

My Superhero

Everyone has a hero—someone he admires, who has had an impact on his life. My brother, John, is my hero. He is the most compassionate, sweet and funny person I have ever met. John is also mentally retarded and has a developmental disability known as autism.

I used to be ashamed of John when I was little. When he first started talking, he had a hard time with pronunciation and understanding the meaning of words. He called me May-Me for most of my childhood because he could not pronounce Amy. As John grew older, his language ability gradually increased. I went from May-Me to Amy, and hammer burgers became hamburgers.

Now I rather enjoy John's mispronunciations and mixing of phrases. For example, instead of "eagle-eyes," John called himself "four-eyes" once, and rather than getting something "off his chest," he prefers to get things "over his back." Instead of people getting their ears boxed, John thinks people get books put on their ears.

When I was younger, I was embarrassed by John. He used to gallop around in stores talking to himself, flicking his ears and putting his hands in his mouth. He had a hard time swallowing and would have drool running down his face. John was very loud, and it seemed to me that he would always find the quietest moments to talk.

All I ever wanted was a normal brother. I would look at other brothers and sisters, see their relationships and turn green with envy. Why did my brother have to be so different? I was very self-conscious of what people thought. I felt as if the entire world was laughing at me because of the way John was acting. I was outraged at times that I could not have a normal brother.

John has changed significantly over the past eighteen years. As he grew older, he became social and adopted an upbeat and positive attitude. John began to see things for what they really are.

Most people feel sorry for John, and they feel as if they should be the one helping him. John, however, does not even see that he has a problem, only that there are problems out there that people need help with, and he wants to help. If my mentally handicapped brother can have so many problems of his own, overcome these problems as if they are nothing and want to help others, then surely I can overcome obstacles of my own.

The siblings of an autistic child can have many reactions to the amount of attention the autistic child receives. Some feel as if they are not receiving enough attention and may become superachievers to get their share. I hate to admit it, but I definitely fall into this category. I feel the need to excel in everything I do. I cannot help but think that this comes from having a disabled brother. I do not feel it comes so much from the need for attention, but instead from the need to do it because John cannot. I need to seize every opportunity I can because I know some people will never have that opportunity. John has taught me to do as much as I can with what I have.

The name John means "gift from God." No one knows for sure what causes autism, and there is no cure. I do not, however, ask God anymore why he did this to John. Instead, I thank him for making John the way he did.

As I grow older, I'm no longer ashamed of my brother; instead, I am ashamed that I used to be. There is no one I would rather walk through a store with, no one I would rather have a "quiet" conversation with in the midst of a quiet restaurant. I beam with pride when someone tells me they love my brother, because I know I am truly blessed to have John in my life to keep me real and remind me of what is important. John has taught me to live life, to love life and, no matter what, that life goes on. So maybe John is no Clark Kent, but he is definitely a superhero and a gift from God.

~Amy Rene Byrne
Chicken Soup for the Christian Teenage Soul

34

In God's Eyes

To love another person is to see the face of God.
~Victor Hugo

By the time I was ten, I was totally ashamed of my father. All my friends called him names: Quasimodo, hunchback, monster, little Frankenstein, the crooked little man with the crooked little cane. At first it hurt when they called him those things, but soon I found myself agreeing with them. He was ugly, and I knew it.

My father was born with something called parastremmatic dwarfism. The disease made him stop growing when he was about thirteen and caused his body to twist and turn into a grotesque shape. It wasn't too bad when he was a kid. I saw pictures of him when he was about my age. He was a little short but quite good-looking. Even when he met my mother and married her when he was nineteen, he looked pretty normal. He was still short and walked with a slight limp, but he was able to do just about anything. Mother said, "He even used to be a great dancer."

Soon after my birth, however, things started getting worse for my father. Another genetic disorder took over, and his left foot started turning out, almost backward. His head and neck shifted over to the right; his neck became rigid and he had to look over his left shoulder a bit. His right arm curled in and up, and his index finger almost touched his elbow. His spine warped to look something like a big, old roller coaster and it caused his torso to lie sideways, instead of straight up and down like a normal person. His walk became slow, awkward and deliberate. He dragged his left foot and used his deformed right arm to balance his gait.

I hated to be seen with him. Everyone stared. They seemed to pity me. I knew he must have done something really bad to have God hate him that much.

By the time I was seventeen, I was blaming all my problems on my father. I didn't have the right boyfriends because of him. I didn't drive the right car because of him. I wasn't pretty enough because of him. I didn't have the right jobs because of him. I wasn't happy because of him.

Anything that was wrong with me or my life was because of him. If my father had been good-looking like Jane's father, or successful like Paul's father, or worldly like Terry's father, I would be perfect! I knew that for sure.

The night of my senior prom came, and my father had to place one more nail in my coffin; he had volunteered to be one of the chaperones at the dance. My heart just sank when he told me. I stormed into my room, slammed the door, threw myself on the bed and cried.

"Three more weeks and I'll be out of here!" I screamed into my pillow. "Three more weeks, and I will have graduated and be moving away to college." I sat up and took a deep breath. "God, please make my father go away and leave me alone. He keeps sticking his big nose in everything I do. Just make him disappear, so that I can have a good time at the dance."

I got dressed, my date picked me up, and we went to the prom. My father followed in his car behind us. When we arrived, he seemed to vanish into the pink chiffon drapes that hung everywhere in the auditorium. I thanked God for answering my prayer. At least now I could have some fun.

Midway through the dance, my father came out from behind the drapes and decided to embarrass me again. He started dancing with my girlfriends. One by one, he took their hand and led them to the dance floor. He then clumsily moved them in circles as the band played. Now I tried to vanish into the drapes.

After Jane had danced with him, she headed my way.

Oh, no! I thought. She's going to tell me he stomped on her foot or something.

"Grace," she called, "you have the greatest father."

My jaw dropped. "What?"

She smiled at me and grabbed my shoulders. "Your father's just the best. He's funny, and kind, and he always finds the time to be where you need him. I wish my father was more like that."

For one of the first times in my life, I couldn't talk. Her words confused me.

"What do you mean?" I asked her.

Jane looked at me really strangely. "What do you mean, what do I mean? Your father's wonderful. I remember when we were kids and I'd sleep over at your house. He'd always come into your room, sit down in the chair between the twin beds, and read us a book. I'm not sure my father can even read," she sighed, and then smiled. "Thanks for sharing him."

Then, Jane ran off to dance with her boyfriend.

I stood there in silence.

A few minutes later, Paul came to stand beside me.

"He's sure having a lot of fun."

"What? Who? Who is having a lot of fun?" I asked.

"Your father. He's having a ball."

"Yeah. I guess." I didn't know what else to say.

"You know, he's always been there," Paul said. "I remember when you and I were on the mixed-double co-ed soccer team. He tried out as the coach, but he couldn't run up and down the field, remember? So they picked Jackie's father instead. That didn't stop him. He showed up for every game and did whatever needed to be done. He was the team's biggest fan. I think he's the reason we won so many games. Without him, it just would have been Jackie's father running up and down the field yelling at us. Your father made it fun. I wish my father had been able to show up to at least one of our games. He was always too busy."

Paul's girlfriend came out of the restroom, and he went to her side, leaving me once again speechless.

My boyfriend came back with two glasses of punch and handed me one.

"Well, what do you think of my father?" I asked out of the blue.

Terry looked surprised. "I like him. I always have."

"Then why did you call him names when we were kids?"

"I don't know. Because he was different, and I was a dumb kid."

"When did you stop calling him names?" I asked, trying to search my own memory.

Terry didn't even have to think about the answer. "The day he sat down with me outside by the pool and held me while I cried about my mother and father's divorce. No one else would let me talk about it. I was hurting inside, and he could feel it. He cried with me that day. I thought you knew."

I looked at Terry and a tear rolled down my cheek as long-forgotten memories started cascading into my consciousness.

When I was three, my puppy got killed by another dog, and my father was there to hold me and teach me what happens when the pets we love die. When I was five, my father took me to my first day of school. I was so scared. So was he. We cried and held each other that first day. The next day he became a teacher's helper. When I was eight, I just couldn't do math. Father sat down with me night after night, and we worked on math problems until math became easy for me. When I was ten, my father bought me a brand-new bike. When it was stolen, because I didn't lock it up like I was taught to do, my father gave me jobs to do around the house so I could make enough money to purchase another one. When I was thirteen and my first love broke up with me, my father was there to yell at, to blame, and to cry with. When I was fifteen, and I got to be in the honor society, my father was there to see me get the accolades. Now, when I was seventeen, he put up with me no matter how nasty I became or how high my hormones raged.

As I looked at my father dancing gaily with my friends, a big toothy grin on his face, I suddenly saw him differently. The handicaps weren't his, they were mine! I had spent a great deal of my life hating the man who loved me. I had hated the exterior that I saw, and I had ignored the interior that contained his God-given heart. I suddenly felt very ashamed.

I asked Terry to take me home. I was too overcome with feelings to remain.

On graduation day, at my Christian high school, my name was called, and I stood behind the podium as the valedictorian of my class. As I looked out over the people in the audience, my gaze rested on my father, sitting next to my mother in the front row. He sat there in his one and only specially made suit, holding my mother's hand and smiling.

Overcome with emotions, my prepared speech was to become a landmark in my life.

"Today I stand here as an honor student, able to graduate with a 4.0 average. Yes, I was in the honor society for three years and was elected class president for the last two years. I led our school to a championship in the debate club, and yes, I even won a full scholarship to Kenton State University so that I can continue to study physics and someday become a college professor.

"What I'm here to tell you today, fellow graduates, is that I didn't do it alone. God was there, and I had a whole bunch of friends, teachers and counselors who helped. Up until three weeks ago, I thought they were the only ones I would be thanking this evening. If I had thanked just them, I would have been leaving out the most important person in my life. My father."

I looked down at my father and at the look of complete shock that covered his face.

I stepped out from behind the podium and motioned for my father to join me onstage. He made his way slowly, awkwardly and deliberately. He had to drag his left foot up the stairs as he used his deformed right arm to balance his gait. As he stood next to me at the podium, I took his small, crippled hand in mine and held it tight.

"Sometimes we only see the silhouette of the people around us," I said. "For years I was as shallow as the silhouettes I saw. For almost my entire life, I saw my father as someone to make fun of, someone to blame and someone to be ashamed of. He wasn't perfect, like the fathers my friends had.

"Well, fellow graduates, what I found out three weeks ago is that while I was envying my friends' fathers, my friends were envying mine. That realization hit me hard and made me look at who I was and what I had become. I was brought up to pray to God and hold high principles for others and myself. What I've done most of my life is read between the lines of the 'Good Book' so I could justify my hatred."

Then, I turned to look my father in the face.

"Father, I owe you a big apology. I based my love for you on what I saw and not what I felt. I forgot to look at the one part of you that meant the most, the big, big heart God gave you. As I move out of high school and into life, I want you to know I could not have had a better father. You were always there for me, and no matter how badly I hurt you, you still showed up. Thank you!"

I took off my mortar board and placed it on his head, moving the tassel just so.

"You are the reason I am standing here today. You deserve this honor, not me."

And as the audience applauded and cried with us, I felt God's light shining down upon me as I embraced my father more warmly than I ever had before, tears unashamedly falling down both our faces.

For the first time, I saw my father through God's eyes, and I felt honored to be seen with him.

~Candace Carteen
Chicken Soup for the Christian Woman's Soul

35

My Light

My mom is a never ending song in my heart of comfort, happiness, and being.
I may sometimes forget the words but I always remember the tune.
~Graycie Harmon

You are the light in my darkness,
my shelter in a storm.
You give me strength when I am weak,
and your love to keep me warm.
When I was hurting, lost, abused,
it was then your faith that I had used.
When I was cold, depressed and lonely,
I stayed alive by your love only.
When I felt pushed or shunned away,
it was then your friendship made me stay.
When I was sick and felt like dying,
I knew you loved me by your crying.
I knew you loved me, knew you cared,
you did what no one else had dared.
You took the time to learn, to see,
just what I really am in me.
You listened to my thoughts and fears,
and helped me wipe away my tears.

You helped me learn, respect and love,
to pray to God my Lord above.
You're the light in my darkness, I hope you'll see,
I'll love you, Mom, for eternity.

~Robyn Robertson
Chicken Soup for the Christian Teenage Soul

36

"One Day You'll Look Back on This..."

I've learned to take time for myself and to treat myself with a great deal of love and respect 'cause I like me... I think I'm kind of cool.
~Whoopi Goldberg

"I can't go to school like this!" I wailed as I stared into my mirror, hating my face, my body and life in general. A river of salty tears traced a path down my cheeks. Summoned from the kitchen by my shrieking, my mother appeared at my side a second later.

"What's the problem?" she asked patiently.

"Everything... just everything!" I complained and continued to stare horrified into the mirror.

At almost thirteen, the problems that I felt I had were overwhelming. I had a hideous new crop of angry, red pimples that had erupted on my forehead and chin overnight—every night. My hair suddenly looked greasy all the time, even though I washed it every second day. My aching tummy signaled that my newfound "friend" was about to visit once again, causing my jeans to fit too snugly and make me appear as though I had been eating nothing but hot fudge sundaes. And to top it off, my chewed-up fingernails were torn and bloody, since biting them seemed to go along with the way I worried about how other people perceived me. But everything that was bothering me wasn't just on the surface—I also had a broken heart. The guy I had been going out with had recently dumped me in favor of an older, more developed girl. Everything combined, I was a physical and emotional wreck.

"Come on, now, Honey. Try not to cry," my mother said with a smile. "I remember what it was like to be your age. It was awkward and frustrating, and I got my heart stomped on, too, but I came through it—and so will you! It's not as bad as you think, and once you get to school with all your friends, you'll forget all about your pimples and what's-his-name, and one day you'll look back on this and wonder why you were ever so upset."

Convinced that she didn't know what she was talking about, I gave her a dirty look and headed off for school, greeting my girlfriends on the sidewalk while my mother waved encouragingly from the front door. Later, as much as I hated to admit it, I found out that my mother was right. As I spent time with my friends, who were going through the same things that I was, my mind wasn't on my troubles anymore, and soon I was laughing.

When I returned home later that day, I was in a much better mood and because I had put my best foot forward, my mother rewarded me with a bag of goodies she had purchased from the drugstore. On my bed was a bag that included shampoo and conditioner, some acne medication, a gift certificate to a hair salon and, surprisingly, some hot, new shades of nail polish.

"What on earth is this?" I asked bewildered, thinking that my mother had to be out of her mind if she thought I was going to flaunt my gnarled nails.

As it turned out, she had a plan. I thought that it was cruel at the time, yet it turned out to be highly effective. I wasn't allowed to have any of the stuff in the bag, nor was I allowed to keep my ever-so-important stick of concealer. The deal was that for each week that I didn't bite my fingernails, one item of my choice would be returned to me.

Desperate to retrieve my make-up and to get my hands on everything in the drugstore bag, I concentrated heavily on my schoolwork, instead of biting my nails and worrying about what people thought of me. Over the next few weeks, I was thrilled to watch my nails grow. By the time I earned the certificate to have my hair cut and restyled, my nails were so long that my mother also treated me to a manicure while we were at the salon. And as time wore on, I began to see that I was getting through the rough spot, just as she had promised I would.

I liked that I received so many compliments on my hands and hair, but more than that, I was proud of myself for sticking with the deal and improving myself in the process—so proud, as a matter of fact, that I failed to notice my acne slowly clearing up. And I couldn't have cared less about what's-his-name. He quickly became a distant memory as I began to date many different boys, some of whom broke my heart and others whose hearts I broke.

Though it certainly wasn't my last acne outbreak, bad hair day or crushed spirit, I did learn something. I will hold with me forever my mother's words of wisdom: "One day you'll look back on this and wonder why you were ever so upset."

Years later, after several ups and downs in my life, I look back and realize that I did come through it all and I am the better for it. I only hope that if one day I have a daughter who is experiencing the struggles of adolescence, I will be as understanding, helpful and creative as my mother was with me.

~Laurie Lonsdale
Chicken Soup for the Girl's Soul

A Farewell Gift

The price of wisdom is above rubies.
~Job 28:18

My wife and I had just finished the 150-mile trip home from our daughter's college. It was the first time in our lives that she would be gone for any length of time. We wondered how other people had survived it.

Later in bed, I thought of the time I started college. My father had driven me too. We rode in the farm truck. In the back was the trunk I had bought with money earned by pitching hay that summer. My mother had to stay behind to keep the cattle from getting into the crops. I, the fourth in a line of brothers, was the first to go away to college. My mother cried, and I cried; after we were out of sight of the farm, I began to feel jelly-like and scared.

The truck was slow, and I was glad. I didn't want to get to the city too soon. I remembered how my father and I stopped by a stream and ate the sandwiches my mother had prepared.

My daughter's day was different, of course. We stopped at a classy roadside place and ordered fried chicken. Then we went to the dormitory, and my wife talked with the housemother. When she came back, she was wiping her eyes. It wasn't until we were passing through the next town that she discovered our daughter had forgotten to take out the portable radio and record player. I told her she should have put it in the trunk with the other things, not in the back seat.

Now I heard a sob beside me. I knew that my wife was thinking about the new kind of loneliness before us.

My father didn't let me stay at the dormitory. A room in a private home was cheaper and better if a student wanted to work his way through. But I didn't have a room. My father told me that we'd leave my trunk at a filling station. I could come for it the next day after I had found a place to stay. We toured the town a bit, but the traffic confused him. I said maybe I'd better go on my own.

I shook hands with my father in the truck. For a long, haunting moment he looked straight ahead, not saying a word, but I knew he was going to make a little speech. "I can't tell you nothing," he finally said. "I never went to college, and none of your brothers went to college. I can't say don't do this and do that, because everything is different and I don't know what is going to come up. I can't help you much with money either, but I think things will work out."

He gave me a brand-new checkbook. "If things get pushing, write a small check. But when you write one, send me a letter and let me know how much. There are some things we can always sell." In four years, the total of all the checks I wrote was less than a thousand dollars. My jobs chauffeuring a rich lady, janitoring at the library, reading to a blind student and babysitting professors' kids filled in the financial gaps.

"You know what you want to be, and they'll tell you what to take," my father continued. "When you get a job, be sure it's honest and work hard." I knew that soon I would be alone in the big town, and I would be missing the furrowed ground, cool breezes and a life where your thinking was done for you.

Then my dad reached down beside his seat and brought out the old, dingy Bible that he had read so often, the one he used when he wanted to look something up in a friendly argument with one of the neighbors. I knew he would miss it. I also knew, though, that I must take it.

He didn't tell me to read it every morning. He just said, "This can help you if you will let it."

Did it help? I got through college without being a burden on my family. I have had a good earning capacity ever since.

When I finished school, I took the Bible back to my father, but he said he wanted me to keep it. "You will have a kid in school some day," he told me. "Let the first one take that Bible along."

Now, too late, I remember. It would have been so nice to have given it to my daughter when she got out of the car. But I didn't. Things were different. I was prosperous and my father wasn't. I had gone places. I could give her everything. My father could give me only a battered, old Bible. I'd been able to give my daughter what she needed.

Or had I? I don't really believe now that I gave her half as much as my father gave me. So the next morning I wrapped up the book and sent it to her. I wrote a note. "This can help you," I penned, "if you will let it."

~Jim Comstock
Chicken Soup for the Christian Family Soul

38

Outstretched Arms

You don't choose your family. They are God's gift to you, as you are to them.
~Desmond Tutu

The morning started off in the usual way. Our daughter, Annie, pulled away from the curb of our home in her little black Mustang and headed off to school just like she had every other morning of that fall semester. She was a senior at our suburban Dallas high school and would be in the first graduating class of the new century. Annie was really enjoying her senior year and looking forward to going to college, where she planned to become a second grade schoolteacher.

At 9:30 A.M., I was having my second cup of coffee (okay, it was really my third!) and checking my e-mail in my home office. The home phone rang. The school nurse said, "Annie is here in my office, and she has something she needs to tell you." Well, a huge lump jumped up in my throat as my daughter got on the phone. Between her sobs I could barely make out what she was saying, but there was no mistake about what I heard, "Mom, I'm pregnant."

I stifled a sob of my own and said, "Come home, Honey, just come home." I immediately called my husband, Tim, on his cell phone. He was en route to the church where he is the pastor of worship and administration. Through tears I told him the news, and he headed back home.

A few minutes later I heard the garage door open, signaling Tim's arrival. I looked out the living room window, and that little black

Mustang was pulling up to the front curb. Tim rushed in from the garage and opened the front door just in time for Annie to run up the steps and into her father's outstretched arms. I stood there in tearful amazement, watching the two of them in a silent embrace that truly said it all: "I love you. I forgive you. I'm here for you."

Our daughter graduated with her class on May 19th, and gave birth to our first grandchild, an eight-and-a-half-pound boy, on July 12th. Within minutes after he was born, she handed him to her daddy, who extended his arms for him. As we caressed him we knew, without a doubt, that sometimes our greatest blessings come through circumstances we never dreamed we'd experience. But it's up to us to love unconditionally and to be there with outstretched arms.

~LaDonna Gatlin
Chicken Soup for the Father & Daughter Soul

39

Our Wonderful "Tragedy"

Four years before I was born, my mom gave birth to a baby boy with Down syndrome. In 1958, children with Down syndrome were a rare breed and were often kept hidden and out of the public eye because they brought shame to their families. Little was known about this condition, but Mom and Dad took it in stride and were determined to make the best of the situation. The fragile little baby was nicknamed Chispo, Spanish for "tiny bit." He was only three pounds when he entered the world. Doctors didn't give Chispo much of a chance—a year at the most. After a few months in the hospital, my parents brought their physically challenged child home, determined to give Chispo the best year they could provide.

A year turned into two, and my mom had another child, a healthy baby girl. And two years after that, I came along. Chispo was now four and still couldn't walk on his own, but that didn't stop him from using me as his personal human teddy bear. We spent a great deal of time in my playpen where he would prop me up, lay me down, toss me around and, when mom wasn't looking, he would insert foreign objects up my nostrils and into my ears. I'm told that with the aid of his walker, he would drag me around the house.

Maybe because I got tired of being his personal mop, I opted for walking sooner than usual—they tell me I took my first steps when I turned eight months old. The little boy in the walker taught me how to walk, and from then on we became a dynamic duo who drove my parents insane. Chispo finally started walking on his own when he was six, just in time to torment our younger brother, who had come along two years after me.

As my siblings and I grew older, we grew closer. There are five of us: Irene, Chispo, Maggie, Carlos and Miguel. My parents treated all of us the same; there were no extra points for higher intelligence, athletic ability, mental retardation or physical handicap. Four of us shared the first two of the above, but Chispo — the only one lacking those two other qualities — was by far the leader of the pack. During the years we attended the same school, we all lived in Chispo's shadow. Even when he didn't attend our school, he managed to somehow become the physical education teacher's assistant. Every kid from first to ninth grade knew Chispo and thought he was way cool. When we tried to cash in on his popularity, kids wouldn't believe that we were related. We would argue the point until the Phys. Ed. teacher confirmed that we were indeed related — something I will treasure for as long as I live.

At one point, doctors predicted that Chispo wouldn't live past the age of eighteen. At the time, I was ten and figured that I had four years to prepare. Well, Chispo's eighteenth birthday came and went. Today he's forty-five — alive and kicking. My parents are now up in age, and their health is failing a bit. My little brother and I live far away in California, and my sisters have their own families to attend to, but every day when Mom and Dad wake up, there's an angel from heaven at their bedside encouraging them to go on. The "tragedy" that my parents brought into the world on February 2, 1958 grew up to become their most trusted and loyal companion.

My family has never felt an ounce of shame or regret about Chispo's condition. We've always believed he's an angel God sent to teach everyone who came in contact with him a lesson on how to live life. He's good, pure and honest, incapable of causing harm. He has affected the lives of many with his unconditional love, which flows freely and doesn't discriminate. Ironically, Chispo, who many in our world might judge as less than "normal," has taught us the dignity, nobility and virtue of being fully human. For as long as we live, we will proudly carry his example and his legacy in our hearts.

~Carlos R. Bermúdez
Chicken Soup for the Latino Soul

The Perfect Brother

You had better live your best and act your best and think your best today;
for today is the sure preparation for tomorrow
and all the other tomorrows that follow.
~Harriet Martineau

I've never had a very good relationship with my nine-year-old brother, Geoff. We started fighting with each other just about as soon as he could talk. For some reason, we enjoyed tormenting each other, and it wasn't a very good pastime. I still wonder why we fought at all, but I think he has a lot going on that I don't know about. He gets angry very easily, so it's hard to talk to him, much less play with him. It's pretty frustrating sometimes. I used to tell him that I hated him and that I never wanted to see him again, but I stopped doing that after what happened just before Christmas last year.

It was around 8:00 in the morning when my parents awoke to noises coming from Geoff's bedroom. My mom went into his room and discovered that he was having a grand mal epileptic seizure. This had never happened before, and of course she was terrified. She woke me and got Dad out of bed. Frantically, we rushed around the house to get Geoff in the car. When we got into the car, with Geoff still having the seizure in Mom's arms, she grabbed the phone and called 911. About five minutes before arriving at the emergency room, Geoff's shaking stopped, and he started breathing rapidly and got really cold. We were all so scared. All of a sudden, I felt guilty for everything bad that I had ever said to my brother. All I wanted right at that moment was for him to be all right, so I could apologize for everything.

We got to the hospital at around 8:20, and they took him right in to a room with Dad. I stayed in the waiting room, crying, while Mom filled out some paperwork. Then she called my aunt Katie, who was visiting with a friend of hers, and our family doctor, who is also a friend of Mom's. Then Mom and I went into Geoff's room and cried. It was so hard seeing my little brother hooked up to all the tubes and machines. Minutes after we got into the room, Katie came and then the doctor came. We all hugged and reassured each other that it was all going to be okay.

After a while, Geoff regained consciousness and started throwing up. He kept throwing up until the doctors gave him some medicine to stop it. He was too weak to talk very well, but my dad filled him in on where he was, since of course he had no idea. I eventually started to break down, so Katie took me out into the waiting room. Katie has been like a second mom to me forever, so I felt totally comfortable with her. I just hugged her and cried for about five minutes. Then she took me home, while Mom and Dad stayed with Geoff.

At home, I tried doing everything possible to get my mind off Geoff, but I couldn't. The next morning, we went back to visit him. By then, he had been transferred to a regular room with a TV and all that stuff. I just sat on the bed with him and talked. It was fun listening to him talk to me about all the cool things he got at the hospital, like cable TV. He also had a little monitor that he snapped onto his finger that would alert nurses if he started having another seizure. He thought that was pretty awesome. I was so happy he was enjoying himself. We watched TV and did a puzzle together, and before I knew it, it was time to go home. The next morning, I snatched a couple of Geoff's Christmas presents from under the tree and took them to the hospital with me. When he opened the one from me, a Palm Pilot, he had the biggest smile on his face. I showed him how to use it, and that's when I realized that he was going to be okay. I lay there and hugged him for so long, and I talked to him about how I was sorry for all the things I had said before. He hugged me back, and I started to cry but forced myself to stop. I was so happy.

The next day was crammed with a bunch of tests. The doctors determined that he had a cyst on his brain, which scared me. It was hard listening to all the talks my parents had with the neurologist and the doctors. Even though they told us that it was nothing serious, I still worried a little. I was happy to hear, though, that Geoff would be released from the hospital that night.

It was so nice to finally be home together again, and Geoffrey was overjoyed to be back for Christmas. We got along really well, and I even started reading up on epilepsy and what to do during seizures. I pulled pages and pages from the Internet and looked at medical books. I even switched my personal research topic at school from computers to epilepsy. I think I know pretty much everything there is to know about seizures, and I feel much more confident about what to do should he ever have another one.

It has now been eight months since Geoff's seizure. He is on medication and has not had another one since. I still worry about him sometimes, but I have gotten a lot better about it. We started fighting again, but I try to avoid phrases like, "I hate you!" or "Get out of my life." Because through it all, I learned that I don't really hate him. I love him. And I have thought about what my life would be like if he wasn't in it. He is such a big part of my life, even if we do fight, and I never want him to leave.

I guess the moral of this story is to love your siblings just the way they are, because you never know when the day might come when they leave your life forever.

~Kacy Gilbert-Gard
Chicken Soup for the Girl's Soul

Unspoken Years

Children begin by loving their parents;
as they grow older they judge them; sometimes they forgive them.
~Oscar Wilde

To an outsider looking in, my life probably looked pretty great. I had what appeared to be a loving family, I lived in a spacious home in a safe neighborhood, and I attended a good school. But what an outsider couldn't see was the cold atmosphere that permeated my house. My endless fights with my parents included the shouting of hurtful words, bitter stares, and at times, unbearable silence. Misunderstandings inevitably led to fights.

This particular fight started just like the others. I packed my bag, preparing to leave for an overnight retreat for my confirmation class. I carefully selected my clothes, folding and refolding them, doing everything I could to stall, thereby avoiding a potential fight. I crept down the stairs into our kitchen, only to find my parents glaring up at me.

"What time should I pick you up tomorrow?" my mom demanded impatiently with folded arms.

I told her that I wasn't certain, but that I thought she should pick me up at approximately 8:00 P.M. I quickly gathered that my reply was not the answer she wanted to hear.

"So you don't know what time?" Her face wrinkled with disapproval.

I tried my best not to explode and release years of repressed feelings of anger, resentment and sorrow. These feelings were trapped inside my confused body. Whenever my parents and I fought, usually about small, insignificant misunderstandings, we seemed to convey more. The fight was not just about the topic of that particular quarrel, but the unspoken emotions that hovered over the sixteen years of my life. My parents and I had issues, and we did not know how to voice them.

"You always run around and never tell me where you are going or when you will be home!" my mom yelled, continuing the argument and inflicting as much guilt on me as humanly possible.

I pretended I didn't know what she was talking about, and I left my house for the retreat on bitter terms with my parents, casting a shadow on my experience at the retreat. I did not want to participate or involve myself in anything that night. I sat by myself, drowning in self-pity. Whenever someone asked me what was wrong, I refused to answer.

The next morning, my instructor approached me and asked if I had received my letter.

"What letter?" I wondered, puzzled. Another leader at the retreat handed me an envelope with my name written on it in my mom's handwriting. I stared at the letter with perplexed eyes and strode to the conference room to open it in privacy.

"Make rainbows with faith in yourself. Many beautiful things will happen in your life. Your shine brightens our lives." As I read these statements, I tried to choke back the river of tears swelling in my eyes. I failed, and the tears trickled down my cheeks. As I made my way toward the tissue box at the other end of the room, three supportive friends hugged me. But wishing to be alone and to finish reading the letter, I broke free from their embrace and rushed toward the exit. I sat in my room, attempting to gather my thoughts and emotions. My instructor then knocked on my door and explained to me that she had asked everyone's parents to write a letter to their son or daughter before we went on the retreat. She then left me alone to sort out my feelings.

After rereading those initial statements, I continued reading the rest of the letter. My mom and dad wrote that they loved me, although it didn't always seem like it and that they needed me in their lives. Their honesty made me think about our relationship, and I began to realize the role I played in instigating the arguments and our lack of communication. In reality, everyone contributed. And now it was time for all of us to work toward a better relationship.

My family was calmer when I returned home from the retreat, and my parents and I had a newfound respect for each other. We still have the occasional run-ins, but they're not like they used to be. There are no more cold stares or hurtful shouting matches. Even though my parents and I cannot change the past and the sixteen years lost to incessant bickering, each day we slowly learn how to communicate as a family, ensuring that another sixteen years won't be lost as well.

~Kristin Sester
Chicken Soup for the Teenage Soul II

Lessons from a Teenager

You cannot do a kindness too soon,
for you never know how soon it will be too late.
~Ralph Waldo Emerson

My dad retired young because of heart problems. To help fill the time, he volunteered at my high school as a hall monitor. He had been doing it for a few years before I entered into ninth grade. I told him I didn't want him to stay there my freshman year. I kind of wanted to go through the school year without having to be known as a daddy's girl because his volunteering there meant seeing him every day before lunch. On the inside I was praying he would ignore everything I said and go anyway because I was a nervous wreck about going into high school.

I liked it when he was there because it kind of made me feel safe knowing he was going to be in the school if I needed him. I was a freshman and not used to the idea of high school yet. He waited outside the cafeteria when he knew I would be going to lunch. We exchanged smiles, once in a while a wave. On rare occasions we actually talked for a few minutes before I caught up with my friends for lunch.

Although in school I acted as though I barely knew him, I loved being known as his daughter.

"Courtney Soucy?" said my art teacher, taking attendance.

"Right here," I answered.

"Any relation to Wayne?" This caught me by surprise because

although my dad had been at the school for a few years, he wasn't actually part of the staff, just a volunteer.

Through my first week as a freshman, almost every one of my teachers asked if I was Wayne's daughter. When I said yes, they usually replied with something along the lines of, "You'll be a pleasure to have in class; your dad's such a nice guy."

I never met any teacher, let alone any person, who said they didn't like my dad. He was very funny and always had a smile on his face. He was the life of every party we went to, always cracking everybody up with his witty remarks and corny jokes. His light blue eyes reflected his cheerful nature—he was never grim or gloomy.

People in our small town referred to him as "the mayor" because on walks around our neighborhood, he made at least ten stops to talk to people. When someone needed a place for their kid to stay while they ran a few errands, my dad volunteered to be the babysitter. In the summertime, our pool became the community pool with my dad as the lifeguard. He was surrounded by screaming kids all day, but he loved every minute of it. My friends soon became my dad's friends; he was such a lovable guy.

I don't remember any specific time when I just came out and told my dad I loved him. Sometimes we'd get into stupid fights about why I couldn't spend the night at Chelsea's, or why I couldn't go to the movies with Kelsey. Even though there was a lot of screaming and yelling, the disagreements never lasted very long.

One night, I stormed up the stairs to my bedroom. "Dad, you're a jerk, and I hate you!" Just another fight, I thought as I cried myself to sleep.

The next day I got myself ready, not even thinking about our fight the night before. Come to think of it, I don't even remember what the fight was about. We always forgot about our arguments because they were pretty meaningless. This fight appeared meaningless, too, until around 4:30 that afternoon.

I had a softball game at 4:00. We warmed up as usual. My dad and sisters, Brianna and Angela, showed up a little early, ready to watch the game. My mom rarely got out of work in time to see my games, but Dad was always there to watch. About five minutes into the game, I heard my mom screaming for a cell phone. She'd gotten out early, only to find Dad unconscious on the side of the field.

The paramedics rushed Dad to the hospital in an ambulance. Mom and I followed them in a police car, holding hands and praying all the way. Ten minutes later, Dad was pronounced dead from a second heart attack.

It was the worst day of my life. I'm sure many people have said that on occasion when they have a bad hair day, when they forget to do their homework, sure it's a rough day. But I've had those days before, and they didn't compare to what May 6th was for me. My mind wandered, nervously thinking about the past weekend, what had gone on, what I did with Dad, trying hard to remember his last few days. My thoughts were blank until tears cascaded endlessly down my cheeks, remembering what my last words were to him: "I hate you." I hadn't realized until then how much I didn't mean that.

People live each day knowing there's always going to be tomorrow to make up for today's mistakes. I thought the same thing. Never did it cross my mind that I would get into another stupid fight and then never get the chance to apologize to my dad.

I'm not writing this for sympathy, because I have enough of that. I'm writing this as a warning to others who still have their dads. It's hard growing up as a young girl with a "crazy" dad. It can be fun at times, and terribly embarrassing at others. Nevertheless, cherish the times you spend with your fathers. There's a small chance that tomorrow won't come. That you won't get that chance to say your "sorrys," your "goodbyes" or your "remember the time whens." Don't disregard this and think that it will never happen to you. I thought the same thing—and it did happen.

Please make it so it isn't too late to say "I love you" to your dad, your mom, your friends, your family; make it so they all know you love them. The world will be a better place when you do.

~Courtney Soucy
Chicken Soup for the Father & Daughter Soul

43

Wise Guy

*Pretty much all the honest truth-telling
there is in the world is done by children.*
~Oliver Wendell Holmes

When I was thirteen, I found out that Jesus was not born on Christmas day. Billy Hollister, who was always reading history, told me that.

When I argued with him to the point of rage, he made me go into his house where he had a lot of books and look it up. Historians said that Jesus was born in the early spring, probably March, because that's when the Romans collected taxes and that's when his parents would have had to return to their native city to pay them. Billy Hollister's book said that their native city was not Bethlehem at all, but probably Nazareth.

All of this confused me and made me sad in a way I can't explain. I liked the idea of Jesus being born in Bethlehem and in the winter, when it was cold and dark and everyone needed some good tidings of great joy. The spring just seemed wrong somehow.

I kept this information to myself until the Christmas when I was fourteen and Aunty Dan came to visit. Aunty Dan came to live with us for a while each winter because she was getting on and her own house was fast becoming a chore for a woman living alone. My mother, who loved her very much, wanted her to stay with us permanently, but Aunty Dan would not hear of it.

She always arrived looking very tidy. Beneath her small black felt hat, her white hair was braided and coiled in a bun at the back of her neck. She carried a very small black suitcase, worn at the handle, and always wore a dark blue dress with a white collar and her best black Chesterfield coat when she came for a visit. She had a very big laugh for such a little woman and liked to play word games.

One night at supper she reminded us all that it was about to be the birthday of Jesus Christ. "I think we should remember that when we give each other gifts," she said.

I missed her point completely—presents were important to me, after all. Besides, I wanted to show off my knowledge of history. So I told her that December 25th was not the birthday of the Lord. Everyone looked up at me as though I'd crawled out from under a rock.

Aunty Dan lowered her eyes for a moment, fussed with her napkin and then looked at me with an expression of such sorrow that I wished I had kept my ideas to myself.

We were all sort of subdued that evening, and I went to bed early to think about things. After my parents came to kiss me good night, I read for a while by the light of my flashlight. Just as I was about to drift into sleep, my door opened and Aunty Dan came into my room and sat on the edge of my bed.

"You have a lovely and inquisitive mind, darlin'."

I don't know what I expected her to say, but certainly not that. I thought I was due for a lecture of some sort. What she said to me really got my attention.

"I've been thinking about the question you brought up about Jesus' birth. You know, there are several months in which scholars believe that holy day could have happened. Many think he was born on January 6th, in fact." She patted my hand with hers. Her fingers felt soft and very warm.

That she knew such things astonished me. I figured she just accepted what everyone believed because it was the thing to do.

"The truth is that it doesn't matter one bit. It only matters that he came to us. And the only important thing about that wonderful moment is that it divided time forever. There is the time before he came to teach, which was a brutal and forlorn world, and the time after, when he showed all mankind by his love that it was possible to live in grace and light and goodness of spirit. For most of the world, time itself has been divided ever since. Now we speak of the time before Christ's birth and the time after he came. I think that is a mighty accomplishment, don't you?"

I started to stammer out something, an objection maybe. Then she said, "Time and dates have nothing to do with important things like love and truth and compassion. You know that in your heart; I am sure you do. That is the message to remember, and it hardly matters on what day you remember it."

And with that, she folded my hands into hers, kissed me on the forehead and left the room so quietly I did not even hear the door close.

~Walker Meade
Chicken Soup for the Christian Teenage Soul

Growing Up

*The turning point in the process of growing up
is when you discover the core of strength within you
that survives all hurt.*
~Max Lerner

44

Choices

When I first met Molly, she instantly became my best friend. We enjoyed the same things, laughed at the same jokes and even had the same love for sunflowers.

It seemed like we had found each other at the right time. Both of us had been in different groups of friends that didn't get along or we didn't feel comfortable in. We were thrilled to find each other.

Our friendship grew very strong. Our families became friends, and everyone knew that wherever you found Molly, you found me, and vice versa. In fifth grade, we were not in the same class, but at lunch we both sat in nearby assigned seats and turned around to talk to each other. The lunch ladies did not like this. We were always blocking the aisle, talking too loudly and not eating our lunches, but we didn't care. The teachers knew we were best friends, but we were also a disturbance. Our big mouths got us into trouble, and we were warned that we would never be in the same classes again if we kept this up.

That summer, Molly and her brother were at my house quite often. My mom took care of them while their mom worked. We went swimming, played outside and practiced playing our flutes. We bought best-friend charms and made sure to wear them as often as possible.

Summer went by very quickly, and middle school began. As the teachers had warned us, we were not in the same classes. We still talked on the phone, went over to each other's houses, sang in choir and practiced our flutes together in band. Nothing could destroy this friendship.

Seventh grade started and, again, we were not in the same classes and could not sit near each other at lunch. It seemed as if we were being put to a test. We both made new friends. Molly started to hang out with a new group of people and was growing very popular.

We spent less time together, and we rarely talked on the phone. At school, I would try to talk to her, but she would just ignore me. When we did take a minute to talk, one of her more popular friends would come up and Molly would just walk away with her, leaving me in the dust. It hurt.

I was so confused. I'm sure she didn't know at the time how badly I felt, but how could I talk to her if she wouldn't listen? I began to hang around with my new friends, but it just wasn't the same. I met Erin, who was also a friend of Molly's. She was in the same situation I was with Molly. She and Molly had been close friends, and lately Molly had been treating Erin the same way as me. We decided to talk to her.

The phone call was not easy. Talking and saying how I felt was difficult. I was so afraid that I would hurt her feelings and make her angry. It was funny, though—when it was just the two of us talking on the phone, we were friends again. It was the old Molly.

I explained how I was feeling, and she did, too. I realized I was not the only one hurting. She was alone without me to talk to. What was she supposed to do, not make new friends? I didn't think about this before, but she was feeling left out by me and my new friends. There were times when I didn't even notice I was ignoring her. We must have talked for a long time, because once we were finished I had used a handful of tissues for my tears, and felt as if I had lifted a heavy weight off my heart. We both decided that we wanted to be with our new friends, but we would never forget the fun and friendship we had shared with each other.

Today, I look back on all of this and smile. Molly and I are finally in the same classes, and you know what? We still get in trouble for talking too loudly. Molly is not my best friend anymore, but more like my sister. We still enjoy the same things, laugh at the same jokes and share the same love for sunflowers. I will never forget her. Molly taught me something very important. She taught me that things change, people change, and it doesn't mean you forget the past or try to cover it up. It simply means that you move on, and treasure all the memories.

~Alicia M. Boxler
Chicken Soup for the Teenage Soul II

45

Inner Sustenance

A ll I ever wanted was to be popular. Have the coolest friends. Be in a hot rock band and date the best-looking men — simple wishes for a young girl. Some of my dreams even came true. I started a rock band. And the cutest guy at Melbourne High School even asked me out.

I answered yes of course, but within a week, he complained, "Your hips are too big. You need to lose weight to look thin like the other girls in your band."

Immediately, I tried several different diets to lose weight. For one, I ate grapefruit and vegetables only. That didn't work; I felt faint and had to eat. The second week I tried skipping breakfast and dinner. When I did that, I became so hungry by the time dinner came, I splurged and eventually started gaining weight. I added ten pounds in a month trying to please my boyfriend. Instead of praising my efforts, he cut me down even more. "You look like a whale," he said, making me feel less pretty than my other friends who wanted to date him. I felt self-conscious and didn't want to lose him as a boyfriend, so I desperately searched for another way to lose the pounds that were keeping him at bay.

I didn't even think that he was the problem: just me, it was just me. Whatever I ate made me fatter. Whatever I wore, I looked hideous. I was now 110 pounds, a complete blimp!

One evening after a date, he made me so angry with his "whale" remarks that I ate an enormous piece of cake. The guilt made me want to try something I had seen other girls in my school doing at lunch break: throw up. I went to my bathroom and without even thinking of the consequences, stuck my finger down my throat and threw up in the toilet.

All I ever wanted was to be as pretty as a model. I wanted my boyfriend to look at me the same way as he did those bikini-poster girls.

It was so easy. That cake I just enjoyed didn't cost me any unwanted calories.

Once a day soon turned into three forced vomits. Becoming malnourished, I was constantly hungry, so I ate more and threw up more. It wasn't until I strangely gained another fifteen pounds and tried to quit a month later that I realized I couldn't stop. I fought to, for several weeks. As soon as I got up from the table, my stomach began convulsing. Now my own stomach somehow believed that was what it was supposed to do. I had to run from the table. I was throwing up without even sticking my finger down my throat or even wanting to!

I wasn't in control anymore. I was caught in a whirlwind. I thought bulimia would help me lose pounds, but after several months, it had failed to control my weight and the purging had opened up the pits of hell.

I needed help. My boyfriend's comments and my weight were the least of my problems now and I knew it. At age fifteen, I didn't know what to do. Desperate for a solution, I broke down into tears and confided in the only person I could trust: my mom. Unsure of how she would react and wondering if she'd stop loving me if she knew, I mustered up the courage to write the truth on a note and leave it on her dresser:

"Mom, I'm sick. I tried forcing myself to throw up to lose weight. Now I am vomiting every day. I can't stop. I'm afraid I'm going to die."

I locked myself in my room the entire night. My mother knocked on my door several times. I could hear her crying. The next morning she pounded harder and told me she had made a doctor's appointment for me. "Get out here before we're late!" she said.

I opened the door. Instead of a hard and loud scolding, I received a hug. Being in her understanding arms, I had the confidence to go to the doctor with her.

I'll never forget that first meeting with the doctor. He told me that by using bulimia to lose weight, I was actually retaining water, losing hair, ruining the enamel on my teeth and was now developing a very serious stomach condition called gastritis. He informed me I was malnourished and in danger of losing my life. He strongly recommended that I check myself into a hospital for treatment.

Knowing that I would be apart from my friends and my mother, I didn't want to agree. Going to the hospital seemed to be a way of walking away from everything I've ever known. I was terrified about leaving home. I'd never been away from my house, my school or my friends before. I was wondering if anyone would even stay my friend or if they all would think I was a freak. I thought about telling the doctor I wouldn't even consider it, but my conscience reminded me: If I don't go, I'll be spending the rest of my days (however many more I have left) throwing my life away, literally down the toilet. I told the doctor I would go.

The first day and night were the hardest. Nurses gave me a study schedule for both educational and counseling activities. I would attend six different classes each day: math, English, science, group counseling, PE and a personal session with my doctor. All the people were complete strangers. Most of the patients my age weren't there for eating disorders but for severe mental illnesses or violent behaviors. In my first class, math, I sat down and said hello to the girl sitting next to me. She turned her head and ignored me. I shifted in my chair and waved to the girl on my left and asked what her problem was. She didn't answer and mumbled something about needing medicine. I quickly learned that the other patients were hard to relate to or on heavy medication. They didn't seem to have any desire to make friends. That night, I cried myself to sleep, feeling more alone than I ever had.

The next morning, I was told that my blood work revealed that I was not only dehydrated but also starving. The doctor said he wouldn't release me until I was strong inside and out. Months passed like this and I continued attending classes with screaming, irrational kids. I felt so isolated. The doctors tried several types of medicines; none of them seemed to be working to keep my food down. They started feeding me intravenously. A needle was stuck in the top of my hand and stayed there, taped, twenty-four hours a day. It was so gross, having a big needle sticking out in my hand. Every morning they would attach a liquid-filled bag that dripped nutrients into my bloodstream. Each night they gave me pills that made me nauseous. I was becoming more and more discouraged. "Will I ever be normal again?" I wondered. Still, I wouldn't give up. I knew what I had to do and I tried yet another medication.

When that didn't seem to do anything, a nurse came into my room, took that morning's medication out of my hand and suggested that I stand in front of the mirror one hour after each meal and repeat to myself these words, "Yes, I am perfect because God made me."

I thought she was nuts! If modern medicine couldn't work, how could saying a few words do the trick? Still, I knew I had to try it. It couldn't hurt and if it got me off the feeding tube, it was worth it no matter how crazy it sounded. Beside, if it didn't work, I could tell the nurse that it wasn't the cure and that at least I tried.

The next meal, I said the words for several minutes. Religiously. I said them for an entire week, extending the time every day. After a while, I realized that since I'd been saying them as if I meant them, I had been keeping my food down. I was getting my bulimia under control because my mind stopped focusing on throwing up, and started focusing on saying those words! Within a week I stopped needing to be fed through tubes, my stomach had stopped rejecting food and my compulsion to vomit ceased. My mind had been tricked into more positive thinking!

With the support of my counselors and nurses, I continued searching for ways to bolster my self-esteem, so that I would never again be so vulnerable to the judgment of others. I began to read self-esteem books and the Bible to further my self-image. By then, my boyfriend had dumped me. Most of my friends had stopped coming to see me. Even on the day I celebrated my newfound ability to keep my food down, I called my brother to tell him the good news and he said, "You're making all this up for attention, aren't you?"

I can't tell you how much that hurt. Still, I wouldn't let the outside world's cruelty diminish my victory or my newly found self-esteem no matter what my weight was. Finally, I realized with this new strength, I was well.

I began feeding myself and choosing to be full—literally, spiritually, emotionally and physically. My self-esteem strengthened as I ate, repeated those words, and learned to love myself. By gulping down food, I became the vessel God had created me to be. I was special regardless of what others thought. And I saw that old boyfriend for what he really was: shallow, close-minded, inconsiderate, and not even worthy of my love in the first place.

It had taken months in the hospital with nurses and counseling to learn a lesson I'll never forget. Being popular is just an illusion. If you love yourself, you are in the "in" crowd. You are an individual gift from God to the world. It's comforting to know joy comes from being who I am instead of trying to become somebody else's perfect model.

My first day back to school, my ex-boyfriend actually came up to me and asked me out again. "Wow, you look great. You're so thin! You want to go to the football game on Friday?"

"No," I answered, without regret. "I'd rather date someone who loves my heart."

Me! Accepting me suddenly became a daily celebration of life. I love me! Those three words sound so simple, but living them, believing them makes living so tantalizingly delicious!

~Michele Wallace Campanelli
Chicken Soup for the Teenage Soul III

46

Sweet-and-Sour Sixteen

Then I did the simplest thing in the world. I leaned down... and kissed her.
And the world cracked open.
~Agnes de Mille

I was fifteen, soon to turn sixteen, and I felt pressured. I had never been kissed. I was certain I had to be one of the most backward, late-blooming teenagers there was, carrying around this terrible secret that might reveal itself at any moment—if I ever got a date.

My only consolation was that my best friend, Carol, was in the same predicament. She, too, feared the label "sweet sixteen and never been kissed."

We spent that summer plotting ways to absolve ourselves by meeting guys and getting dates. We even went so far as to sign ourselves up for corn detasseling. For three hot, sweaty weeks in humid Iowa, we walked up and down cornfields with a busload of teenagers, mostly guys, and picked corn. There were water fights, romps through the fields, heady compliments and serious flirtations—but no dates.

Carol had her sights set on one promising candidate (he was at her side constantly), but when the last day of work came, he still had not asked her out. I think it was sheer frustration that drove her to tell him that she would be sixteen in two months and had never been kissed.

"You haven't?" he asked. "That's great! If you can go another two months without a kiss, you'll be sweet sixteen, not sour sixteen!"

So much for that candidate.

By the end of the summer, we had pretty much given up on our quest. We went out for pizza with a group of girls in another town. We were sitting there laughing and having a good time when two of the girls noticed a group of guys at a nearby table. Before long, all the other girls had joined in and it was a full-on flirting party.

Carol and I became annoyed. Sure, the guys were cute. Sure, they were looking at us, but this was our last night of the summer! We weren't about to waste it on a group of guys who might send all kinds of positive signals then never make it to our table. We stomped outside to the parking lot to talk in peace. The guys followed us and asked if we knew the time.

They were even cuter close up. I tried not to stare at the one with dark, wavy hair and hazel eyes, but my eyes kept wandering back to him. His name was Cody.

The other girls soon joined us, and we talked with the guys as late as our curfews would allow. They arranged to meet us the next night at a park.

Somehow, the next night, we ended up paired off as couples. I found myself with Cody. He and I walked over to a monument in the park and sat down on it. Suddenly, anxiety overcame me. I realized that I was about to receive my first kiss, and I simply wasn't ready for it. I burst into tears. Cody put his arm around me and asked what was wrong. I blurted out the whole tragic story of being sixteen and having never been kissed. Then, realizing how lame this must have sounded, I went for broke. I blurted out every negative thing that had ever happened in my life. By the time I was done, I was convinced he must have thought I was a total nutcase.

He looked at me for a few moments from under those long, dark eyelashes, then slowly brushed his lips against mine. The kiss was soft, quick and moist. I was just glad when it was over—and that I was away from home. No one needed to know the embarrassment I had just put myself through. I never bothered to tell him how he could reach me again, and he never asked.

The next day, the phone rang and my mom answered. "It's for

you," she said, a startled look in her eyes. As I walked over she whispered, "It's a boy!"

My heart went crazy. I managed to mumble a hello, and a male voice started talking. Cody! I felt as if my heart might burst out of my chest. Mom stared at me. I stared back. This was the first time that a boy who I cared about had called me.

I asked how he had gotten my number. He told me my girlfriend had given it to him and asked if I wanted to go out with him that weekend. He told me my girlfriend and his friend would be coming with us. "Would you like to go out with them?" he asked.

I'm not sure how I responded, but I know I accepted. I also said, "I never expected to hear from you again."

"Why not?" he asked.

"Well, after last night..."

"After last night, I think you're the sweetest girl I ever met," he said. There was a pause, then he added, "Someone has to sour you."

~Ronica Stromberg
Chicken Soup for the Teenage Soul on Love & Friendship

Dear Child —
A Sister's Message

Train a child in the way he should go,
and when he is old he will not turn from it.
~Proverbs 22:6

Today I look into your tender young face. You're all of eleven years old, and I shudder at that thought. Perhaps I am trying to relive my adolescence through you and I recall how tough that age was for me. It was about the time Mom and Dad divorced, the year I had my first real crush and the beginning of junior high — three hard-hitting blows to a confused, awkward kid. That is possibly why I want to write a letter that could somehow condense all my experiences and all my sufferings in one neat page, for you to look at and say, "my mistakes — never!" You see, my experiences weren't unusual or extraordinary, but at the time they took place, I felt as if the world would sooner swallow me whole than allow me to overcome it with some sense of self intact.

So, somehow, I want to call upon that girl I once was and ask her to help me find the words that will give you the armor, that will make all the cruel insults you will surely encounter simply roll off your back. I want to find the potion that will make you see how extraordinary you are so that when that first heartbreak comes along, although you may doubt the love of others, you will never once doubt the love you hold for yourself. I want to make you aware of the beauty that is woman, so that you will always be proud and bold, never flinching in the eye of a man, or most likely a boy, who will try with all his might to convince you that you have a lesser place in the world.

I want to show you how to adore this temple in which you house your mind and soul, always respect it and treat it as the jewel that is you. Remember, dear child, that whomever you allow near this temple, this possession that is solely yours, is completely your choice. No amount of convincing or begging could ever change that. Don't allow your heart—the treasure box that holds dreams and secret wishes—to become a house for fear. Fear will consume you; it will beckon you to keep from shining, to step down for the light on the horizon. Don't hesitate, not even for a moment, because in that moment you may be draining the life of your spirit. Instead, walk with firm, steady steps into the glare of failure and humiliation, two of your greatest foes—believe me, they are no match.

Friends will test your best judgment. You will ask yourself if you chose wisely, or perhaps you will not choose carefully enough and, desperate not to walk alone, you will allow yourself to be surrounded by meaningless acquaintances, who have little interest in your true self. These friendships could at times prove to be soul-killing and exhausting, and although this may seem out of touch right now, I want you to know that at times there is more dignity in marching alone. Loneliness is what you will feel if you build your friendships on longings of being mirrored by visions of your self.

There will always be those that are different from you, in aspects ranging from ethnic background to physical challenges. I wonder "will she be gracious and kind, an angel cloaked in a child's disguise, or will she be cruel and sharp with a tongue solely shaped to stab at the heart?" Who will you be, sister? Will those around you regard you as boring and snotty for not wanting to partake in the spirit-bashing of those unaccepted souls? Or will you be a leader of such tragic slander? Although you may be cast out for any goodness you exhibit, will you have the commanding strength to remain true to what you've been taught? True to yourself?

Dear child, I know this is huge and unsettling, and perhaps too much to digest at this place and time, but will you tuck this away in a safe, unrelenting place so that its presence will always peer into your conscience? Perhaps you will have a question someday and you will remember these words, my words, which today seem unfitting, uncompromising. I don't think I've covered every possible adolescent terror that you will be struck with, but I can't possibly anticipate all the life that will come your way. What I can say is that you will survive, but not without scars in the most unimaginable place—your heart. Wear them like a badge of courage once you have survived this battle referred to as "growing up." You will be all the wiser, dear child—I know I am.

~Danette Julene Gomez
Chicken Soup for the Teenage Soul III

My Secret in Silence

You came into my life
Quietly, simply, placidly
And my words stood still.

I couldn't express in words
Or even in simple gestures
The secret I kept in my heart.

So I loved in silence,
Admired you from a distance,
Dreamt of you from afar.

I wanted to say I love you....
I wanted to say I care.
But cowardly, maybe, you'll only laugh at me.

In silence then I will love you....
In silence then I will care....

~Lorelei Pablo
Chicken Soup for the Teenage Soul on Love & Friendship

The Importance of Conscience

Be careful how you interpret the world: It is like that.
~Erich Heller

I was faced with a decision. While delivering laundry into the appropriate bedrooms, I stumbled upon my thirteen-year-old sister's diary, a modern-day Pandora's box, suffused with temptation. What was I to do? I had always been jealous of my little sister. Her charming smile, endearing personality and many talents threatened my place as leading lady. I competed with her tacitly and grew to resent her natural abilities. I felt it necessary to shatter her shadow with achievements of my own. As a result, we seldom spoke. I sought opportunities to criticize her and relished surpassing her achievements.

Her diary lay at my feet, and I didn't think about the consequences of opening it. I considered not her privacy, the morality of my actions, nor her consequential pain. I merely savored the possibility of digging up enough dirt to soil my competitor's spotless record. I reasoned my iniquity as sisterly duty. It was my responsibility to keep a check on her activities. It would be wrong of me not to.

I tentatively plucked the book from the floor and opened it, fanning through the pages, searching for my name, convinced that I would discover scheming and slander. As I read, the blood ran from my face. It was worse than I suspected. I felt faint and slouched to the floor. There was neither conspiracy nor defamation. There was a succinct description of herself, her goals and her dreams followed by a short portrayal of the person who has inspired her most. I started to cry.

I was her hero. She admired me for my personality, my achievements and, ironically, my integrity. She wanted to be like me. She had been watching me for years, quietly marveling over my choices and actions. I ceased reading, struck with the crime I had committed. I had expended so much energy into pushing her away that I had missed out on her.

I had wasted years resenting someone capable of magic—and now I had violated her trust. It was I who had lost something beautiful, and it was I who would never allow myself to do such a thing again.

Reading the earnest words my sister had written seemed to melt an icy barrier around my heart, and I longed to know her again. I was finally able to put aside the petty insecurity that kept me from her. On that fateful afternoon, as I put aside the laundry and rose to my feet, I decided to go to her—this time to experience instead of to judge, to embrace instead of to fight. After all, she was my sister.

~Elisha M. Webster
Chicken Soup for the Sister's Soul

Desperate to Fit In

I'm not exactly sure when I realized my life was spinning out of control. I'd grown up in a Christian family. I thought I had my act together—until I hit high school. That's when things started happening, things that led to some major changes in my life—and some bad decisions on my part.

First, we started building a new house, and the only time we could work on it was on weekends. We stopped going to church regularly. Eventually, we spent less and less time praying and reading the Bible.

Second, my best friend moved away the summer before I started ninth grade. I felt really lost and alone, so when school started that fall, I was desperate for some new friends. And it was that desperation—my intense desire to "fit in" with the right group—that ultimately led me down the path of self-destruction.

I met Kathy during the first week of ninth grade. She was one of the most popular students, so when she befriended me, I was pretty excited. I'd never been part of the "in" group before.

It wasn't long before Kathy invited me to spend the night with her at another friend's house. But that night turned out to be much more than I'd expected. It was a major party, with lots of alcohol.

I'd never been to anything like that before. And before the night was over, I started feeling excited about everything—the sense of freedom, of having no limits, of trying something new and grown-up.

I didn't get drunk that night, but a pattern had begun. Before long, I was partying and getting drunk every weekend. I was staying out later and later. And since our house was still under construction, we didn't have a phone. So I would stay out as late as I wanted, then I'd lie about where I'd been. What could my folks do? They couldn't say, "Well, you should have called."

By that time, I wanted to be as thin as the other girls in my group of friends. So I started forcing myself to throw up after meals. In fact, I became so obsessed with my weight that when I was at a party, I'd drink until I'd get sick and throw up, just so those calories wouldn't be in my body.

And then there was shoplifting. Since it was a part of the "fun" my friends were into, I felt I had to join in, too. I enjoyed the thrill of getting away with it. At first, I mostly took small things that didn't cost much. But soon, I was taking clothes and other expensive items.

So there I was, a freshman in high school, a common thief with a drinking problem and an eating disorder. And all because I wanted so badly to "fit in."

As much as I loved being part of the in-crowd, I knew my life was out of control. I wanted things to change, but I couldn't do it on my own. If I said I wanted to change, my friends would immediately dump me. But secretly, I wanted to get caught. I felt that would be my only way out.

Then it happened.

First, my folks found the wine bottle. My mom and I were up all night yelling and fighting.

Then I got caught shoplifting. The cops came and took me away in the squad car. I had to call my parents to come and get me at the police station. The ride home was awful. My mom and dad sat together in the front seat, holding hands and crying. I sat by the window, staring outside, not believing what had just happened.

How could this be? I felt so ashamed.

Shortly after that, one of my friends caught me throwing up. She called my parents to tell them. Even though I was angry at my friend for squealing on me, it was the best thing anyone did for me. My mom confronted me, and we really had it out that night. At that point, my mom realized my problems weren't going to go away on their own, and that I was really putting myself in danger.

My mom made an appointment for me to see a counselor, and I thought it was a good idea. Those counseling sessions helped a lot. We talked about the drinking, the stealing, the bulimia, my friends, how I was feeling and what I wanted my life to be like.

I later learned how much my folks had worried about me and loved me through all the garbage I was doing. I found out my dad had been getting up at four o'clock every morning to pray for me. I cried when I heard that.

I knew I needed to make some changes in my life. I wanted to stop the drinking and throwing up and stealing because I was scared for my health and safety.

Also, I wanted to stop living a lie. I'd been lying to my parents all along. I'd been lying to my friends about what kind of person I was. And I'd been lying to myself about what was important to me. I was ashamed of the way I'd been living, and I knew it wasn't what God wanted for my life.

I had some big fears about changing, though. I knew I'd have to find some new friends who wouldn't pressure me to act a certain way. I was so afraid I'd end up with no friends at all. But God was already working on that. Within a short time, I met a group of girls who accepted me and cared about me for who I was. They also shared my Christian values, so I was free to be myself.

A couple years have gone by. I'm not interested in the party scene anymore. My shoplifting days ended after that run-in with the police. And after a lot of counseling, I'm no longer fighting my eating disorder—although I still struggle with how I feel about my body.

I'm so much happier now. I'm hanging with a good group of friends, people who love me for who I am—not for somebody I'm pretending to be. And even though I care and worry about my old friends, I've decided not to spend time with them. I've learned the hard way that I can't handle it very well.

When I last saw my old friends, one of them asked me, "What

happened to you? You used to be so much fun at parties, but we never see you anymore. You should hang out with us again."

I just smiled and said, "No, thanks. I'm much happier now."

~Colleen Holmes as told to Jake Swanson
Chicken Soup for the Christian Teenage Soul

51

My Sister's First Love

Dear *Chicken Soup for the Teenage Soul*,

I am sending you a story my sister wrote for your consideration for a *Chicken Soup for the Soul* book. My sister, Jodi, underwent a very emotional, psychological and spiritual struggle as she dealt with the fact that her long-term boyfriend, Tim, was dying from an inoperable brain tumor. She helped Tim fight his cancer in every way imaginable, but unfortunately on Valentine's Day in 1997, Jodi sat by Tim's side as he took his last breath.

Although her story is tragic, she was able to gain a whole new outlook on the meaning of life and death. She wrote this story about her experience, and it touched me deeply. The power of her words is simply breathtaking, and I wanted to share them with you, and, hopefully, others, as well.

Sincerely,

~Kristi Vesterby

Immortal

His dizziness and headaches began during the summer; they worried me a little, but I never thought they would amount to anything serious. I look back now and wonder if he knew they were signs of what was to come. Tim and I had been dating for over a year; we'd become best friends. We were in that phase of our lives when we thought nothing could go wrong. We were going to be together forever and live our perfect high-school-sweetheart love story with a white picket fence and all. When his symptoms persisted, I think we both knew that something was wrong, but I never could have imagined just how wrong.

By basketball season, things were considerably worse. It was his junior year, and Tim had hoped he would finally be starting on the varsity team. I would sit in the stands and cheer with the rest of my friends, but inside I was constantly wondering who this impostor was that was taking over Tim's body. He bobbled the ball as he'd dribble up the court, or tip over on the backs of his heels while attempting to play defense. His frustration increased with each day of practice, so when his mother, Ann, suggested he see a doctor, Tim agreed. The local clinic scheduled an appointment for him to have a scan of his brain the next time the "MRI-Mobile" came to Olivia, our small, unequipped town. The scan later showed a tumor growing on the base of Tim's brain, and from then on our lives were never the same.

We all sat crammed in an incredibly small room they called a doctor's office, waiting for the arrival of some overly busy neuro-oncologist. He was going to interpret the complicated X-rays that were beyond the capability of the doctors at Prairie Family Practice. This room was as close to hell as I've ever been, and without even knowing what was ahead of me, it was difficult to find a way to pass the time. None of us wanted to think about why we were there, so we mostly occupied the passing minutes with the idle talk of basketball and history class. The oncologist finally graced us with his presence as he walked into our crowded room. He introduced himself and started discussing what we already knew from the scans. Tim had a tumor invading his brain stem. He went on to say that it was inoperable, which meant very little to me at the time. As he went into medical jargon, his words became mere background noise as I turned my attention toward Tim.

He sat in the chair directly across from me, listening to every word the doctor was saying. He was motionless; even his eyes seemed to be staring into a place that had somehow captured his whole being. Tim hated his eyes. He often joked about their "ugly" tint, which he called green-brown-yellow-orange. I always had to remind him that despite their lack of definite color, his eyes were one of his best features. They disclosed his every emotion. All I had to do was look at them and I could actually see his love for me. His eyes revealed his kindness, his cocky and somewhat rebellious nature, and, of course, his spark of determination. Now they were vacant.

Ann, Tim's mother, asked a question, and I was thrown back into the conversation at hand. Dr. So-and-So answered by discussing the options that could be attempted to shrink the tumor. I wondered why none of his so-called options sounded promising. As this thought meandered through my mind, his mother, with a voice that attempted to hide the quivering, asked how long Tim was expected to live. Her words snuck up from behind me and grabbed my throat. I looked at her as though she was a murderer with no conscience. How could she ask such a question? Tim was not going to die, and she had no right to even suggest that he might. In a detached voice void of all emotion the doctor said, "One year to eighteen months with treatment."

As he spoke these words, the grip around my neck tightened to the point of choking me. I struggled for a breath, and the already tiny room closed even more. I needed space, and the first thought that crossed my mind was to run, not only from the room, but from the whole situation. I could escape now before I got hurt. I was confused and angry, but most of all I was consumed by the incredible fear of losing someone I loved so much.

I looked at Tim, who sat motionless; he didn't say anything and neither did anyone else. The room was filled with an uncomfortable silence, and I could feel the pulse of my heart pounding in my ears. I was sure that everyone could hear me sucking in each breath. I don't remember what the doctor said before he left the room—I couldn't even look at this man who had just sentenced Tim to death. When we were alone, Ann crossed the room and gave Tim a hug. The rest of us sat and cried. Tim looked up and with a smile said, "I'm not going anywhere." It was his declaration of war.

I was nervous, and I didn't know what I should do. I was just the girlfriend; I didn't know if I had any business being a part of this ordeal. As I was thinking that this was a time their family should be alone, Ann left Tim's side and he motioned for me to come over. I sat down on his knee and, wrapping my arms around his neck, rested my forehead against his. When I opened my eyes they met his, and I saw the emotion in them that had been missing up to that point. Water welled up on the brim of his lids, and finally a single tear fell, gliding down his cheek in slow motion.

Tim had always had the fighter attitude, and I believed him completely when he said he was going to beat the odds that were stacked against him. The battle was on. He was going to do everything he could in order to conquer the cancer threatening to overtake the life that he wasn't done living. His life became a quest to find a physical cure. He viewed it as a challenge he needed to overcome, and there was no doubt in his mind that he would do it.

His battle was viewed as courageous; he became a local hero. Why is it that people with terminal illness are so respected for fighting for a cure until the end? Do they even have a choice? The focus always lies in finding a physical remedy. Do everything and anything you can to battle the disease. What have you got to lose? Don't give up. Rarely do you find people looking for a type of healing that restores the soul. I guess that's just not good enough. Death meant failure, and that was unacceptable. So along with everything else, I encouraged Tim to stay strong and fight. I wanted him to do whatever he could to beat the cancer. I didn't realize that it didn't have to be a war. Nobody had to be the loser. I wish I had known that then.

He was bombarded by alternative healing options, some more "far out" than others, but all promising a miraculous cure. There was no way he could try all of them. Tim choked down over seventy pills a day: shark cartilage, herbal remedies, beta this and turbo that, each one offering a way to fight his growing tumor. He forced himself to drink glass after glass of carrot juice despite the thick texture, pungent odor and lingering aftertaste. He tried some positive-imagery techniques and then there was that magnetic contraption. The list goes on.

The traditional medical world was also involved in the battle, despite their lack of confidence in a cure. Surgery was out of the question because of the tumor's location, so the doctors suggested other treatment options. The Duke University brain tumor team provided a protocol that involved heavy doses of radiation therapy, shooting directly at the base of his brain stem two times a day for several months. The tumor shrunk by half, but it wasn't annihilated; in fact, it was fighting back. Eventually chemotherapy, a word that had quickly became as taboo as profanity in church, was attempted as a last resort. It didn't work.

I was included in Tim's battle against cancer in almost every way possible, and the Orth family always made me feel welcome. I went where Tim went. I don't know if his parents always approved (or mine for that matter), but as long as it kept Tim happy, they didn't complain. I went along on all the hospital visits. I went on family trips. I spent more time at their house than I should admit, but it was worth it. I rapidly evolved from my "just a girlfriend" status to member of their clan. I loved them, and still do.

Tim's health declined rapidly during the last months of his life. His former physique was reduced to a loose layer of skin covering his skeleton. It was difficult to keep him comfortable, and he spent most of his days hunched on the reclining sofa in his living room. I spent most of my days in the seat beside him watching him sleep. Sometimes the selfishness in me would overpower my good sense, and I would wake him from a peaceful sleep so that I could talk to him.

In a matter of months, I watched my boyfriend turn into an eighty-year-old man. He went blind, he couldn't walk, he couldn't remember, but he could still laugh. I experienced a crash course in Nursing 101, quickly learning all of the details involved in caring for someone who is terminally ill.

However, I soon realized that my most important "job responsibility" was to keep a smile on Tim's face. It's difficult to maintain dignity when you can't do anything for yourself. He had to cope with issues of aging as a teenager. He was nineteen years old and had to deal with the fact that his girlfriend had to help him go to the bathroom. I cracked jokes and teased him about silly things to lighten his mood. I basically treated him like I always had; I was the person who didn't minister to him like he was dying. I made him laugh. It was the only thing I could do to help in a seemingly helpless situation, but it wasn't enough. I wanted to help him be at peace, even though I wasn't.

One day after waking up from a regular afternoon nap, I noticed that Tim's eyes were focused in a dreamlike manner on something in the upper-right corner of the living room. He was mesmerized by what he was seeing, and the slight grin across his face suggested it was something awesome. It took me a few seconds to remember that Tim was blind because the tumor was slowly overtaking the optic nerve's space in his brain. I wondered what he could be looking at.

"Tim, what are you staring at?" I asked, though I wasn't sure I was ready to hear his answer.

"Just the light up there," he replied, continuing to stare ahead. The tears raced to my eyes, but I blinked to keep them from falling. I knew in my heart what he was seeing, but I wasn't satisfied with his vague answer. I wanted more.

"I can't see it. What is it like?" I asked.

"It's beautiful. You're not supposed to see it, though."

"Tell me about it," I probed with a combination of curiosity and fear. Tim didn't take his eyes off the spot in the corner of the room. He had several false starts before he was finally able to form the words he was searching for.

"I'm going up there... soon." The tears that had been welling in my eyes up to that point were released like floodgates. For the first time, I was grateful for Tim's blindness; I didn't want him to see me cry. I cleared my throat, in an attempt to get rid of the lump that had formed there, and took a deep breath, letting it out slowly to help me relax. This might be my last opportunity to talk to Tim about facing death, and I wasn't going to allow my emotions to let it slip away. I had so much I needed to tell him, for my own sake and for his. I wanted Tim to experience a peaceful death, and I did not want to be the one who was holding him back. I told him he could leave whenever he was ready. I explained that I would be okay after he left.

"I love you so much," I said, "and I am going to miss you more than you could possibly imagine. It will be so hard to live the rest of my life without you here, but I know that one day I'll see you again." Tim's attention was finally diverted from the heavenly focus. He reached over and held his hand out for me to hold. A smirk took over the peaceful expression that had been occupying his face and he let out a weak chuckle.

"That part is up to you," he said, completely amused with his insinuation that I had better be good while he was gone if I wanted to join him in eternity. He could never pass up a good smart remark. I laughed and cried. I felt a sense of relief. There was no way I could have said everything that needed to be said, and of course, everything didn't come out the way I intended it to. However, Tim and I were able to share an experience that offered us both a sense of closure. It was the closest to heaven that I have been in my lifetime, and I'll never forget it.

I left Tim's house on February 13th feeling disheartened. I always got a kiss from Tim before leaving; it was a custom I'd grown used to. He would sit with his eyes closed and his lips puckered, waiting for me to bend down and say good night. Tonight things were different. Tim had slipped into a coma-like state and was still incoherent as I prepared to leave. I bent down to kiss him goodbye, and his labored breathing was magnified. My lips touched his, and all hope for a response was lost. As I put on my coat and boots, I remembered that the next day was Valentine's Day. I had told him earlier that the best gift he could give me was for him to be at peace. As I closed the front door behind me, I wondered if he heard.

With a bunch of red and white balloons in hand, I entered the Orths' house the next morning. I knew he wouldn't be able to see the gift I'd brought, but I needed to bring something. Tim was lying lifeless in his high-tech hospice bed, but I could see his chest moving as he took each breath, and was relieved that he hadn't gone without me by his side. I spent the morning curled up next to him in his bed, holding his hand. Around 12:30, Tim took his last breath. I don't recall the exact moment he died; I only remember opening my eyes and he was gone. His mother proclaimed, "Oh, Tim, no more seizures, no more headaches. Now you can see. Now you can laugh. Now you can run. Now you can fly! We love you!"

I didn't have any profound words; I'm not good with goodbyes. I whispered, "See ya later."

Although Tim's life on earth ended on February 14, 1997, he continues to live on in so many other ways. Tim helped me to be the person that I am today. He taught me that the most important part of living is to find happiness in everything. I look back on all the memorable moments we shared together, and I recall his immortality. I remember all the fishless fishing trips. I remember eating popcorn and playing endless games of cribbage at my kitchen table. I remember cringing every time a song by Prince came on the radio because I knew he would sing along. I remember keeping my parents up all night with our outbursts of laughter, and I remember falling asleep on the couch listening to his heartbeat.

I know I will experience love again, but I will never find a replacement for what I had. Instead, I will take Tim with me as I continue to live my life. He will be with me when I graduate from college. He will be with me when my father walks me down the aisle at my wedding. He will be with me when I teach my first child to throw a softball. Eventually we will be together again when it's my time to leave this Earth.

~Jodi Vesterby
Chicken Soup for the Teenage Soul Letters

Miracles Great and Small

*Miracles are a retelling in small letters
of the very same story which is written across the whole world
in letters too large for some of us to see.*
~C.S. Lewis

52

Sadie Hawkins Day

I was squinting into the camcorder lens at a baseball game, our eight-year-old Vincent trotting past second base, when I noticed the limp. No one could have known, as Vincent began to favor one leg, that his strained gait was the first symptom of Fibrodysplasia Ossificans Progressiva (FOP), a rare genetic disorder that turns muscle into bone and leads, over time, to catastrophic immobility. No one could have known that FOP would go on to prevent our active son from combing his hair or tying his shoes. No one could have known, on that mild San Joaquin Valley afternoon, as I pointed my camera at a spring green schoolyard, that Vincent would have no more seasons of sports.

We have lived with FOP for six years now, always hoping for a cure, for scientific miracles at the University of Pennsylvania, the focal point for FOP research. But until a cure appears, we pray for an average teenage life for Vincent, who has traded sports for trigonometry and a trumpet. And though a sense of loss stays with him, with all of us, this loss throws the small miracles of life, its happy coincidences, into sharp relief.

Last year, Vincent was invited to his first Sadie Hawkins dance by Clemencia, a pretty freshman girl in band, with shy brown eyes. One cold, clear February night before the dance, Clemencia's family came by to take Vincent on a Sadie Hawkins shopping trip. Clemencia's parents, I discovered, were from Mexico, so we spent a good while rattling off in Spanish, and by the time I had to explain FOP precautions, the teenagers had tuned us out, sparing Vincent the embarrassment of my recitations. A few hours later, he and Clemencia returned from a trip to Old Navy, happily holding up matching khaki camouflage gear.

The Saturday morning of Sadie Hawkins, the phone rang. It was Leonor, Clemencia's mother, with distress in her voice: "My daughter wants to apologize," she said. Clemencia had the flu.

Vincent quietly hung up the phone and retreated to the family room computer. Our oldest son, Brian, was on his way to a friend's to have cornrows woven in his hair for the dance, and his younger brother Lucas was at a basketball game. While I was glad for our other sons, my throat tightened for Vincent.

But it was a sunny day, at least, a clear one in our normally white-skied valley, with the Sierra Nevada's dark rock suddenly visible, its snow shining like a grace. The day was so pretty that my husband, Walt, decided to cheer up our son with an outing.

"Come on, Vincent," he said. "We're going to the park to feed the ducks!"

"No, thanks," said Vincent, expressionless, at the computer screen.

"Come on!" called my husband, moving our eight-year-old daughter Celine and our four-year-old, Isabel, toward the garage with baggies of bread.

He extended the invitation again. Vincent refused again. Walt tried again. No answer. Almost out the door, my husband asked once more.

"Okay," said Vincent abruptly, "but I'm staying in the car."

We found a spot for the van on the park perimeter, and my husband, the girls and I walked down a grassy rise to the oily olive lake patrolled by ducks and geese. Vincent stayed in the car. Our daughters had just started flinging bread chunks at the bustling birds when a swarm of seagulls began to loop and dive furiously for every tossed crust, setting off a family laughing fit. "Vincent has to see this!" said Walt after a while, and he jogged back to the parking area.

From where I stood by the rocks of the lake, I could see Walt rap on the car window and Vincent swing out his legs stiffly from the passenger side. A pretty young Latina with long dark hair and wearing sweats was running past. She stopped.

I could tell by his posture that Vincent knew the girl, and I saw my husband discreetly leave our son and his friend in conversation. After a while, the girl jogged off, and Vincent appeared at the lakeside. His face was transformed, radiant: "I'm going to Sadie Hawkins!" he announced.

The young jogger Vincent had just seen by chance was a friend from school. She had asked him if he would be at the dance, and when he explained that his date was sick, she invited him to join her large group, which was meeting at a brand-new arcade restaurant, John's Incredible Pizza, for a pre-party.

Vincent wore his khaki camouflage pants to Sadie Hawkins, and that night, instead of a first awkward couple's pose, our son brought home a professional photo of himself in the center of a crowd of friends.

I should add that—of course—Vincent never goes to the park, which happens to be on the other end of the city from his Catholic high school, far from our house. And the friend who jogged by lives in another town. The high school itself is a freeway drive away from our home, so, with the exception of Sadie Hawkins Dance day, Vincent has never coincidentally run into any classmates—many of whom live in different or distant San Joaquin Valley towns.

I said to my husband on that afternoon at the park that I know Vincent is surrounded by angels. Then Walt told me the name of the girl who jogged by at just the right moment: Angelica!

~C. M. Zapata
Chicken Soup for the Latino Soul

The Accident

Insight is better than eyesight when it comes to seeing an angel.
~Eileen Elias Freeman,
The Angels' Little Instruction Book

This was the call every parent dreads. I picked up the phone to hear our sixteen-year-old daughter, Whitney, in absolute hysteria. She'd had a head-on collision in a busy Dallas/Ft. Worth intersection, six hundred miles away. To make things worse, she had our two- and three-year-old nieces she was babysitting in the car with her.

"Are you hurt?" I kept asking.

"Just my wrists, because of the airbag, and my head hurts and my shoulder hurts and my back..."

"What about Abby and Hallie?"

"They're absolutely fine. They're eating snow cones right now on the sidewalk. Dad, this is my worst nightmare!"

I stayed on the phone and did my best to calm her as the police and emergency medical technicians arrived and began treating the injured. The other driver, trapped in her car, had to be freed from the mangled mess of metal by the Jaws of Life.

Finally I spoke with the attending police officer, the EMT and anyone else who would listen to my long-distance plea for help. They treated Whitney at the scene of the accident, Abby and Hallie were without a scratch, and the other driver was taken in an ambulance to a local hospital. Whitney's car was totaled.

As the police were investigating the accident, the officer's first question was, "Who was driving this gray car?"

"I was," said Whitney.

"Well, how did you get out of the car?"

"I don't remember. All I remember is the crash, the airbag deploying, and then my two little nieces and I were standing on the sidewalk."

"I don't see how that's possible," replied the officer. "The impact of the crash has jammed the front doors, and the rear doors were childproofed. You couldn't get out of this car from the inside."

We thought this was curious, but were so absorbed in the trauma of it all that we didn't think about it too much.

In the days after the crash, we learned Whitney's injuries were painful, but not life threatening—one broken wrist, the other badly sprained, a whiplash injury and a large contusion where the seatbelt had grabbed her. Abby and Hallie were literally and miraculously unscathed.

A few days after the accident, their mom, Julie, asked Abby if she remembered the crash and, recalling what the police officer had said, asked her if Whitney had gotten them out of their car seats.

Abby recounted the impact in great detail, then replied, "No, Mom, the angel opened the door and then Whitney got us out."

In one of our many conversations with their parents after the accident, this is the sentence that stopped us in our tracks. Julie said to my wife, "We really don't talk about angels in our house. In fact, I didn't know Abby really even knew what an angel was."

We do. Psalm 91:11-12 says, "For He will command His angels concerning you to guard you in all your ways; they will lift you up in their hands, so that you will not strike your foot against a stone."

Yes, we know, now more than ever before.

~Dick and Mel Tunney
Chicken Soup for the Christian Soul 2

54

Mrs. Tree and Her Gentleman Caller

*Those who bring sunshine to the lives of others
cannot keep it from themselves.*
~James Matthew Barrie

rs. Tree had lived alone since becoming a widow a quarter-century before. Like most people in our neighborhood, she had little. But what she did have was enough for her meager needs—rent, a little food, electricity and a donation each week to her church.

But she had not attended services for some time. Mrs. Tree was almost blind and, once her husband died, could not manage the two block walk alone. One of her friends did her shopping, and Mrs. Tree's occasional trips to the doctor were made possible by a visiting nurse who came and picked her up.

We called her Mrs. Tree because her German name, Baum, she told us, meant tree. "Tannenbaum is a Christmas tree," she taught me patiently when I delivered papers with my brother Kevin on his paper route, "and Rosenbaum means rose tree."

Kevin had met the old woman one day while collecting for his route. She was sitting on a back stoop enjoying the sun. Of course she had no need for a newspaper, but Kevin's outright friendliness did not depend on whether one was a customer.

"What do you do by yourself, Mrs. Tree?" he asked, realizing how lonely she was.

"I listen to my radio," she replied. "I love some of the stories on it, like Ma Perkins and Helen Trent. Then there is fine music in the evenings or sometimes a play or a show with that funny gentleman and that little wooden puppet, Charlie McCarthy."

To be sure, Mrs. Tree was a proud woman who seldom asked for help with anything. But Kevin had a way about him that invited confidences, and, one day after finishing his paper route, he announced he was accompanying Mrs. Tree to church on Sunday.

"You'll have your hands full!" Mama laughed. "I still remember when the Ladies' Guild went to see if they could help her and she told them to mind their own business!"

Mrs. Tree, Mama added, had been a very attractive woman; her husband, a dapper gentleman, had worked for the gas company in the office. Though they were not wealthy, they enjoyed a social life, and Mrs. Tree sort of considered herself the belle of the ball.

"Perhaps," Mama speculated with a light laugh, "being helped by ladies was not her cup of tea!"

"She seems nice enough to me," Kevin said quietly.

I giggled, secretly referring to the coming Sunday as "Kev's date."

When the first church date grew into a second and then, a third, Kevin showed no sign of quitting. Nor did Mrs. Tree. Each Sunday, she'd be ready and waiting, dressed in her best, for the walk to church. For his part, Kevin, in his Sunday clothes, would help her with her coat—which she always wore, even in the heat of summer.

All the way to church, Mrs. Tree clung lightly to Kevin's arm. Once inside, she insisted on sitting in front where she'd sat with her husband.

When Kevin led Mrs. Tree out of the church, the crowd on the sidewalks parted politely. They did not, however, disguise their interest in seeing the mysterious parishioner on the arm of my older brother.

During the week, Kevin told us that Mrs. Tree had invited him in for tea and they'd sat at a comfortable old table covered with a linen cloth. They drank the tea from china cups, he said, and ate little cookies made of shortbread. Kevin promised to ask Mrs. Tree next time if he could bring some cookies home for us to enjoy, too. The dates continued through the summer and into fall.

Though Kevin was not very talkative about his friendship with the elderly widow, he did confide that she often told him stories of her husband and how they had wished for children but had not been so blessed. She also showed him photographs of herself and her husband in their younger days. Kevin told us she was a "Corker indeed," which meant, in his practiced eye, she was very attractive.

As the leaves began to fall in earnest, Mrs. Tree seemed to slow a bit. Kev said she remarked more often about "these tired old bones" and how the winter days seemed to hang in her loneliness.

"I'll still come here for you!" Kevin protested. "And my brothers can come, too."

She smiled and told him he was a kind lad, and she thanked God for bringing him to help her.

As Kevin got up to leave, Mrs. Tree pointed out a crumb on his lip and handed him a handkerchief. He dabbed his lip and went to the door, absentmindedly taking with him the lace-bordered cloth.

"I forgot to give her the hanky!" he said, still clutching the sweet-smelling linen when he got home.

"How did she know you had a crumb there," Mama asked, "with no eyes to see?"

Kevin stood thunderstruck. He turned to go out the door, intent on returning the hanky. But Mama told him she thought perhaps it was all right to stay put, and so he stashed the handkerchief in his drawer, planning to return it on Sunday.

A few days later, Father O'Phelan informed us that Mrs. Tree had passed on the night before. Mama, though, was not surprised when we brought her the news. Indeed, she seemed to think that the handkerchief was the old woman's way of saying goodbye to my brother.

A funeral was held on Saturday morning, and Kevin sat next to Mama in the pew usually reserved for family. He was, for what it was worth, all she had.

It turned out that, shortly before she died, Mrs. Tree had bundled a few books and an old framed picture of her and her late husband with a note to give the items to Kevin. But the remembrance he cherished most was the old woman's sweet-smelling handkerchief. It was, he's said in the years since, her personal goodbye and a thank you far and above anything he ever expected.

~Sean Patrick
Chicken Soup for the Christian Family Soul

55

A Voice in the Woods

I remember the first time I got close enough to smell his cologne. We were playing "pass the orange" at youth group. He stepped up to me, brushed his cheek against mine and began to move the orange awkwardly from under my chin to his without using his hands. I could feel his breath and the scent of his Old Spice. He intoxicated me. He was shy and mysterious, maneuvering around my neck, millimeters away from my lips, smiling up at me sheepishly. I wanted to kiss him right there in front of everyone. Dear God, just an inch higher, let me kiss you! He was beautiful. Long brown hair, bell bottoms and Beatle boots that made him look hip and mysterious. I must have written his name a hundred times. I kissed my pillow at night, pretending it was him. And when "Crimson and Clover" came on my radio in the darkness, all I could think about was Mark. I had fantasized about him for two years and he didn't even know it.

Now he was lying in a casket. It was the first time I had ever been to a funeral or seen a coffin. I took a step back in horror. He lay so frozen. The church filled up quickly, and I made my way through the crowd to the front. I tossed my song down on the music stand. I had never written a song for a funeral before. Getting through it without crying was going to be the challenge. His coffin was right in front of me. Two men wearing carnations closed the heavy lid as his parents sat down in the front row. The cheerleaders in the back sobbed and clung to each other. When a teenager dies, girls come out of the woodwork to help grieve. Looking back, I think every adult in that place wished they could have allowed themselves to show their feelings as openly as those girls did. He deserved it, and someone needed to weep for him, weep loud and long and without apology. He was the first boy I ever loved. Now half the sophomore class was waiting for me to sing his eulogy.

I glanced at the front row as I sang and saw his mother's face, hanging on my every word. His sister broke down, hiding behind her long, black hair. She was off to college next fall. I noticed a chain around her neck with Mark's high school ring dangling from it, as if they had been going steady. Girls are like that with their brothers.

I strummed the last chord on my guitar and sat down behind the casket. The minister stood up, pale and thin-lipped.

"God had a reason to take him," he began. "He had only sixteen short years on this Earth, but God had a reason."

I stared down at my lap, refusing to look at this clergyman I was beginning to hate. "You're a liar," I thought. "God wouldn't kill Mark. The drunk driver killed Mark. God wouldn't do that."

He rambled on about God needing Mark in heaven, as the two women in Mark's life, his mother and sister, squeezed each other's hands until their knuckles turned white. His little brother sat there, staring straight ahead in a JCPenney's suit that was too big.

Norma Peterson ended the service on the organ as the casket was wheeled down the center aisle and then loaded, like air freight, into the back of the hearse. The limo drove off to the cemetery, and the rest of us stood in front, chatting about nothing. Marge Sherman took a smoke break, and some of the football players stood with their hands in their pockets, talking about Saturday's game. I couldn't handle it. This was it? That's all? I couldn't process it. I didn't know what to do.

So I ran. I ran down the hill to my house; ran across my yard to the woods at the end of my street. I ran through the purple flowers and wild onions, to the thick of the woods near the stream. I stopped breathlessly by the water, wrapped my arms around a huge tree and sobbed into the bark, sobbed from somewhere so deep, I couldn't open my eyes for a long time.

Then I looked around at this magical chapel in the woods I had stepped into. I felt calm. Honeysuckle filled the air, and a ladybug landed on my arm. I bent down and picked one of the white lilies that covered the forest floor. I grabbed an armful of purple stems until I held a whole bouquet. Standing there in the dappling sunlight, a voice spoke to me. It came from inside my own heart, but it was louder than the rush of the water racing in the creek beside me.

"I didn't kill him. I only resurrected him."

I noticed a butterfly hovering over the water, gold and black wings sparkling in the sunlight. All around me was life: flowers, hummingbirds and bees buzzing in the orange daylilies. It was then that I realized how wrong he was, that minister. God didn't "take" Mark. God didn't bend down and kill this boy and break his mother's heart.

I carried my flowers to the edge of the water and let them fall. They twirled down into the rushing stream, and then spun down a waterfall. The last petal floated out of sight, and I stood back and felt something, someone, behind me, covering me with a warmth that I had never felt before.

"God, take my flowers to Mark," I whispered. "Comfort him."

And in that moment I knew that He would, because He had already comforted me.

There would be times in the future when I would attend other funerals; tragic deaths and untimely losses that made no sense. People would rationalize with the same idea of a Supreme Being who cut down innocents in the middle of their prime. "God took him," they would say.

And I would answer unwaveringly: "God doesn't kill people. Years ago He told me so. And I believe Him."

~Carla Riehl
Chicken Soup for the Christian Soul 2

56

Two Percent Is Enough

F rom the day I was born, I was a sickly, weak child who never had as much energy as a child my age should. When I turned four, everything seemed to go wrong. I had asthma and for the most part I was in constant pain. Every day, I had a nagging side pain that seemed to never go away and I was in and out of doctors' offices many times, but they could never figure out what was wrong. "Simply growing pains," they told my parents.

One night, I had a fever, high blood pressure, nonstop vomiting and my feet were purple. My parents rushed me to the emergency room, where they were told that I needed my appendix taken out. I lay there that night, getting worse by the minute. Finally, purple feet became numb and my stomach was empty of everything. My parents lost control of their emotions. The next morning, my urine was brown. At that point, the doctors knew it was more than my appendix.

The next day, I was taken by ambulance to Children's Hospital under the care of Dr. Kohen, a kidney specialist. I was diagnosed with a rare form of kidney disease called glumerulonephritis. After two weeks of treatment, I was still not responding. My kidneys were only functioning two percent of the time and if something wasn't done, I would die.

My parents were faced with choices they never thought they would have to make: steroids, dialysis or a transplant. They were told that their only daughter was dying and without vast improvement would be put on a waiting list for a kidney transplant.

That night, my dad sat down by my bed and told me that I was going to have to fight harder than I had ever fought before. All of a sudden, I reached up and—mustering all the energy I had—I punched him in the nose! He knew then that I was not going to give up without a fight.

The next morning I was evaluated for a transplant. I was put on a steroid. Within a couple of days, I started showing steady signs of improvement, but my parents were told, "Krissy will never have as much energy as a normal kid, even if she pulls through."

Within four days I was strong enough to return home. For the next couple of months, I was under constant supervision. As a four-year-old little girl, I was taking fourteen pills a day and having my blood taken every other day. Gradually, I was taken off the medicine and my doctors' visits grew further apart. But still, I was given no chance of a full recovery.

Well, ten years later, I can proudly say, "Look at me now!" I am fourteen years old, I play four sports, I am a member of the National Junior Honor Society at my school, vice president of Student Council, have a 3.5 grade point average, and I am a living miracle to my doctors, family and friends. I thank God every day for giving me my life. Even if you are only given a two percent chance of survival, that's all you really need.

~Krissy Creager
Chicken Soup for the Preteen Soul

57

Passing the Torch

How glorious a greeting the sun gives the mountains!
~John Muir

Summer 1964, a northwoods lake.

"**G**et up! Get up!" my mother whispers.

My eyes flash open. Confusion clouds my brain. Where am I? Is something wrong? I quickly look around.

I'm sandwiched between frayed woolen blankets and the sagging mattress of an old metal bed on the porch of our family log cabin. Looking almost exactly as it did when my grandparents built it in 1929, it sits high on a hill surrounded by the pine and musty fragrance of the woods.

Through sleepy eyes, I take in the dark-green porch swing, the birch leg table, and the smoky glass of the corner kerosene lantern reflecting the stillness of the lake below.

Having escaped the steamy cornland of my home for a few summer weeks, I believe I'm in heaven on Earth. My face feels the coolness of the early morning air. I relax and curl deeper beneath the blankets' warmth.

"Get up!" my mother's voice whispers again. "You must come now. The sunrise is simply glorious!"

The sunrise? Get up to see the sunrise? Who's she kidding? The last thing this fourteen-year-old wants to do is leave a warm bed to go see a sunrise, glorious or otherwise. It's 5:00 A.M. and freezing out there.

"Hurry!" my mother urges.

Careful not to let the screen door slam, she sets off down the forty-nine long steps at a determined rate of speed to the lake below.

In the twin bed opposite me, my seventeen-year-old sister Nancy stirs. She pushes back the covers and plops to the floor. Not to be outdone, I make a supreme effort and struggle out of bed as well. In our thin cotton nighties, we grab my father's WWII pea-green army blankets from the foot of our beds and wrap them tightly around our shoulders.

As our bare feet touch the cold porch floor, we are thunderbolted awake. Our pace quickens. One of us misses catching the screen door. It slams. Like a couple of water bugs hopscotching across the lake in avoidance of fish jaws, we gingerly pick our way over slippery rocks and prickly pine needles down the forty-nine dew-covered log steps to the lake shore.

When we feel we've saved our feet from any horny toads or big black spiders that might be crazy enough to be up this early, we catch our breath and look up. Our mother's silhouette is outlined against a rosy dawn, the first light catching the soft red of her hair. She is right. It is a glorious sunrise.

Across the lake, a sliver of the most brilliant red crests the top of the shadowed forest. Hues of lavender, rose and amber begin to pulsate in the sky like a heavenly kaleidoscope. High above in the soft blueness, a lone star still sparkles. Silver mist rises gently from the smoothness of the lake. All is still. In the sacred silence, my mother, sister and I stand reverently together against a backdrop of tall pine and watch the magic of God's dawning unfold.

Suddenly, the curve of a brilliant sun bursts through the dark forest. The world begins to wake. We watch a blue heron rise up from a distant shore and gently fan its way over still waters. Two ducks make a rippled landing near our dock while the black and white beauty of a loon skims along the edge of a nearby island, hunting for its morning food.

Breathing in the chill air, the three of us draw our blankets closer. The soft hues of the sunrise turn into the brightness of a new day and the last of the stars fades. My sister and I take one more look, race up the steps, and jump into our beds to grab a few more hours of sleep.

My mother is more reluctant to leave the sunrise's amphitheater. From the renewed warmth of my bed, it is a while longer before I hear her reach the top step and gently close the porch door.

Summer 1994, a northwoods lake.

"Get up! Get up!" I whisper to my adolescent sons sleeping dreamily in the same old metal beds of our family's cabin porch.

"Come see the sunrise! It's awesome!"

Amazed, I watch as this fourth generation of cabin snoozers rouse themselves from cozy comfort. They snatch the WWII pea-green army blankets from the foot of their beds and stumble out the porch door. It slams. Gingerly they maneuver slippery rocks and prickly pine needles down forty-nine dew-covered log steps to the lakeshore.

Their seventy-four-year-old grandmother is already there. Her red hair, now streaked with white, reflects the first light.

She greets her grandsons with the quiet of a bright smile, gathers her blanket closer, and turns toward the east to observe once again God's dawning.

My sons' faces watch intently as the rich colors of the sunrise soar up into the sky like the brilliant plumage of a great bird. It isn't long before the flap of a blue heron's wing and the melodic call of a loon awaken the lake with activity.

"Isn't it beautiful?" I whisper.

The boys nod in silent agreement. Their grandmother smiles at them. Before long, they grab the tails of their frayed blankets and race back up the steps to the welcoming warmth of their beds.

My mother and I stay a little longer. Standing close, we watch the swirls of pearl mist rise and the sky bloom into the shades of a morning rose. We are rewarded this morning by the graceful glide of an eagle high overhead. The gentle rays of the early sun warm our faces.

Eventually, we turn to begin our slow climb up the old log stairs. Halfway up, I catch my breath and look back to see how my mother is doing. But she is not there. She has changed her mind, and through the treetops I can see her, still on the lakeshore, lingering in the light.

~Marnie O. Mamminga
Chicken Soup for the Grandparent's Soul

He Sees

What we are is God's gift to us.
What we become is our gift to God.
~Eleanor Powell

Recently in church, the sermon was about Jesus' challenge to his people: "Do you see what I see?" The pastor spoke about using the eyes of Jesus to identify the needs of a person, rather than focusing on outward appearance only.

When I was growing up, I often felt different. My parents were missionaries, and we moved between Austria, Turkey, Germany and our home base in Illinois more than eleven times. I attended twelve different schools before college. After depositing me in Indiana at a small Christian university, my parents were on their way back to Germany for the next four years. I was emotionally exhausted.

I wasn't close to God, although I had had some spiritual experiences that assured me of my connection with God. I felt tired by the time I started college. I was tired of starting over all the time, tired of always being told what to do and tired of years of never feeling rooted in a place I could call home. I spent a lot of time in my dorm room, consumed by increasingly depressed thoughts.

As a true missionary kid, at first I tried to make friends with people. But I longed for one true friend I could trust. Finally, I gave up and kept to my room. I felt unloved and deserted.

I was shocked by how dark my thoughts had become. I actually entertained thoughts of wondering how many pills it would take to get me out of the terrible spot I was in. I became physically run down and developed a terrible cold, which was what drove me out of my room to the campus clinic.

While I was waiting my turn to see the doctor, Mike approached me. The only contact I'd had with Mike was when he had helped my roommate's father set up loft beds for my roommate and me. I had to actually concentrate on remembering his name as he approached. He sat down beside me. Looking vaguely uncomfortable, he said, "When you're done with the doctor, I'd like to speak with you. Will you have a minute?"

I agreed without much enthusiasm. There was a school banquet coming up, and I distractedly thought he looked uncomfortable because he was going to ask me to attend the banquet with him. I spent the entire time being examined by the doctor, dreading the prospect of being asked to go to an event I had no desire of attending with someone I barely knew. When I was finished, Mike reappeared. We stood outside the clinic, and the awkwardness was almost palpable.

He looked at me and said, "I have something to tell you, and I feel a little weird about saying this, but if you could bear with me until I'm finished... I really think God wants me to tell you this."

There was an uncomfortable pause as he waited for my permission to go on. I must have nodded some sort of assent, thinking this was easily one of the weirdest ways anyone had ever asked me out on a date. What came next was very much unexpected.

He told me, "I've been praying for you. God has really put your name on my heart. He's been guiding me to tell you he knows you've been having suicidal thoughts. I know this sounds crazy, but he wanted me to tell you that you are not alone, and he loves you."

I suddenly felt exposed. I didn't even know this guy, and here he was telling me not to end my life. Who did he think he was? What gave him the right to talk to me like I had lost my mind? I wasn't crazy, just tired of feeling like nobody understood me.

Then I took a deep breath and tried to open my heart to what was happening. From a place of calm, I suddenly realized Mike was

God's messenger. God understood! Mike had taken a huge personal risk approaching me, a person he didn't even know, with a message he didn't really understand. I gathered myself together enough to thank him and ask him to keep praying because I needed it, then I made my escape back to my room.

As I sat on my bed and examined the conversation, I was overcome by the amazing fact that God knew where I was and had used one of his servants to deliver hope. I felt warmed and encouraged. Although I didn't immediately snap out of my depression, I felt comfort in the realization that God knew how badly I was hurting.

I have been through hard times since, but I've realized that through all of the inevitable ups and downs of life, God reaches out to individuals when they need him. I remember that encounter often, and I feel incredibly blessed to have been the recipient of such a message of love. The world is a better place because of people like Mike—people willing to see others through the eyes of Jesus.

~Kristina J. Adams
Chicken Soup for the Christian Teenage Soul

Life Lessons

Difficult times have helped me understand better than before, how infinitely rich and beautiful life is in every way, and that so many things that one goes worrying about are of no importance whatsoever.

~Isak Dinisen

59

In-VINCE-ible Lessons

I believe in the sun even if it isn't shining.
I believe in love even when I am alone.
I believe in God even when He is silent.
~Author Unknown

Just looking at my vivacious, seven-year-old brother, Vincent, no one would know the painful struggle he went through just three years ago, nor would they know about the invincible way in which he fought and overcame his terminal disease.

"Mommy, my leg hurts," Vincent said three years ago. Having used all his energy to limp to the couch, he lay down for a rest. For a very busy four-year-old who never sat still, this was not normal. His sudden inability to walk up or down stairs and go about his usual playful activities concerned us. My family thought it might be an injury from roughhousing with my other younger brother. The doctor said it was his left hip and advised temporary bed rest, which seemed to help at first.

Soon it was time for Vincent's Halloween party at preschool. The children formed a parade circle outside the school to show off all their cute costumes. When an adorable panda trailed far behind the rest of the class as they walked around, we were abruptly reminded that something was seriously wrong.

It's been three years since Vincent was diagnosed with

neuroblastoma, a fast-growing malignant childhood cancer. The cancer in his abdomen had already spread to other parts of his body, including his left hip. The day I was told, I was overwhelmed with confusing emotions. I saw how young, innocent and weak Vincent looked, and all I could do was watch and hope. I prayed that he could handle chemotherapy, surgery, radiation and two stem cell transplants.

Even through his pain, loss of hair, mouth sores, isolation from friends, stomach cramps and other complications, Vincent never complained. He continued to enjoy the simple things of childhood—jokes, arts and crafts, teasing and goofing off. As the months went on, Vincent's smile and sense of playfulness remained. Vincent made me feel more secure that God would protect him and be there through everything.

Vincent made it through a number of treatments and both his bone marrow transplants. However, following his three-month isolation period at home, Vincent came down with post-transplant kidney problems. After a six-day hospital stay, he was stabilized and able to still go with us on his Dream Come True trip to Disney World. My family received our dream come true, as well. Vince was clear of cancer and finished with his treatments. Within five months, his kidneys were ninety percent healed. Vincent has proven himself invincible. He is now almost three years cancer-free and still maintains a wonderful, spirited attitude. We are so thankful to God that he is a survivor.

Vincent taught me important lessons through his suffering. Not only did I learn to trust in God, but also that the Holy Spirit and His gifts will always be here for me in times of spiritual or emotional challenge. Patience, the presence of God and an inspirational little boy have made an everlasting impact on my life.

~Casey Glynn Patriarco
Chicken Soup for the Christian Teenage Soul

60

"Yes, Daddy, I Promise"

*As the feeling of betrayal is the worst feeling ever for me,
forgiveness is probably the best.*
~Rae B. Ramos

The security guard grabbed my arm. "Come with me," he barked, leading me back inside the discount store and into the office. Then he pointed to a lime green chair. "Sit down!"

I sat. He glared at me. "You can give it to me or I can take it, your choice. What'll it be?"

As I pulled the package of hair ribbons from the waistband of my jeans, I could feel the sharp corner of the cardboard cutting into my skin. I handed it to him and pleaded, "You're not going to call my dad, are you?"

"I'm calling the police. They will call your father."

My head dropped onto my hands and I sobbed, "No, please! Can't you just let me go? I can pay you. I have money in my pocket. I'm only fourteen years old. Please, I won't ever shoplift again!"

"Save your tears, they won't work on me. I'm sick of you bratty kids stealing, just for the thrill of it."

I sat, trembling with fear and shame.

The police arrived, and they exchanged muffled words with the guard and the office manager. I overheard one of the policemen say, "I know her father." I also heard, "Teach her a lesson."

The policemen walked me to their black-and-white car and opened the back door. I got in, and they drove me through the middle of our small town. I slouched down into the seat so no one could see me as I looked out the window at the evening sky. Then I saw the steeple of my family's church, and the guilt pierced me like a dagger. I thought, "How could I have been so stupid? I've broken my father's heart... and God's."

We arrived at the station, and a round woman with a square face asked me questions until I ran out of answers. She pointed to the door of a large open cell and said, "Sit. Wait."

I walked in, and my footsteps made an echo that bounced off the bars. The tears started again as I sat down on a hard bench and heard her dial the telephone and say, "I have your daughter in a cell at the police station. No, she's not hurt. She was caught shoplifting. Can you come and get her? Okay. You're welcome, goodbye." She yelled, "Hey kid, your father's on his way."

About one hundred years later, I heard his voice say my name. The woman called me up to the desk at three times the necessary volume. I kept my eyes on the floor as I walked toward them. I saw my dad's shoes, but I didn't speak to him or look at him. And, thankfully, he didn't ask me to. He signed some papers and my jailer told us, "You're free to go."

The air was dark and cold as we walked to the car in heavy silence. I got in and closed the door. Dad started the engine and drove out of the parking lot as he looked straight ahead. Then he whispered in a sad and faraway voice, "My daughter... a thief."

I melted into repentant tears. The five mile drive felt like forever. As we drove into our driveway, I saw my mom's silhouette at the back door.

More shame came in a tidal wave.

After we entered the house, Dad finally spoke to me. "Let's go into the living room." Mom and Dad sat together on the couch, and I sat, alone, in the stiff wingback chair.

Dad ran his fingers through his hair, linked our eyes and asked me, "Why?"

I told him about the first time I stole a tube of lipstick and how I felt equal amounts of thrill and guilt. Then the second time, when I took a teen magazine, the guilt faded as the thrill grew. I told them about the third time, and the fourth and the tenth. Part of me wanted to stop the confession, but it gushed out like an open fire hydrant. I said, "Each time I stole, it got easier—until now. I can see how wrong it was." Hot tears bit my face as I said, "Please forgive me. I'll never do it again. Stealing was easy; getting caught is hard."

Dad said, "Yes, and it's going to get even harder." He asked Mom to hand me the notepad and pen that were sitting by the telephone. She walked over and patted my hand as she placed them in my lap. Dad continued, "I want you to make a list of all the places you stole from. Write down what you took and how much it cost. This is your one chance for a full confession and our forgiveness. If you ever steal anything again, I will not defend you or bail you out. We will always love you, but this behavior will stop. Here. Tonight. Correct?"

I looked at his face, which had suddenly aged, and said, "Yes, Daddy, I promise." As I wrote my list of offenses, Mom warned, "Make sure you haven't forgotten any; this is your only chance."

I finished writing. "Here's the list." I went to the couch and handed it to him, and I asked, "What are you going to do with it?"

Dad looked at the paper and sighed. He patted the cushion, and I sat down between my parents. "Tomorrow morning, we will go to all the places on your list, and you will ask to speak to the manager. You will tell him that you are a shoplifter. You will tell him what items you stole from his store, apologize, and then repay him. I'll loan you the money, and you will work all summer to pay me back. Do you understand?"

With my heart slamming and my palms sweating, I nodded.

The next morning, I did exactly as he asked. It was impossibly hard, but I did it. That summer, I repaid my father the money, but I will never be able to repay him for the valuable lesson he taught me. Thanks to his courage, I never stole again.

~Nancy C. Anderson
Chicken Soup for the Father & Daughter Soul

The Bridge Builder

"America! I'm really here," Ursina had murmured. "If only my family could visit this wonderful land. My dream all my life is to come here." Her eyes glistened slightly with tears. "I'm really here!" She opened her arms as if to hug someone. When she talked about America with such intensity, I would look around at my small hometown of Elberton, Georgia, wondering if Ursina saw something I had missed.

She often spoke about her mother, brother and sister, and her country fondly, but if she suffered from homesickness, she never let any of us know. Ursina's father had died in a Russian prison in 1945.

She knew a lot about American history, but she never flaunted her knowledge. Always though, she wanted to learn more about our land and customs. She listened enraptured as we answered her never-ending questions.

"I want to learn all about America." Ursina pronounced "America" in a special, almost reverent way. Nothing ever seemed too small to captivate her attention.

Ursina's accent fascinated me. I hadn't met many people from other countries, and no one my own age. I watched her mouth closely as she pronounced my name precisely.

Sometimes now I don't think about her for months—even years. Then something stirs my memory—an old song, a ballerina skirt pulled out of mothballs, or a photograph of our graduating class. Then I recall vividly my senior year of high school in 1953, and Ursina Stahnke, the German exchange student who had come to live in America for a year and to graduate with our class.

The stubborn memory has remained in my heart all these years, and with bittersweet fondness, I remember Ursina. She could have easily been a beauty queen with her long, thick hair and dark eyes. Her flawless complexion seemed to be as perfect as a doll's. When she smiled, it happened slowly, like a velvet curtain being drawn back. She seemed completely unaware of her deep beauty.

The Halls, the family she was living with in Elberton, fell in love with Ursina almost instantly. Mrs. Hall sewed beautifully, and as a school party approached, she began making Ursina an exquisite formal gown. Ursina told me about it. "So lovely, new, green net, wonderfully soft..." she had whispered, with tears sparkling in her eyes. "I'm going to have my picture made in it for my family."

One bright September day, when Ursina had been here only four weeks, some of us girls in the senior class decided to have a party for her. We called it a Coca-Cola party. We planned to have the get-together at Shirley's home. We all brought something special we had baked and there was an air of excitement.

Ursina came into the room a bit breathless, a little nervous, looked around at us, then slowly smiled that wonderful smile of hers, obviously pleased at our efforts. She tasted the cakes and cookies with great fanfare, as though she was judging a cooking contest, and she raved over each morsel. I watched her lift a Coke bottle to her mouth. She swallowed slowly, then smiled approvingly. Ursina got the most out of everything. I had gulped mine down without even tasting it. When all of her Coke was gone, she shut one eye and looked into the empty bottle with the other eye as though she peered into a microscope and saw something fascinating.

Ursina planned to ride Shirley's pet horse that afternoon. She was a skilled rider. As I left the party, she called out, "Bye. See ya tomorrow." Ursina had started to pick up our Southern slang, and it pleased us all.

That night I received a telephone call. One of my girlfriends spoke in a strange, tight voice. "Marion, Ursina fell or was thrown off the horse this afternoon. She's in the hospital, unconscious. They're going to operate, I think. They... they... shaved her head."

Back in bed I rationalized and hoped. Since they've shaved her head, I thought, they surely will operate and she will be fine. I went to sleep imagining a smiling Ursina with short, curly hair.

The next morning I learned the agonizing truth as the grim news spread throughout our shocked town.

Ursina had died.

I shut my eyes, remembering her peeping down into the empty Coke bottle and grinning. I recalled how her eyes sparkled when tears threatened. I thought about how coming to America had been her life's dream. My small hometown had been America for Ursina.

I couldn't cry. I ached inside, unable to shed tears. Then I began to think about her mother—what bitterness she must have for people in Elberton, America.

Elberton mourned. At the funeral home, Ursina's body was never left alone. They had dressed her in the new green evening gown she had never gotten to wear. Later at a memorial service, a granite statue of Ursina, chiseled by a gifted artist from Elberton, was placed in the schoolyard and a well-known columnist from Atlanta spoke. She wrote about Ursina and Elberton in her column. Our senior class dedicated the annual to Ursina's memory. We used the picture of her in the new green dress. She would never see that photograph. Underneath the picture it said, "Ursina Stahnke, beloved German exchange student who was accidentally killed while horseback riding on September 17, 1953—to know her was to love her."

Many people from Elberton sent messages of sympathy to Ursina's family in Hamburg, Germany. I couldn't write a letter. It seemed incredible to me that her mother wanted to hear from Americans. How she must hate us!

I tried to pray for them. Maybe prayer is an attitude of the heart after all and God understands a silent, aching heart that doesn't know the exact words to say to Him.

A prayer that I hadn't known how to express was answered through a letter from Ursina's mother. Our local newspaper published it. Reading the letter, feelings I couldn't put into words welled up inside me and I finally cried for a long time.

> The weeks in America were the crown of Ursina's life. She loved America before she had seen it. America had always been the goal of her thoughts and desires. I had only jubilant letters from her. She seemed to live in a dream; she was drunk with joy about the lovable people in Elberton. Ursina drank in all the beauty and was enjoying life in a manner that she never had been able to in our narrow circumstances. It could not have become any more beautiful perhaps — therefore, my beloved child had to go. She came home very much differently from what we had pictured. On the 25th of September we saw the child once more — like Snow White lying in her coffin, but already quite distant and sublime. We became quiet and prayerful at her sight.

> The chapel had been turned into a sea of sunflowers at my wish and it was filled with music, "Andante" by Hayden. I chose the twenty-third Psalm for the minister to read, and later learned that you also had chosen that Scripture for her in Elberton.

> I don't feel anything but gratitude for the people of Elberton for helping Ursina realize her dream. How beautifully and how lovely you sent me my child! Your acts of love are a wall around my heart. I have become quiet. God would have taken her here too — I know this for certain.

> Please give Ursina's clothes to poor children in Elberton.

> I will by and by write more letters to Elberton. We don't ever want to miss the love of friends that spoke to us from letters. My children and I greet all the dear people of Elberton. We are more often with you now than here, as if we could still reach Ursina there. There shall remain a bridge of affection which my beloved child has built between our people.

Ursina's family later crossed that bridge and came to Elberton for a visit. I was out of town and didn't meet them. But I already knew them. They were people, like Ursina, with amazing love for my country. They were people who simply would not turn their backs on my town, my country.

As time passed, I often caught myself looking for beauty in the simplest places, expecting happiness out of heartache, and experiencing forgiveness where bitterness might have grown.

~Marion Bond West
Chicken Soup for the Christian Family Soul

The Mirror

If you want others to be happy, practice compassion.
If you want to be happy, practice compassion.
~Dalai Lama

At fourteen, I was the new girl at a rural school in an apple orchard valley. There were twenty-eight kids in my class, which was equally divided between boys and girls. It was the tightly knit group of twelve girls that kept me an outsider. They teased me about my bright red hair, my height, my clothes, my shoe size, my accent and anything else they could think of. I cried myself to sleep after my parents' pep talk. They said all the right things like "Give it time" and "Once they get to know you, they'll love you." I wanted to believe them, but the evidence proved otherwise.

Then, a few months into the school year, my parents' predictions came true. I was playing out in left field for the girls' baseball team when a ball rocketed right at me. I put my mitt up as a shield, and the ball packed itself right into my glove. That play saved the game, and we beat the boys' team for the first time. Well, after that, the girls couldn't just exclude me from the victory party. It turned out they liked my sense of humor, and a few actually said they wished they had my mass of auburn hair. Suddenly, I was "in." Friendships grew, and soon I was included in the overnights and birthday parties.

Spring break came and went, and we returned to a school of freshly waxed floors, redone bulletin boards and one new girl. Rosa was petite and quiet. Her family had come to work in the apple orchards. I knew how she felt, so I smiled at her and helped her find her way around. The final weeks of school passed, and we came to our last day and the traditional eighth grade graduation dance.

I decided it would be a nice gesture to invite Rosa over to help her get ready for the dance. It was fun getting ready together and being each other's support when those insecurities would creep in.

We stood side by side in front of the mirror.

"Oh, thank you, Cindy!" Rosa said. We smiled at each other's reflection. "I only wish my friend Tracie could see me now. I wish she could come to the dance. She said she's never gone to one. She made me promise to have the best time ever and to remember every moment so I could tell her all about it tomorrow. She was so excited for me."

Tracie! I had never even thought of her.

Tracie was one of the fourteen girls in our class. I was so happy when the twelve welcomed me into their inner circle that I had never looked back or looked around. I never looked at or thought about Tracie, the one who stood alone until Rosa had become her friend.

That night at the dance, Rosa was a hit. It was great to see her so happy. Yet I couldn't stop thinking about Tracie. For the first time I was aware of her absence. Tracie didn't make it to the dance that night, but she affected me more than anyone who did. Tracie's example of wanting her friend to be happy even though she had been excluded far outshined me taking such pride in a small kindness to another. I might have done a nice thing, but for whose gain did I do it?

These moments when we are humbled enough to learn are when God really teaches us. That night I learned my own happiness is only part of the big picture. I learned it is just as important to make sure others are loved and accepted as it is to feel that way ourselves.

~Cynthia M. Hamond
Chicken Soup for the Christian Teenage Soul

Forever Changed

He is a wise man who does not grieve for the things which he has not,
but rejoices for those which he has.
~Epictetus

Every morning when I wake up, I peel back the blankets that keep my body warmth hostage and look around my room. I see cherished family photos, my favorite mahogany dresser and of course my love beads that hang from the windows. I can't imagine my life without a loving family surrounding me or a roof shielding me from the night.

This past July, I went on a mission trip to Monterrey, Mexico, with my youth group. I sat on a bus for two days, not knowing what to expect. My friends on the bus described all the bugs that had infested the orphanages we were to work at for the next week. They told me how dirty everything would be and how dangerous the streets were. Secretly, I was hoping the bus would turn around somehow. But it did not. The first night we arrived, a man said, "We have come here to change Mexico, but instead, Mexico will change us."

Each morning during the hour-and-a-half bus ride to the orphanage, I would think of how little I had slept the night before, how tired I was, and how there was no air conditioning on the bus. But, as soon as the orphanage came into view, all those feelings melted away. The children would run up to the gates, scream, and jump up and down because we had finally arrived. The first day I walked cautiously inside the metal gates. I saw one girl with a huge smile on her face. When I walked over to her, she gave me a hug. I looked around at all the other children. All were smiling. All were laughing. They were not upset, nor complaining about their lives and living conditions.

I met a little girl at the orphanage named Erica. She had short black hair and a big scar beneath her nose. I picked her up and swung her around. She squealed with laughter. Every day when we arrived, she always ran up to me, gave me a hug and kissed my cheeks. I began looking forward to this.

The whole time, I was thinking, "Who would give such a wonderful child up?"

I saw other children in the orphanage. They did not fight over the toys we brought them. Instead, they shared them because they wanted everyone to experience the joy of the new toys.

On the last day, the kids were singing songs to us. Rose, the lady in charge, told us that one of the children wanted to share her story with us. To my amazement, Erica went up to speak. She smiled at me and began her story: "I am so happy to be here in the orphanage." Happy, I thought. Who would be happy to be in an orphanage? "When I was in my house," she continued, "my parents used to beat me. They threw me against the wall and hurt me."

When she was done, I ran over to tell her how proud I was of her. I looked down and saw the scar near her nose. Now I knew how she got it.

The day we left is a day I'll never forget. Everyone was crying. I held Erica for fifteen minutes, too scared to put her down. I kissed her scar, hoping, once more, to erase her memories. I told her I loved her. She stopped crying and smiled. When our time with the children was done, they waved once again through the gates. This time it was goodbye.

When I came home, I looked in my room while unpacking. I looked at all my clothes hanging in my closet on multicolored hangers. The visions of Erica's closet with two shirts in it flashed before my eyes. She tried to give me one of her stuffed animals in return for my friendship. I told her I did not need one. She said she didn't either because she had two. Erica is only seven. It will take me a long time to learn what she already knows.

~JoLynn Shopteese
Chicken Soup for the Teenage Soul III

Michael

It's lunch hour, and the cafeteria is a zoo. At a round table near the edge of the room, I'm brown-bagging it with six of my friends. We almost always sit together at the same table in the same seats.

Lunch hour for us is a safe and predictable routine. There's never any stress or worry about where we'll sit, who we'll sit with or what we'll talk about.

But across the way, a guy named Michael sits alone. Every day. I've never seen him sitting with anyone. For that matter, I've never seen him walking in the hall with anyone, talking to anyone between classes or hanging out with anyone after school.

I only see Michael alone.

Michael is tall and thin. His shoulders sag. He walks slowly. His brown hair is straight and long. His face looks sad and hurt. Michael doesn't hide his loneliness very well.

Michael is in my P.E. class. He is not athletic. He can't throw well, he runs awkwardly, and he obviously doesn't enjoy the class. By the end of the semester, after being laughed at and ridiculed by nearly everyone, Michael's face begins to look more guarded. He seems to be learning to hide his feelings.

When I see Michael in the hall, he seems lost and confused. Instead of going to his locker between classes, he carries all his books, so he's always dropping stuff. He walks along the wall where he can avoid all the crowds.

Sometimes I wonder if anybody ever even notices him.

Sometimes I notice, but I don't do anything about it. What does it matter, anyway? I don't have any obligations toward him. He's just another kid in school who really has nothing to do with me. Right?

My youth director wouldn't agree. His big themes this year are, "Reaching Out to Others," "Being a Good Christian Witness," "Stretching Beyond Your Comfort Zone," stuff like that. My youth director talks about it all the time, challenging us to be the kind of people he knows we are capable of being.

I have no problem with these ideas. Hey, my close friends are from different faiths and backgrounds. I tell them what I believe. Some have even come with me to youth group. Isn't that reaching out?

But how could I even begin to reach out to Michael? I didn't even know if he would want me to.

Halfway through the year, while I sat in the lunchroom with my friends, I glanced up and noticed Michael sitting alone—again. And I realized I wasn't really reaching out or stretching beyond my comfort zone.

Silently, I pleaded with God to leave me alone, to not bug me about Michael because surely there was someone else who could befriend him. For me, it would be so inconvenient, so uncomfortable, so embarrassing.

But God didn't leave me alone.

And so after a few miserable days, I walked into the lunchroom. I walked past my table of friends, without telling them what I was up to. And I sat down across from Michael.

My heart was pounding. My face was burning. I felt like everyone was staring at me. And for some reason, I was afraid.

I said, "Hi."

Michael said nothing.

I said, "How are you?"

Michael said nothing.

I wanted to shrivel up and die, but I ate my lunch and made small talk while Michael just ate his lunch in silence.

I did this the next day and the next. Soon several days had passed, and I was beginning to feel a little resentful because, after all, I was doing my part. I was reaching out. I was talking about school and classes and stuff. But Michael was not doing his part by being grateful or friendly or nice.

The next week, I no longer saw Michael in the lunchroom. His schedule changed, and now he had fifth-hour lunch.

So my lunches with Michael ended.

I went back to sitting with my friends. We talked about school and classes and teachers and what we'd do after school or over the weekend. They never pried about the whole Michael thing. I just told them it seemed like maybe he needed a friend.

Michael never stopped me in the hall to say thanks. He never acknowledged the fact that, for a few days, we were lunch partners. He never said I really changed his life and now he's a brand-new person because someone took the time to reach out to him. I have no idea how he felt about the whole thing or if he even noticed me.

But as I think about it, I realize that I've learned something important.

God is asking me to be a better person all the time, in all kinds of ways, even ways that aren't obvious at first. It isn't always easy, comfortable or fun. But when it's the right thing, I know what I need to do.

With this experience I learned that doing the right thing doesn't always come with an obvious reward or even recognition. But knowing inside that you did what you knew was right, even though it was uncomfortable, is all the recognition you really need.

~Jake Swanson as told to Crystal Kirgiss
Chicken Soup for the Christian Teenage Soul

65

The Helpful Stranger

With Christmas vacation coming up, I was hoping that we would get a lot of snow, so I could go tobogganing with my friends. I had also asked for a snowboard for Christmas, so I was really hoping for snow to try it out.

On Christmas morning, not only did I awaken to find that it was snowing outside, but I also found an awesome new snowboard under the tree. I begged my mom and dad to take me to the toboggan hill, so I could try out my new snowboard. They agreed, so off we went through snow so thick that we could barely see where we were going.

I got on my board for the first time and made it only a quarter of the way down the hill when I fell off. I became very discouraged and didn't think that I was any good.

I made an instant decision that I didn't want to do it any more.

A few days after Christmas, my friend Zachary came over with his snowboard to go to the hill near my house with me. Zachary was very good at snowboarding, and since I could barely do it at all, that made me feel even worse. I wondered if maybe my new board wasn't the right size for me, so I tried riding Zachary's board. I still wasn't able to get very far. Finally I just gave up and said, "I can't do it."

But while I struggled with my new board, Zachary was making run after run down the hill and having a great time. He asked me if we could go to our favorite hill a little farther away to do some more runs, and not wanting to spoil his fun, I reluctantly said I would go.

While out on the new hill, I still struggled to stay up. I had fallen a few times when a teenager that I had never met before noticed that I was getting frustrated. He called over to me to give me some advice about how to snowboard. I don't talk to strangers as a rule, but my mom was with me so I felt safe. So I listened to what he had to say, and then I tried again. I was able to go farther down the hill than I had before. He watched as I made one more run, and then he came over to give me more pointers, like where to place my feet and what to do with my hands. He also told me that I should lean a little bit forward once I got up. I tried what he told me to do, and I was able to go all the way down the hill without falling! It seemed so much easier with the instructions that he gave me. He continued to help me a number of times and gave me lots of encouragement.

I find it hard sometimes to listen to other people when they are telling me what to do, but this guy was very helpful and nice about the way he instructed me. He could have chosen to make a few more runs for the day, instead of taking time to help me—a kid he didn't even know.

As younger preteens, sometimes when we think of teenagers, we think about those that are "trouble makers," or some who intimidate us. But this teenager was not like that at all. He made me feel comfortable around him and was really helpful and kind to me.

I'm a much better snowboarder now, thanks to a very helpful and considerate teenage stranger.

~Alex Judge
Chicken Soup for the Preteen Soul 2

66

Born to Win

The doctor called my mom and dad and me into his office. He said, "Jake, you have angiosarcoma, a very rare form of cancer. You have thirty tumors in your foot. In the last fifteen years, there have only been a few instances in the United States in which this form of cancer occurred only in an extremity. It is usually found in the internal organs, but for some reason yours started at your foot and spread to your ankle."

How could this be? During a basketball game—a summer league—I had come down wrong on my ankle. After limping around all month, I decided to get it checked out. School was starting, and I needed to be in top condition for basketball season. I thought at worst that I had fractured my ankle.

The doctor continued, "You really don't have a choice here. The biggest problem with this type of cancer is there is no cure. Chemo and radiation won't work. We need to perform a below-the-knee amputation."

I went home and went right to my room where I had a really, really good cry. I thought, "Why me? I'm only sixteen years old. I'm a good kid; I haven't done anything wrong in my life."

That afternoon was the only time I felt sorry for myself. I thought about my grandmother, Baba—she had passed away a couple of years before—and how brave she was. She had diabetes. Because of complications, her leg was amputated. No matter how sick Baba felt, she always smiled and never complained.

I talked to God for a while that day. I said, "I'll try to be as strong as Baba was. If this means giving part of my right leg so I can keep my life, then I'm completely game, because I'm not about to lose my life."

The morning of the surgery I listened to a song from my favorite group, the Beastie Boys. I told myself to be strong, to just get it over with.

The first few days after the surgery were the hardest. I experienced phantom pains. Those really hurt. The brain doesn't understand at first that a body part is gone. I would wake up in the middle of the night having to scratch my toe, and I couldn't. This would go on for three hours—it was torture.

I was up on crutches right away. The next step was to get my prosthesis—an artificial leg. I'll never forget that day. The physical therapist told me that walking with my prosthesis would be difficult. I should expect it to take one and a half to two months to learn to walk without crutches. I looked at him and said, "You know what? I'm going to learn to walk without crutches in two weeks."

It ended up that I was half a week off. When I walked into the therapy clinic, my therapist held up a basketball. He said, "Here, Jake, since you proved to me you could walk in record time, let's shoot a round."

I slowly walked outside to the court. I stood at the free-throw line, and he threw me the basketball. I threw it up and sunk it. You can't imagine the feeling when I heard the swoosh. I thought, "I've still got it. I'm still the same person."

From then on, my progress just took off. A month later, I learned how to jog. I was already playing basketball again, and during my free period at lunch, I was shooting baskets with my friends.

My dad took me to San Antonio to meet Thomas Bourgeois, the number-one pentathlete in the United States. A pentathlete is an athlete participating in five events at the Paralympics, elite sport events for athletes from six different disability groups. They emphasize the participants' athletic achievements rather than their disabilities. The Paralympic Games have always been held the same year as the Olympic Games. In Atlanta in 1996, 3,195 athletes participated.

Thomas won a bronze medal in 1992 in Barcelona and a silver medal in Atlanta in 1996. When we met up with him, I couldn't help but stare. Here was this professional athlete wearing shorts exposing his prosthesis—a black, robotic-looking device—and totally confident. He even had a sandal on his foot. And here I was wearing long pants trying my best to hide my leg.

After lunch, we went to the basketball courts. He and I played three college kids and beat them. I couldn't believe his moves. He made those guys look like little kids.

Thomas said, "Jake, it's unbelievable that in six months you are playing ball like this. You have a future in athletics." I went with Thomas to the Summer Nationals to watch him compete. To see all those athletes with prostheses was mind-boggling.

I ended up taking a clinic with Dennis Oehler, a gold medal winner in the 1988 Paralympics. He puts on clinics for new amputees and teaches them how to run again. We started with a fast walk and then a jog. He told me to sprint like I normally would. I took off running. It was nine months after my leg was amputated, and I was sprinting. Tears filled my eyes—I felt like I was flying.

Dennis told me he had never seen anyone run so soon after an amputation. He entered me in the amateur one-hundred-meter race. I ran a fifteen-second hundred, which is pretty bad. But I finished the race and felt incredible.

I came home and told my parents I wanted to start running—but a sprinting prosthesis costs twenty thousand dollars. Luckily, Nova Care, the manufacturer, was so amazed with my progress that they sent me a leg for free.

I trained for the Nationals. I wasn't ready to compete with my old school team, but I got to train with them. The Nationals were awesome. This time I ran a 13.5-second hundred, qualifying me for the World Championships.

I went to the Olympic Training Center in California. Only U.S. Olympic and Paralympic athletes can train there. I worked really hard, knowing I only had two weeks to get ready.

The World Championships were held in Birmingham, England.

There were sixteen hundred athletes from more than sixty countries. My parents and sister came to see me compete for the first time. I made it to the semifinals, but once there I got totally blown away. I was just happy I was even there in the first place, with people who shared my philosophy. The feeling at those games—the spirit—was all about athletes from all over the world overcoming adversity and giving everything we have.

When I got back home, I tried out for the track team at my school and made the varsity squad. I think I'm one of the first amputees to ever run varsity track against non-amputees.

At the first race, as I lined up against two-legged strangers, I felt I had to break the ice. My dad told me, from the beginning, that people were going to act the way I act. He said to go into every situation with a positive attitude.

I looked at the other guys in my heat and said, "Am I at the wrong meet? I thought I was supposed to be at a disabled meet. You guys are going to kill me."

One guy said, "I've seen you in the newspaper. You're supposed to be fast. We heard about you. You can't pull that on us."

I thought if I could beat just one of them, I'd be happy. I ended up finishing fourth and beating three or four guys. They told me I was the fastest one-legged guy they'd ever seen.

My goal is to compete in the Paralympics this year. In the meantime, I train hard. I also go to the hospital and hang out with little kids. It's the greatest when I see a little guy, five years old, with his prosthesis, and I can lift up my pant leg and say, "Oh, look, I've got one, too!"

I am one of the lucky ones. My parents, coaches and friends supported me from the moment I was diagnosed. I met Thomas, who believed in me, and then Dennis, who taught me how to run. I'm going to see where my running takes me, but when that's over, I'd love to do what Dennis does—go out and teach young amputees how to run again. I also want to continue to tell my story to kids and adults who are suffering—anyone who's lost faith and thinks life is over—that if you look for something good to come from something bad, you'll find it every time. With the right attitude, you always win.

~Jake Repp
Chicken Soup for the Teenage Soul on Tough Stuff

Tough Stuff

Give sorrow words; the grief that does not speak whispers the o'er-fraught heart and bids it break.

~William Shakespeare

67

Life Is a Gift

my hands trembled as I let the phone fall carelessly on my unmade bed; this had to be a mistake. There was no way Gray could be dead!

At that moment, everything in my life seemed insignificant. How could anything else matter when my best friend—someone I had known, trusted and loved since eighth grade—was gone forever? I looked down at the clothes I was folding and saw Gray's national soccer team jersey lying on my bed. My whole body froze. How could this be true? I wanted to cry, but I was in complete shock.

It took a month after Gray's death before I was emotionally ready to visit his gravesite. It was a cold Sunday afternoon and the rain bounced off the pavement as I stared at my muddy black boots. The fifty feet from the car to the grave seemed like fifty miles. I looked around at all the different tombstones and flowers, and I thought about just how many people must have done exactly what I was here to do. They had all endured the pain of visiting loved ones who had passed away.

Tears streamed down my face as I began to walk toward my best friend's grave. My legs felt like they weighed one hundred pounds each, and my stomach twisted into a knot so tight that I thought I was going to be sick. I did not want to look up and see his name written on the temporary headstone. I wanted to savor my last moments of hope that he would come back.

The rained turned into a downpour, and it was cold enough

that I could see my breath. I did not feel a thing; my entire body was numb. I shut my eyes, hoping, praying this was all some horrible dream. When I opened them, I was still in the cemetery, blurred by the shield of tears that covered my eyes. Taking a deep breath, I glanced up to the sky and made one last desperate wish that I would wake up from this nightmare. Then I slowly turned my eyes downward and looked at his name written on the headstone, the fresh hay lying over his body, the wilting flowers with water dripping off their petals and splashing into the soil covering his casket. The moment I saw his grave, I finally stopped fantasizing that he would come back, and the reality sank in that I would never again see my best friend. I knew this was goodbye, but I could not leave. I did not want to walk away; I yearned to stay by his side forever. I stood there and let my mind drift to all of our experiences together, from the time we fell in love to our first real fight. The memories came in crystal clear torrents.

"Do not tell him that I like him! Pinky swear?" I told my best friend Falon in eighth grade. I was in love. He was taller than all the other boys and had shoulder-length blond hair just like Taylor Hanson, from my all-time favorite band, Hanson. Sure enough, by the end of the day Falon had told him how I felt. Word was now out that I had a very serious crush on Gray. Every time we passed in the hallways, my cheeks would turn a soft pink. I had no idea what was happening; this was definitely not like me. I never liked guys; I was always "one of the guys." My friends would try to get me to talk to him, but no words would come out. Then our eighth grade dance made all my dreams about him come true. Gray dedicated "All My Life" by K-Ci & JoJo to me and asked me to dance. I was on cloud nine. We dated for about three weeks and then broke up. (In middle school, a week was considered a long-term relationship.)

After we got through the soap opera breakup, Gray and I were inseparable. Even distance did not hurt our friendship. In the tenth grade, Gray was offered the opportunity of his lifetime; he was asked to be the captain of the United States Junior National Soccer Team. He had to move to Florida to attend a special training center. He frequently traveled to tournaments in Italy, China, France and other locations throughout the world. Despite his distance and hectic schedule, he was there for me during all of my most difficult hours, and he always took the time to call with encouraging words.

I'll never forget the time I spent the night at Falon's house in tenth grade. We were lying in bed talking about our past relationships, teasing each other about our old boyfriends and laughing for hours. It was around 3:30 A.M., and right as we were about to drift off to sleep, Falon said something that will stay with me forever. "LP, you know that Gray loves you more than anybody ever will. You are lucky to have such a good friend." At the time, I didn't think much of this statement, as I took our friendship for granted. I never recognized just how lucky I was to have a friend who I could call at any time of the night, who would talk with me until I fell back asleep. Only now, in his absence, do I realize what an incredible friend and person Gray truly was.

Just two months ago, I approached Gray for advice, as I had frequently in the past. I was caught in a dilemma, debating whether or not I should transfer to Appalachian State University. Gray's words were simple and wise; he told me to follow my heart and that, no matter what, he would always be there to support and guide me. I then asked if he knew that I loved him, and he told me that he never doubted it. If I only knew that this was the last time I would talk to him, I would have driven to Furman and spent the entire night with him! However, I know I can't live regretting the past or wishing I had done more.

I have learned to cherish every moment I have with the people I love. I take time to fully enjoy life, and I try to appreciate each minute I am given on this planet. I did not "lose" Gray. He is still my best friend, only now he is guiding me from above. I can talk to him every night and know he is listening, and I still see him in my dreams. Gray was my angel on earth, and now he is my angel in heaven.

~Lindsay Ann Parker
Chicken Soup for the Teenage Soul IV

68

The Worst Day of My Life

I was sitting in class with about twenty-five other first-graders, listening to our teacher go on and on about the kinds of words that sound alike. The only thing I could think about was getting out of class for recess.

Then my name was called over the intercom to go to the school office.

When I got there, my brother, William, was waiting for me with my dad.

That's when I really started to wonder. Dad never picked me up early and it wasn't even his weekend to have me since my parents were divorced and I lived with my mother. I started to get little butterflies in my stomach warning me that something was definitely wrong.

We got in the car and there was my grandfather from my mother's side of the family and my uncle from my father's side of the family. That also was weird. I kept hearing Dad say to my grandfather, "Don't worry, Ray, everything will be all right, I promise." I wondered why he was saying these things. What was going on? Then I started thinking that maybe I really didn't want to know what they were talking about.

We finally got to my grandparents' house and Dad told us to come on inside; we all needed to talk. Right then, William and I looked at each other, both thinking that we were in trouble.

We got inside and no one knew how to bring bad news to a

nine-year old and a six-year old. With tears coming to his eyes, my dad said, "Kids, first we want you both to know that we will all get through this together. It will all be okay. Things happen, and a family must help each other and work through it."

Finally after what seemed like hours, but was actually only a few minutes, Dad said, "Kids, your mother has been in a very bad car accident."

"Well, is she okay?" I asked.

"No, I'm sorry. It killed her. The accident took your mother's life!"

I was so upset that I ran outside crying. I sat on the porch with my face in my hands sobbing. So many things were going through my mind. What will happen? Where will I go? What will happen with William?

At that time I had no idea what the things my dad had said meant, like God doesn't take people from earth unless he believes they are prepared for heaven. I was so angry with God though! He had taken the person who had brought me into this world — one of the most important people in my young life.

Now that I am older I understand what my dad had meant. Losing someone you truly love makes you value life a lot more. After my mother died, I went to live with my father, and he and I became very close. He remarried and we are very happy.

My brother, William, has had a terrible time though. We had different fathers, and he went to live with his own father. Not too long after our mom was killed, his father was run over by a train cart and killed. William now lives with our grandparents and I try to see him as much as possible.

Now I know why people say your life can change with each breath you take. I do regret a few things. I regret being angry with my mother that morning and not telling her that I loved her. One thing I do know is that at her funeral she did hear me tell her I was sorry. I asked her to help me with each day.

I know she heard me because every morning when I wake up I hear my mother in my heart. She tells me to make the best of my life with my new mother. People hear this and say it's weird but I can hear her and I can understand everything that she tells me. I still think about her all the time and I miss her a lot, but I have to live my life and do the things she didn't get to.

I also know God has a reason for everything that he does. You may not understand these things now but when someone this close to you dies it all starts to come together. Hold on to what you love and make the best of it. With life, there aren't second chances.

~Jennifer Kerperien
Chicken Soup for the Preteen Soul 2

69

Faith of an Angel

Prayer is not merely an occasional impulse to which we respond
when we are in trouble:
prayer is a life attitude.
~Walter A. Mueller

Life lessons come in all forms. For me, inspiration came in the shape of a small, forty-pound, five-year-old cousin of mine. I'll be honest, Debra bugged me. I was about to enter my freshman year of high school, and the last thing a teenager wants is a little tag-along cousin. What I didn't realize was that although I felt like I was always the teacher and she was the pupil, roles can be reversed in a matter of seconds. We traded places one hot July afternoon when I discovered that, in the blink of an eye, happiness could be shattered.

We were all gathered at a friend's outdoor wedding reception. The decorations were simple yet elegant, and the setting sun illuminated the bride and groom's already glowing faces. Comadres traveled from table to table, catching up on the latest news, because when you come from a small town in South Texas, everyone is family. The children were running around, playing games of tag and greeting their extended family. The evening could not have been better. My friends and I gathered around and talked about our up-and-coming freshman year and all of the hot guys we would be meeting. After all, we were leaving behind the boys of junior high and looking for the "men" of high school. Debra wanted to join my friends and me, but what could a five-year-old contribute to our stimulating conversations?

I left the table where we were sitting, leaving behind my mother, Tía Jeri, Abuela and Debra. I walked inside the house and greeted everyone before making my way to the bathroom. The line wasn't long, thank God, because one body can take only so much punch! As I was washing my hands, there was a thud and the bathroom door came bursting open. It was an older cousin of mine, Sylvia. I will never forget the look of fear, helplessness and shock on her face. She immediately began opening cabinets in a mad dash to find towels. I figured that one of the kids had hurt themselves playing when she blurted out, "Cristina, there has been a terrible accident. Stay inside!"

What kind of accident? Who was involved? Was anyone hurt? Was it anyone I knew?

The questions flooded my mind. I gathered with my friends in the living room amidst the screams and cries of parents panicking to find their children and more towels. A woman approached and told us that a guest who was leaving the wedding had lost control of his car and plowed through the crowd. I couldn't believe it. How could there be so much joy one minute and tragedy the next?

Then I heard a voice calling my name. It was Paul, a student of my mother's. He told me that I needed to find my mother because she was looking for me. He then told me, "Debbie has been really hurt." My thoughts immediately went to the only "Debbie" I knew, my cousin Debra's babysitter. Oh God, I thought, poor Debbie.

I ran outside. Nothing could have prepared me for the war zone I saw. Bodies on the ground, tables and chairs overturned everywhere, and there, the cause of the destruction: a runaway sedan that had finally been stopped by the fence in front of the tennis courts.

I found my mother. She hugged me with tear-filled eyes and told me that we had to leave immediately—Debra was badly hurt! My heart dropped to my feet. Debra? So the girl who got hit by the car was not "Debbie" the babysitter but Debra, my five-year-old cousin. It was little Debra. I was in shock. My mother quickly drove our van around and laid down the backseat. But where was Debra? I saw two men running from the barn with a piece of board, perfectly Debra's size. I did not see my tiny cousin until she was hoisted onto the board and laid in the van. Her new white dress and shoes were torn and blood-stained, and on her left shoe was a tire mark, clear as day. We covered her with a blanket my mother kept in the van. It had a picture of La Virgen on it; how fitting, I thought. Debra never lost consciousness, but the trip seemed never-ending.

Just as my tía Jeri and I were about to lose it completely, Debra spoke in a quiet voice.

"Let us pray together," she said, and she led us in an Our Father and a Hail Mary. Here she was, a child, broken and bleeding, yet her spirit and faith never strayed. She was trying to comfort us! She asked if she was going to die and told us how much she loved us—it felt like she was saying goodbye.

Upon our arrival at the hospital, we were met by her brother, Jacob, and my tía Stella. I had never seen Jacob cry before. It terrified me! Debra immediately went into surgery, and we prayed for the best. Six hours later, Debra was brought to the recovery room. We were told that she had suffered extensive injuries and might never walk again. My mother entered the room and took Debra's tiny hand in hers. Debra awoke and asked my mother to lean in. In her ear, Debra whispered, "Tía Norma, I saw God with two angels." My mother broke down and held Debra close.

I learned more that summer in a matter of minutes than I have in my whole life. I realized that I was so caught up in my "world" that I had not taken the time to see how precious my cousin was, and how lucky I was to be the object of her attention. I also learned from Debra to accept gracefully what life gives you, but to never give up, and to keep on loving and caring for those around you. Above all, I learned from Debra to hold tightly to my faith. Debra's example that day showed all of us that the size of one's heart and the depth of one's soul cannot be judged by age, but only by actions.

Thank you, Debra, for waking me up, and for sharing your lion's heart with us.

~Cristina Cornejo
Chicken Soup for the Latino Soul

EDITORS' NOTE: Debra's recovery was long and painful, but, not surprisingly, she persevered. She not only learned to walk again, but also to dance the ballet folklorico!

70

Smiles in My Heart

What children need most are the essentials
that grandparents provide in abundance.
They give unconditional love, kindness, patience,
humor, comfort, lessons in life.
And, most importantly, cookies.
~Rudolph Giuliani

One of my first memories is of my Gramma cuddling with me in the rocking chair in her kitchen. She would sing in my ear, call me Dolly and tell me how much she loved me, her first-born grandchild. Whenever I stayed overnight, she would give me a bath with warm, white bubbles and then wrap me in the fluffiest towels she had. She made me feel safe.

She would peel the skin off apples, cut them into little pieces and sprinkle cinnamon and sugar on them because that was the way I loved them. She let me put as many different kinds of sprinkles and syrups on my ice cream as I wanted. She would buy root beer when I was coming to visit and always made sure the glass was at least half-full of foam because that was my favorite part. Then she would refill it again and again until I was full of root-beer foam. She made me feel special.

I remember sitting on her bed watching her get ready to go out and being amazed by her rituals. She smelled of Dove soap and Noxzema cream. She wore a red shade of lipstick that came in a green tube. On Saturday nights she would wash her hair in the kitchen sink, twist it into little waves, and hold them together with bobby pins so that in the morning she would have curls in her hair. She was beautiful.

Her voice was warm and made me feel safe, like fireplace fires and hot chocolate on snowy days. Her laugh was strong and clear; when she laughed with me the rest of the world didn't exist. I felt like I was the only thing she cared about. In the same way, her tears when I was sad made me feel like I would never be alone. She yelled at me once when I was mad at my mom. When I went storming out the door, all she said was, "I love you."

She let me ruin those tubes of lipstick when I'd play dress-up in her clothes and shoes. She taught me how to play bingo, and when I sat with her, staying up way past my bedtime, playing with her in a smoke-filled room of old ladies, I felt so cool.

When I was seventeen, I knew she was dying. I would spend the night at her house, and she would still wait up for me to get in, half-asleep and snoring on the couch.

When she lay dying in her hospital bed, she called me to come to her from where I stood hiding in the corner, and though her grip was weak and her lips pale, she held my hand and kissed me. She was dying, yet she comforted me.

She passed away four years ago. Sometimes it feels like it was yesterday. Entering her house, I sometimes expect to find her sitting at the table. There are times when it occurs to me that I have skipped thinking of her for one day or that I have misplaced the sound of her laugh or the healing of her touch, and it frightens me. I thank God when I remember. I thank God when I am able to cry because that means I have not forgotten her. I thank God that she was my Gramma, and I will always love her.

~Sara Tylutki
Chicken Soup for the Teenage Soul on Tough Stuff

71

Love Lives Forever

Consult not your fears, but your hopes and dreams.
Think not about your frustrations,
but about your unfulfilled potential.
Concern yourself not with what you tried and failed at,
but with what it is still possible for you to do.
~Pope John XXIII

My mouth felt dry as I followed my mother into the doctor's private office and sank into a padded chair next to hers. This doctor didn't carry a stethoscope. He had a room full of gadgets and gizmos to analyze the learning abilities of failing students. That day he had analyzed me.

He shuffled papers and jabbed his wire frame glasses with a forefinger. "I'm sorry to tell you this, Mrs. Dow, but Peter has dyslexia. A fairly severe case."

I swallowed and tried to breathe. The doctor went on. "He'll never read above the fourth-grade level. Since he won't be able to complete high school requirements, I suggest you enroll him in a trade school where he can learn to work with his hands."

I didn't want to go to trade school. I wanted to be a preacher, like my dad. My eyes filled with tears, but I forced them back. A twelve-year-old was too big to cry.

Mom stood up, so I jumped to my feet, too. "Thank you, Doctor," she said. "Come along, Peter."

We drove home without saying much. I felt numb. Dyslexia? I'd never heard the word until last week. Sure, I was always the slowest kid in my class. During recess I had a special hiding place behind a shrub. There I would cry because I couldn't do my lessons no matter how hard I tried.

Of course, I never told my mom about that part of school. I was too ashamed. I didn't want to worry her, either. She had enough on her mind with teaching school full-time and taking care of Dad, my two brothers, my sister and me.

Mom and I arrived home before the rest of the family. I was glad. I wanted some time alone. With my chin almost touching my chest, I pulled off my coat and hung it in the closet. When I turned around my mother was standing right in front of me. She didn't say anything. She just stood there looking into my eyes with tears running down her cheeks. Seeing her cry was too much for me. Before I knew what was happening, I was in her arms bawling like a big baby. A few minutes later, she led me into the living room to the couch.

"Sit down, honey. I want to talk to you."

I rubbed my eyes with my sleeve and waited, plucking at the crease in my trousers.

"You heard what the doctor said about your not finishing school. I don't believe him."

I stopped sniffling and looked at her. Her mild blue eyes smiled into mine. Behind them lay an iron will. "We'll have to work very hard, you and I, but I think we can do it. Now that I know what the problem is, we can try to overcome it. I'm going to hire a tutor who knows about dyslexia. I'll work with you myself evenings and weekends." Her eyebrows drew down as she peered at me. "Are you willing to work, Peter? Do you want to try?"

A ray of hope shone through the hazy future. "Yes, Mom. I want to real bad."

The next six years were an endurance run for both of us. I studied with a tutor twice a week until I could haltingly read my lessons. Each night, my mom and I sat at my little desk and rehearsed that day's schoolwork for at least two hours, sometimes until midnight. We drilled for tests until my head pounded and the print blurred before my eyes. At least twice a week, I wanted to quit. I had the strength of a kitten, but my mom's courage never wavered.

She'd rise early to pray over my school day. A thousand times I heard her say, "Lord, open Peter's mind today. Help him remember the things we studied."

Her vision reached beyond the three R's. Twice I won at statewide speech competitions. I participated in school programs and earned a license to work as an announcer on a local radio station.

Then my mother developed chronic migraines during my senior year. She blamed the headaches on stress. Some days the intense pain kept her in bed. Still she'd come to my room in the evening, wearing her robe, an ice pack in her hand, to study with me.

We laughed and cried when I passed my senior finals. Two days before graduation I talked to my mother and father about Bible college. I wanted to go, but I was afraid.

Mom said, "Apply at the Bible Institute in our town. You can live at home, and I'll help you."

I put my arms around her and hugged her close, a baseball-sized lump in my throat.

A week after graduation, my mom felt a stabbing pain in her head. She became disoriented for just a moment, but seemed to be all right. It was another migraine, she thought, so she went to bed. That night Dad tried to wake her. She was unconscious.

A few hours later, a white-coated doctor told us Mom had an aneurysm that had burst. A massive hemorrhage left us no hope. She died two days later.

My grief almost drowned me. For weeks I walked the floor all night, sometimes weeping, sometimes staring at nothing. Did I have a future without my mother? She was my eyes, my understanding, my life. Should I still enroll in Bible school? The thought of going on alone filled me with terror. But, deep inside, I knew I had to move on to the next step, for her.

When I brought home the first semester's books and course outlines, I sat in the chair at my little desk. With trembling fingers, I opened my history book and began to read the first chapter. Suddenly,

I looked over at the chair she used to sit in. It was empty, but my heart was full.

Mom's prayers still followed me. I could feel her presence. I could sense her faith.

In my graduation testimony I said, "Many people had a part in making Bible college a success for me. The person who helped me most is watching from Heaven tonight. To her I say, 'Thank you, Mom, for having faith in God and faith in me. You will always be with me.'"

~Peter Dow as told to Rosey Dow
Chicken Soup for the Christian Woman's Soul

My Most Memorable Christmas

I don't think of all the misery but of the beauty that still remains.
~Anne Frank

The fall of 1978, our daughter Carol, age thirteen, was thrown from a motorcycle on which she had been a passenger. She sailed eighty-nine feet through the air and landed in a ditch, where she almost died. My wife and I were on a mission in Korea when we got the news that the doctors were in the process of amputating her left leg.

Our flight home took twenty-two hours. I suppose I did more crying on that flight than I ever have in my entire life. When my wife and I arrived at our daughter's side, unable to think of adequate words of comfort, surprisingly enough, Carol began the conversation.

"Dad," she said, "I think God has a special ministry for my life to help people who have been hurt as I have." She saw possibilities—positive ones—in tragedy! What a lift those words gave me. But we were just beginning what would prove to be a long, exhausting battle.

Carol's femur had broken in four places and plunged through the thigh bone into the ditch of an Iowa farm, next to a slaughterhouse. There, it picked up a form of bacteria that had previously been resistant to any known antibiotics.

In November, Carol went back into the hospital for surgery that would, hopefully, release muscles in her knee that might make her leg more usable. The doctor was delighted when he opened her thigh and knee and discovered no pus pockets. But the hidden bacteria, which until that time had remained dormant, erupted like a prairie fire when exposed to the open air. Three days after surgery, she was the sickest little girl I've ever seen.

Each passing day, the bacteria multiplied with increasing impatience. Carol's fever soared to 104 degrees and lingered there day after day, night after night. Her leg continued to swell and the infection raged out of control.

About that time, we were blessed with a minor miracle. With no knowledge of my daughter's need, the Federal Drug Administration released, for the first time, an antibiotic that was declared significantly effective against the specific strain of bacteria that Carol contracted while lying in that Iowa ditch. She was the first human being in Children's Hospital, Orange County, California, to receive it. In a matter of hours after the first dosage, her temperature went down. Each successive culture reading showed fewer and fewer bacteria. Finally, about three weeks before Christmas, a culture came back that showed no bacteria growth.

Lying in her hospital bed with the intravenous tubes still in her hands, Carol asked the visiting doctor, who was standing in for her own surgeon, when she would be released. "Will I be home for Christmas, Doctor?" she asked.

"I don't know," he replied cautiously.

"Will I be able to get my new prosthesis?" she asked.

"Well," the doctor cautioned, "I don't believe you can get it yet."

But when her own doctor returned, he checked her over. That same day Carol called me at my office. "Daddy, I have good news," she announced.

"What is it?" I asked.

"Doctor Masters is an angel," she exclaimed. "He said I can come home for Christmas!"

On December 16th, a Saturday night, Carol was released from the hospital. I was told to stay home and await a surprise. My wife went to pick her up. I saw the lights of the car as it rolled up the driveway, and I ran to the front door. My wife barred my way and said, "Bob, you have to go back in and wait. Carol wants you to wait by the Christmas tree."

So I waited nervously by the Christmas tree, counting the seemingly interminable seconds. Then I heard the front door open and the squeak of rubber on the wooden floor. I knew the sound came from the rubber tips of Carol's crutches. She stepped into the open door, ten feet away from my seat by the Christmas tree. She had gone straight from the hospital to the beauty parlor, where her hair stylist gave her a beautiful permanent. There she stood with lovely curls framing her face. Then I looked down and saw two shoes, two ankles, two legs and a beautiful girl.

She had come home and, because of it, made that Christmas my most memorable.

~Reverend Robert Schuller
Chicken Soup for the Teenage Soul II

Dealing with My Mother's Death

Dear Teenage Chicken Soup,

Thank you for the uplifting stories that you have published. I own two inspirational books: *Chicken Soup for the Teenage Soul* and *Chicken Soup for the Christian Soul*. The stories in both books are filled with what this world should be more like.

I used to be a drug and alcohol abuser at the age of thirteen. I felt invincible and I rebelled. I didn't understand the method of discipline my parents used at that time. They believed that if you misbehaved, you should pay the consequences for your actions. Some months down the road, a tragedy struck our household. My mother, who was suffering from congestive heart failure, passed away. I felt cut off from the world and that God had turned his back on me. My friends helped me relieve the pain, but it would come back like a wave washing over me. All I had to do was look around at home. It was a constant reminder. It was so bad that I ended up staying at a friend's house for close to six months. I was always able to cover up the pain with distractions that would seem to keep my mind off her. I knew deep down inside at some point I would have to deal with my real feelings and emotions surrounding my mother's death. That time came very recently.

It started out as a normal day, until I turned on the radio. "Amazing Grace" blared into my ears. It was the song sung at my mother's funeral. I instantly broke down. At first, I began blaming my mom, then myself, then God. The barricades blocking my memory broke down and I had to finally face that my mother was no longer here. She was never going to return and there was nothing I could do about it. I cried, then prayed, then cried some more. I couldn't take it. It wasn't fair. Everyone else I knew had mommies. I didn't want to be different in that aspect of my life. Yet, the harsh fact still remains: I am motherless. It still hurts to look back on those memories, but it made me who am I today. Her golden smile is my favorite memory of her, and I know she is keeping heaven radiant with that same smile.

The books you have written are truly special. I would like to tell you from the bottom of my heart, THANK YOU!!!! This world is full of tragedy, disaster, fear, hatred, anger and remorse. The books you have published have shown me that this world is also full of goodness.

Love,

~Amanda L. Poff
Chicken Soup for the Teenage Soul Letters

Chapter
10

CHRISTIAN Teen Talk

Reaching Out

*Do nothing from selfishness or empty conceit, but with humility of mind
let each of you regard one another as more important than himself.*
~Philippians 2:3

One Single Rose

Kindness, like a boomerang, always returns.
~Author Unknown

It was Valentine's Day, my freshman year of high school. I was so young, the romantic type, and I longed for a boyfriend or secret admirer. I walked the halls seeing couples holding hands, girls with huge smiles on their faces, and dozens of roses being delivered to "that special someone." All I wanted was a rose. A single rose to brighten up my Valentine's Day. But I was picky. I didn't want the rose from my parents, my sister or even my best friend. I wanted it from a secret admirer.

When school ended, I had no rose to hang in my locker as I had hoped. I came home a little sad and hoped next year's Valentine's Day would be better. I sat in my room dreaming about next year's romantic Valentine's Day when the doorbell rang. There at the front door was a deliveryman bringing one single rose to my house. Surely this rose wasn't for me. I didn't have such luck. I closed the front door with the rose in my hand and gave it to my mother. "Open the card!" she insisted when I told her it must be for her. I unsealed the envelope as my hands were shaking. Why were my hands shaking? I knew it wasn't for me. I slowly lifted the card and read what it said:

To Amanda
From someone who cares

I must have read it twenty times in a matter of seconds, praying my eyes weren't playing tricks on me. But they weren't. The rose was for me. I must have been happy for about five minutes, until I started calling the obvious people and accusing them of sending me a rose and playing a joke on my hopelessly romantic heart. No one knew who sent it to me. My friends, family and relatives were as surprised to hear I got a rose from a secret someone as much as I was. I was on cloud nine for weeks. Every time in high school that I felt down, I would think about my freshman year's Valentine's Day and a smile would appear.

Senior year rolled around and the dreaded February fourteenth was once again upon us. This year I received at least six carnations (a carnation-selling fundraiser was held at school that year), all from my best friends. I walked around with a big smile on my face, holding my flowers. Even though they were just from friends, they made me happy.

The end of the day was drawing to a close, and I had two classes left to show off my flowers. I walked into my French class and noticed one of my closest French class friends looking upset. I had grown to know my French classmates pretty well, since I had spent three of my high school years with the same people in one class. We'd turned into a little French family. Well, my friend saw me walk in with my six flowers and lowered her head with tears in her eyes. She hadn't received a single flower, not even from her best friend.

We talked a few minutes before class, and some very familiar words came out of her mouth. "All I wanted was one single rose." My heart ached as I heard those words. The familiar sense of loneliness I had felt as a freshman, she was feeling now. I wanted to do something. It was too late to purchase carnations and I couldn't get her anything on a break because school was almost over. Finally, I figured it out. My freshman year. The single rose. That was it; that was what I had to do.

I told my mom about my plan and asked her if we could try to find a rose after our Valentine's dinner out. She remembered having seen a bucket of roses at a local drug store, so we rushed over and purchased the last good-looking rose and a small card. In order to preserve my identity, my mom wrote what I dictated to her in the card:

To Kristen
From someone who cares

We drove to her house, trying to be discreet. I ran up to the front door, put the rose in her mailbox, rang the doorbell, ran back to the car and drove away. All the feelings of happiness I had felt my freshman year had come flooding back. I just kept thinking that I was going to make someone feel as special as I had three years earlier.

The next day in school, Kristen came up to me and gave me a hug with tears in her eyes. She had realized it was me by the handwriting. I guess my mom and I are more alike than I thought. She cried and said it was the nicest thing anyone had done for her in a while.

I never did figure out who it was who sent me that rose. But I did figure something else out. It didn't matter if it was a guy who secretly loved me, my mom trying to make me feel loved or an acquaintance who knew what I needed. What matters was that it was from someone who cared about me and who went out of their way to brighten up my day.

~Amanda Bertrand
Chicken Soup for the Teenage Soul on Love & Friendship

Angel

Two days before my birthday, I got an e-mail that would first make me cry and then make me smile.

Patrick was a kid that I knew from 4-H. We became friends when I taught him how to show horses and he showed my horse in the Junior Division at the county horse show. We weren't "close" friends, but he was a pretty cool guy. I mean, how many guys like to show horses and will let a girl teach them how to do it? Not very many.

After he left the club, we kind of lost contact. He sent me a Christmas card with his e-mail address in it, but I put off e-mailing him. I thought, "How much stuff would we be able to talk about anyway?"

His e-mail address was in my address book, and when I changed servers, my new address went to everyone on my list. A few days later I got a reply from Patrick. It was brief; he asked me how I was and told me that he had started riding lessons again. He also asked me how Theo, my horse, was and he gave me his e-mail address. He ended with:

Hope you have a nice day. Patrick.

I replied to his e-mail, just small talk, and my e-mail looked something like this:

*Hi! Nice to hear from you. That's so cool you're taking lessons.
I'm really sorry that I didn't e-mail you at all during the winter.
School has been really busy for me this year. Theo is doing well.
He still knocks my radio off the stall door when I have the music
on too loud. You'll have to come out and visit sometime.*

A few more lines ended my e-mail. When his came back, he had
some questions for me.

*That's cool. What kind of music do you listen to? I like country.
Do you like hunting?*

Turns out, country music is the only thing I will listen to! And hunting is one of my favorite pastimes. I had no idea we had so much in common. I thought, "This is cool, we actually like the same stuff!"

Those e-mails were the start of a two-month correspondence that covered a wide variety of subjects. Having a lot in common made it easy to just chat. And to tell you the truth, I enjoyed getting his e-mails.

Toward the end of June, I wrote him a reply to an e-mail I had received four days earlier from him. I felt bad about not getting back to him right away and my e-mail wasn't much more than a note, but what I got back from him took my breath away.

Patrick's e-mail was short. He started off by telling me he was going to be on vacation for three weeks and other stuff like that. But the postscript is what got me. It read:

*P.S. I really wanted to say thank you for talking to me through
e-mail. I'm usually really shy and am afraid to tell people what
my likes are and all, plus I really have been bored since school
let out. E-mailing you, at least I can talk to someone. You like
everything I like so far, and as long as I have lived I have never
met anyone so much like me. I've been used to a lot of people
picking on me, and I've been pretty down the past few years.*

When I read that people picked on him, my thoughts were, "Why in the world are kids so mean? Don't they realize how they are making him feel?" It broke my heart to hear him say that he had been down the past few years. I actually started crying when I read how the other kids treated him. It was then that I understood that Patrick was a kid who had needed a friend. My taking the time to e-mail him had made him feel important, like someone really cared enough to talk to him instead of just picking on him.

> *I want to thank you again. You like just about everything I like—hunting, cars, country music, horses. To me you're like an angel.*

Those last six words touched my heart. It made me feel so good I just can't explain it! No one had ever said anything that nice to me before, and to be called an "angel" just made my day! When I e-mailed him back, I sincerely thanked him for what he said and told him to hang on.

That day, I learned a lesson that would stay with me for the rest of my life. From now on, I will take the time to do the little things, like replying to an e-mail or card, even if it's just a line or two. You never know how you might help someone and become his or her "angel."

~Jena Pallone
Chicken Soup for the Preteen Soul 2

76

Troubled

Christmas waves a magic wand over this world,
and behold, everything is softer and more beautiful.
~Norman Vincent Peale

A song sung by Faith Hill in the blockbuster movie *The Grinch* asks: "Where are you, Christmas? Why can't I find you?" Well, sometimes the Christmas spirit is like a misplaced sock—you find it when you aren't looking and where you'd least expect it to show up.

I found it at a quarter past one in the morning.

On my way home from work, I stopped at the neighborhood doughnut shop. After parking in its ghost town of a parking lot, I was headed toward the door when I spotted trouble.

What lit a warning light on my intuition radar was a group of teenagers—three boys and a girl. Understand, I wasn't alarmed by their tattoos (the girl included) or their earrings (boys included—eyebrows as well as each of their ears). Rather, it was the extremely late hour and the fact they loitered on the sidewalk in a semicircle around an elderly man sitting in a chair. Wearing a tattered flannel shirt and barefoot, the man looked positively cold and probably homeless.

And in trouble with a capital T.

Against my better judgment, I went inside the store and ordered three doughnuts—while keeping a worried eye on the group outside. Nothing seemed to be happening.

Until I headed toward my car.

Something was indeed "going down." As ominously as a pirate ordering a prisoner to the plank, the teens told the old man to stand up and walk.

Oh, no, I thought. Capital tee-are-oh-you-bee-el-ee.

But wait. I had misjudged the situation. And I had misjudged the teens.

"How do those feel?" one of the boys asked. "Do they fit?"

The cold man took a few steps—maybe a dozen. He stopped, looked at his feet, turned around and walked back. "Yeah, they'z about my size," he answered, flashing a smile that, despite needing a dentist's attention, was friendly and warm on this cold night.

The teens, all four, grinned back.

"Keep them. They're yours," one of the boys replied. "I want you to have them."

I looked down. The teen was barefoot. The kid had just given the cold-and-probably-homeless man his expensive skateboarding sneakers—and, apparently his socks, as well.

The other two boys sat on their skateboards by the curb, retying their shoelaces. Apparently, they, too, had let the man try on their sneakers to find which pair fit the best. The girl, meanwhile, gave the cold man her oversized sweatshirt.

With my heart warmed by the unfolding drama, I went back into the shop.

"Could I trouble you for another dozen doughnuts?" I asked, then told the clerk what I had witnessed.

Christmas spirit, it seemed, was more contagious than flu or chicken pox. Indeed, the cold night got even warmer when the woman not only wouldn't let me pay for the doughnuts, but added a large coffee, too.

"These are from the lady inside. Have a nice night," I said as I delivered the warm doughnuts and piping-hot cup. The old man smiled appreciatively.

"You have a nice night, too," the teens said.

I already had.

~Woody Woodburn
Chicken Soup for the Soul The Book of Christmas Virtues

77

The Boy Under the Tree

Act as if what you do makes a difference. It does.
~William James

In the summer recess between freshman and sophomore years in college, I was invited to be an instructor at a high school leadership camp hosted by a college in Michigan. I was already highly involved in most campus activities, and I jumped at the opportunity.

About an hour into the first day of camp, amid the frenzy of icebreakers and forced interactions, I first noticed the boy under the tree. He was small and skinny, and his obvious discomfort and shyness made him appear frail and fragile. Only fifty feet away, two hundred eager campers were bumping bodies, playing, joking and meeting each other, but the boy under the tree seemed to want to be anywhere other than where he was. The desperate loneliness he radiated almost stopped me from approaching him, but I remembered the instructions from the senior staff to stay alert for campers who might feel left out.

As I walked toward him, I said, "Hi, my name is Kevin, and I'm one of the counselors. It's nice to meet you. How are you?" In a shaky, sheepish voice he reluctantly answered, "Okay, I guess." I calmly asked him if he wanted to join the activities and meet some new people. He quietly replied, "No, this is not really my thing."

I could sense that he was in a new world, that this whole

experience was foreign to him. But I somehow knew it wouldn't be right to push him, either. He didn't need a pep talk; he needed a friend. After several silent moments, my first interaction with the boy under the tree was over.

At lunch the next day, I found myself leading camp songs at the top of my lungs for two hundred of my new friends. The campers eagerly participated. My gaze wandered over the mass of noise and movement and was caught by the image of the boy from under the tree, sitting alone, staring out the window. I nearly forgot the words to the song I was supposed to be leading. At my first opportunity, I tried again, with the same questions as before: "How are you doing? Are you okay?" To which he again replied, "Yeah, I'm all right. I just don't really get into this stuff." As I left the cafeteria, I realized this was going to take more time and effort than I had thought—if it was even possible to get through to him at all.

That evening at our nightly staff meeting, I made my concerns about him known. I explained to my fellow staff members my impression of him and asked them to pay special attention and spend time with him when they could.

The days I spent at camp each year flew by faster than any others I have known. Thus, before I knew it, mid-week had dissolved into the final night of camp, and I was chaperoning the "last dance." The students were doing all they could to savor every last moment with their new "best friends"—friends they would probably never see again.

As I watched the campers share their parting moments, I suddenly saw what would be one of the most vivid memories of my life. The boy from under the tree, who had stared blankly out the kitchen window, was now a shirtless dancing wonder. He owned the dance floor as he and two girls proceeded to cut a rug. I watched as he shared meaningful, intimate time with people at whom he couldn't even look just days earlier. I couldn't believe it was the same person.

In October of my sophomore year, a late-night phone call pulled me away from my chemistry book. A soft spoken, unfamiliar voice asked politely, "Is Kevin there?"

"You're talking to him. Who's this?"

"This is Tom Johnson's mom. Do you remember Tommy from leadership camp?"

The boy under the tree. How could I not remember?

"Yes, I do," I said. "He's a very nice young man. How is he?"

An abnormally long pause followed, then Mrs. Johnson said, "My Tommy was walking home from school this week when he was hit by a car and killed." Shocked, I offered my condolences.

"I just wanted to call you," she said, "because Tommy mentioned you so many times. I wanted you to know that he went back to school this fall with confidence. He made new friends. His grades went up. And he even went out on a few dates. I just wanted to thank you for making a difference for Tom. The last few months were the best few months of his life."

In that instant, I realized how easy it is to give a bit of yourself every day. You may never know how much each gesture may mean to someone else. I tell this story as often as I can, and when I do, I urge others to look out for their own "boy under the tree."

~David Coleman and Kevin Randall
Chicken Soup for the College Soul

78

Give Random Acts of Kindness a Try!

One dismal evening, just a few months ago,
When the sky was dark and the streets were covered
 with snow,
I had nothing specific in mind and wasn't sure
 what to do,
Since it was one of those chilly nights that leave you
 feeling a bit blue,
I shuffled through a few papers and picked up a book
And without giving it much thought, decided to
 take a look.
It was one those volumes filled with dozens of stories
That told tales of victories, failures, and
 special glories.
There was an account of a boy who went to school
 and learned,
And another of a girl who got the toy for which she
 yearned.
Then I came to a story about someone just like us
Who decided to spend a day doing random
 acts of kindness.
Every thoughtful gift and kind word said with grace,

Brightened someone's day and left a smile on
    their face.
I sat back to ponder the story and came up with
    a thought—
If everyone tried to share some happiness and
    kindness sought,
Wouldn't our world be so much more pleasant than
    it is now
When a few more smiles and time for others
    we'd allow?
I baked a batch of cookies today, and I know a lady
    down the street
Who I'm sure would love a few moments' company
    and a home-baked treat,
And her lonely neighbor who always seems a bit sad
    and gray—
I think a nice visit from someone would just make
    her day.
Well, it was starting to get late, so I decided to get
    some sleep
After I made a list of things to do the next day and
    appointments to keep.
When I got up in the morning I went to school with
    a goal in mind—
I would try to cheer a few people up and find ways
    to be kind.
I bid "Good morning" and smiled at everybody I met.
A few returned the greeting, then our separate ways
    we went.
Someone dropped their books, so I helped gather
    them willingly,
And I noticed the more I helped others, the more
    they helped me!
After I went home I packaged some cookies to share,
Attaching a note that said, "Just because I care."

When they opened the doors, you should have seen
    their faces light with glee
And watched their smiles as they exclaimed, "You
    mean you came to visit lonely old me!"
Later in the evening, I sat down and wrote
    a few notes
Wishing the recipient a great week, before sealing
    them in envelopes.
Then I took a few moments to think about my day
And realized I received even more joy than I had
    given away;
Because every time you smile or with a
    cheerful word part,
The warmth of that kindness penetrates into your
    own heart.
We're only given a short time to spread some cheer
    before we die,
So why not give random acts of kindness a try?

~Melissa Broeckelman
Chicken Soup for the Teenage Soul II

79

Ivy's Cookies

With every deed you are sowing a seed, though the harvest you may not see.
~Ella Wheeler Wilcox

The clank of the metal door and the echo of their footsteps rang in the ears of Ivy and Joanne as they walked down the dingy corridor behind the prison guard toward the "big room." The aroma of Ivy's homemade chocolate chip cookies wasn't enough to override the stench of ammonia from the recently mopped floor, or the bitterness and anger that hung in the air. Women's Correctional Institute was not the kind of place where most seventeen-year-olds go for an outing, but Ivy had a mission.

She didn't know what she was getting into, but she had to try. With trembling fingers, she had dialed the number for an appointment at the prison. Warden Baylor was receptive to Ivy's desire to visit and referred her to Joanne, another teen who had also expressed interest.

"How do we do this?" Ivy asked.

"Who knows? Maybe homemade cookies would break the ice," Joanne suggested.

So they baked their cookies and came bearing gifts to strangers.

"I put almonds in these," Ivy rambled nervously as they moved along. "The dough was gummier than usual..."

"Don't chatter," the guard snapped. "It gets the prisoners riled."

The harsh words made Ivy jump and her heart pound. She walked the rest of the distance in silence.

"Okay. Here we are," the guard grunted, keys rattling. "You go in. I'll lock the door behind you. Be careful what you say. They have a way of using your words against you. You have fifteen minutes. Holler if you have any trouble." Ivy noted the prisoners' orange jumpsuits and felt overdressed. Maybe we shouldn't have worn heels, she thought. They probably think we're snobs.

Remembering the guard's admonition, the girls put the cookies on the table next to plastic cups of juice, without saying a word. Some prisoners leaned against the wall; others stood around watching, studying, thinking, staring. Nobody talked. Ivy smiled at one of the women, who scowled back. From then on, Ivy avoided eye contact with the inmates. After five minutes of strained silence, Joanne whispered, "Let's move away from the table. Maybe they'll come over."

As they stepped back, one of the prisoners blurted out, "I'm gettin' a cookie." The others followed and began helping themselves. Soon they heard the rattle of keys. Time was up.

"What a relief to get out of there," Joanne sighed as a gust of fresh air caressed their perspiring faces.

"Yeah," Ivy agreed. "But I have a strong feeling that we're not done. Would you be willing to go back?"

Joanne nodded with a half-smile. "How about Thursday after school?"

Week after week they came. And week after week the prisoners ate the cookies, drank the juice and stood around in silence. Gradually, antagonistic looks were replaced by an occasional smile. Still, Ivy couldn't bring herself to speak—not a word.

Then one Thursday, an evangelist walked in. Her step was sure, her chin was high and she glowed with the love of God. But she meant business. "I've come to pray with you," she announced to the inmates. "Let's make a circle."

Ivy was awed by the women's compliance. Only a few resisted. The others, although murmuring, inched their way toward the middle of the room and formed a lopsided circle, looking suspiciously at one another.

"Join hands," the evangelist instructed. "It's not gonna hurt you, and it'll mean more if you do." Slowly, some women clasped hands, others barely touched. "Now, bow your heads."

Except for the orange outfits, it could have been a church meeting.

"Okay. We're gonna pray," the evangelist continued, "and prayer is just like talking, only to God. I want to hear you tell the Lord one thing you're thankful for. Just speak it out. Don't hold back."

Ivy's palms were sweaty. I can't pray aloud, Lord. I can't even talk to these women. I guess I should set an example, but they probably don't even like me—they probably think I'm better than they are because of my clothes.

The words of an inmate jolted her from her thoughts.

"I'm thankful, God, for Miss Ivy bringing us cookies every week."

Another voice compounded the shock. "God, thanks for bringing a black lady to see us."

Ivy's eyes brimmed with tears as she heard, "Thank you, God, for these two young ladies giving their time every week, even though we can't do anything to pay them back."

One by one, every inmate in the circle thanked God for Ivy and Joanne. Then Joanne managed to utter a prayer of gratitude for the prisoners' words. But when it came Ivy's turn, she was too choked up to speak. Her eyes burned in humble remorse over how wrong she'd been about these women. She wished she could blow her nose, but the inmates were squeezing her hands so tightly, she resorted to loud sniffles and an occasional drip.

The following week, Ivy and Joanne returned, bright eyed, to find the prisoners talkative.

"Why do you bring us cookies every week?" a husky voice inquired from the corner of the room. When Ivy explained, the inmate inched a few steps closer. "Can you get me a Bible?" she asked. Others wanted to know more about the Jesus who inspires teenagers to visit prisoners.

A ministry was born from Ivy's cookies. What started as a silent act of kindness and obedience turned into a weekly Bible study at the prison, which eventually grew so big, it split into several groups that continue to this day. After Joanne married and moved away, Ivy continued to minister to the inmates alone for years. Eventually Prison Fellowship picked up the baton.

Ivy is a grandma now. Her radiance has increased over the years, and she brightens any room she enters. But last Thursday afternoon she indulged herself in a good cry. Curled up on the couch, wrapped in the afghan her daughter had made, she wept on the first anniversary of her daughter's death. "Her kids can live with me," Ivy had said. Now they napped as the doorbell rang.

A young woman, about seventeen, stood there with a plate of homemade cookies.

"Are you Ivy Jones?" she asked.

"Yes," she answered, dabbing her eyes with a wadded tissue.

"These are for you," the girl said as she handed the cookies to her. With a shy, sad smile, she turned to leave without another word.

"Thank you," Ivy whispered in a daze. The girl was halfway down the sidewalk when Ivy called out, "But why?"

"My grandmother gave me her Bible before she died last week, and her last words were, 'Find Ivy Jones and take her some homemade cookies.'"

~Candy Abbott
Chicken Soup for the Christian Woman's Soul

Something Worthwhile

Do not wait for extraordinary circumstances to do good action;
try to use ordinary situations.
~Jean Paul Richter

As a busy freshman college student who preferred entertainment and camaraderie, I decided to become a member of the university's Student Activity Committee. This committee was responsible for organizing and carrying out campus events, including community volunteer projects.

One of my first ventures with committee members consisted of boxing food items at the local food bank for delivery to low-income senior citizens. It'll be fun to get away from studies and just hang out with my peers, I thought. Yet, far beyond my wildest imagination, God had something much more meaningful in store for me.

Our first day out, students gathered at the food center. We packed boxes with some staples of life and loaded them into our vehicles. Then, in teams of three, we set out to predetermined destinations. My partners and I were assigned to the senior housing project on the south end of Salt Lake City.

Upon our arrival, we checked in at the monitor's desk and began moving from door to door with our grocery offerings. It quickly became evident to me that, although the residents were grateful for the food items, they were especially pleased to have young visitors. However, I sensed a longing in a few of them, perhaps for days of their youth.

One resident introduced himself as Loki and invited us into his humble dwelling. At the age of ninety-two, he carefully moved about with an aluminum walker. Loki explained that he lived alone since his wife, Ester, died in 1972. Around the small room were photographs of a young Ester and Loki, their children, grandchildren and great-grandchildren. Loki declared that he enjoyed his independence and preferred to live alone, not with family. Then, with downcast eyes, he said, "If life wasn't so hectic, I'd have plenty of family visitors." I wondered if his loved ones had forgotten about him.

We discussed sports, school and hobbies. As I made us some hot cocoa, Loki promised to teach us how to tie a fishing fly, in case we decided to visit again. Upon our departure, Loki smiled and gave us each a little hand-carved hickory flute. "This is to show my appreciation for your commendable service work," he announced proudly. By day's end, my selfish motives for participating in this project had slipped away. The sunlight of an unfamiliar spirit had begun to radiate in my heart.

As a windy fall began to turn into a frosty winter, I found myself returning frequently to the housing project for visits with the residents, especially Loki. Although he had little formal education, his wisdom was profound. Thanks to Loki, aside from mastering the arts of tying fishing flies and whittling flutes, I came to appreciate poetry, nature and God. Loki told me why I was unique and important—something that no one had ever impressed upon me. As my self-esteem increased, I began to gain interest in others. Soon, I felt a usefulness I had never known.

In late December of that year, bearing a Christmas gift, I went to see Loki. Upon my arrival at the senior housing project, John, the front-desk monitor, reluctantly informed me that my friend Loki had died during the night. My heart sank like a stone plummeting into a bottomless pit. I dropped Loki's present on the floor and staggered to a chair in the lobby. "God decides when it's our time to come home," Loki had recently told me, "and until then, we do the best we can on Earth." I vividly remembered his words.

Unaware that John had moved to my side, he placed a letter in my lap. My name was scrawled on the envelope in Loki's unsteady handwriting. "When I found him in bed this morning," John whispered, "he was holding this in his hands."

Trembling, I opened the envelope and removed the single page. As I read, tears welled up in my eyes. I began to cry and was unashamed, "...for this is natural and beneficial," my old friend had said. His letter of farewell was inscribed as follows:

Dear Tony,

It's my time to be with Ester. Although my body is very tired, my soul is soaring. I've lived a lot of years. But it was in my last days that the goodness in your heart, Tony, made for many of the most special moments. You were a good friend to an old man who ended up alone in this world. Thank you for being a valuable part of my life. Remember to always let God guide your journeys, and his angels will forever remain by your side.

I love you,
Loki

My service work allowed me to have a spiritual encounter with a ninety-two-year-old man who changed my attitude and outlook on life. God has blessed me with the gift of being a part of something worthwhile.

~Tony Webb
Chicken Soup for the Volunteer's Soul

81

An Unexpected Customer

*Blessed are those who can give without remembering
and take without forgetting.*
~Elizabeth Bibesco

I had barely made my way around the counter when I saw her.

The moment I established eye contact, a huge smile spread across her face. As the corners of her mouth curved upward to form a lopsided grin, her eyes came alive and danced with light. I smiled back and asked, "Is there anything I can help you with today?"

In an excited, childlike tone, she exclaimed, "My name is Didi!" I watched as she fumbled around in her pocket. After a few seconds the search ended, and she presented me with a tube of lipstick. "I need one of these. Do you have one of these? I need a new one of these."

As I took the lipstick from her dirty hands, I knew my coworkers were staring my way. It was not difficult to conclude what they were thinking. After all, Didi was not our typical customer. Her clothes were slightly wrinkled. Neither of her two shirts was tucked in, and no two articles of clothing even remotely matched. Over her blond, unruly hair she wore a blue baseball hat. Curls peeked from beneath the hat, framing her face.

Although she must have been in her mid-twenties, she acted as if she were a young child. The faces of my coworkers communicated relief in being spared the chore of assisting her, while also revealing the humor they found in watching me take on the challenge.

Feeling slightly uncomfortable, I answered, "Yes, we have that brand. They're right back here." As I led Didi to the back of the store, she walked steadily beside me and asked, "What's your name?"

Once again I smiled and answered, "My name is Ashleigh."

"Ashleigh," she repeated. "That's a pretty name, Ashleigh. You're nice, Ashleigh."

I was unsure how to react to Didi. Politely, I replied, "Thank you."

Upon reaching the back of the store, I attempted to subtly reclaim a portion of my personal space. Moving slightly to the left, I examined the lipstick Didi had handed me earlier. As I focused my attention on it, the temptation to run overwhelmed me. And why not leave her there? After all, there was nothing wrong with allowing her to look for the correct shade. I had shown her where to look and had been friendly. Why should I stick around and continue to feel uncomfortable? Didi would be fine on her own. How hard could it be to match a lipstick shade?

Nearly convinced by my reasoning, I opened my mouth to excuse myself. Before I could form the words, conviction washed over me. Deep down I knew I did not have a good excuse to walk away. Yes, I could justify my reasoning, probably well enough to convince both myself and others. But I realized that no line of excuses or justifications would make it right.

I couldn't simply walk away and leave Didi to search for the lipstick on her own. I was basing my decision to leave Didi on what I saw—a woman who was less than what the world said she should be. I had failed to view Didi through the eyes of Jesus. When Jesus looked at Didi, he didn't see someone of little value or see an uncomfortable situation that he couldn't wait to escape.

I suddenly recalled stories in the gospels where Jesus reached out to and loved those who society rejected and counted as worthless. He loved the beggar and the blind man. He embraced the tax collector and the harlot. He extended healing to the lame and the leper. Jesus recognized and treated each individual as a precious, priceless soul.

It didn't take long for me to locate the correct shade. Removing it from the shelf, I handed the tube to Didi. "Here you go. This is the one."

Excitedly, Didi took the tube from my hands and asked, "This is the right one?"

"Yes, this one will look pretty," I answered as I led Didi to the front of the store. As I reached the counter, I knew my coworkers were still watching me. Yet, this time I was not bothered by their expressions. I saw Didi through new eyes. I no longer focused on her dirty hands or less-than-perfect attire. I saw Didi as I believe Jesus would, as someone made in the image of God.

After I rang up her purchase, Didi smiled at me and said, "Ashleigh, you're sweet."

I simply smiled back, knowing that, because of Didi, I would now view my world just a little bit differently.

~Ashleigh Kittle Slater
Chicken Soup for the Christian Teenage Soul

82

Mr. Gillespie

*Real generosity is doing something nice for someone
who you think will never find out.*
~Frank A. Clark

When I was in seventh grade, I was a candy striper at a local hospital in my town. I volunteered about thirty to forty hours a week during the summer. Most of the time I spent there was with Mr. Gillespie. He never had any visitors, and nobody seemed to care about his condition. I spent many days there holding his hand and talking to him, helping with anything that needed to be done. He became a close friend of mine, even though he responded with only an occasional squeeze of my hand. Mr. Gillespie was in a coma.

I left for a week to vacation with my parents, and when I came back, Mr. Gillespie was gone. I didn't have the nerve to ask any of the nurses where he was, for fear they might tell me he had died. So with many questions unanswered, I continued to volunteer there through my eighth grade year.

Several years later, when I was a junior in high school, I was at the gas station when I noticed a familiar face. When I realized who it was, my eyes filled with tears. He was alive! I got up the nerve to ask him if his name was Mr. Gillespie, and if he had been in a coma about five years ago. With an uncertain look on his face, he replied yes. I explained how I knew, and that I had spent many hours talking with him in the hospital. His eyes welled up with tears, and he gave me the warmest hug I had ever received.

He began to tell me how, as he lay there comatose, he could hear me talking to him and could feel me holding his hand the whole time. He thought it was an angel, not a person, who was there with him. Mr. Gillespie firmly believed that it was my voice and touch that had kept him alive.

Then he told me about his life and what happened to him to put him in the coma. We both cried for a while and exchanged a hug, said our goodbyes and went our separate ways.

Although I haven't seen him since, he fills my heart with joy every day. I know that I made a difference between his life and his death. More important, he has made a tremendous difference in my life. I will never forget him and what he did for me: he made me an angel.

~Angela Sturgill
A 5th Portion of Chicken Soup for the Soul

Coming Together

D ear *Chicken Soup for the Teenage Soul*,
My name is Jen, and I am nineteen years old. In September 1999 I left Sheffield, England, to live and volunteer at a place called Corrymeela in Northern Ireland. I am here for a year. The Corrymeela Community is a diverse community of people of all Christian traditions who are individually and collectively committed to the healing of social, religious and political divisions in Northern Ireland and throughout the world. I am joined by eleven other volunteers: six from Ireland and five from other parts of the world such as Sweden, America and Germany. Together with the permanent staff, they have become my work mates, support structure, friends and family, and the people I have grown to love. I live in a house on-site with the other volunteers. When I first set out for this adventure back in September, the idea of living with eleven complete strangers was a pretty strange thing to comprehend. Now that I have been living, eating, working and socializing with this group for close to a year, I can't imagine our paths not having crossed.

The groups I work with at Corrymeela consist of all different people who come by the hundreds every year to stay at the center. We see all types come through our doors: school groups, single parents, youth groups, families, churches, ex-prisoners, recovering alcoholics, you name it. Most of the people we work with come from Ireland, but we have had people join us from all corners of the world, too. As I write this, we have over thirty countries represented on-site this week as part of a major project. It's amazing!

I help to run all kinds of different programs depending on the group's needs. Our main aim, however, is to bring people together who wouldn't normally come together under any other circumstances. We work on enabling relationships and trust between the groups, building bridges across the many divides that exist in our world today. I help facilitate and mediate different practical and discussion workshops, such as breaking down stereotypes, adventure learning, art therapy, identity work and team building. Corrymeela's work in Northern Ireland has shown that reconciliation is possible. Everyone is accepted for who and what they are. Corrymeela has taught us all so much, and we have all grown because of the experiences we have had here. That is the magic of Corrymeela. But as our motto goes, "Corrymeela begins when you leave!"

In Northern Ireland, there is a big divide between Protestants and Catholics. A lot of issues come down to the Catholics wanting Northern Ireland to stay part of Ireland and the Protestants wanting Ireland to stay part of Britain. The Protestants mostly refer to themselves as British, while the Catholics mostly refer to themselves as Irish. Corrymeela gives people who sometimes even come from the same town a safe environment to meet people from "the other side" and get away from the "struggles." To see them even communicating with each other is a major breakthrough. Even witnessing two young boys playing football and talking about sports together is an amazing experience, especially when you know that the religious differences between the two are so great that their only contact with each other would normally be in the form of name-calling and stones thrown across the road at one another. It makes you realize just how important the simple things are.

Because Corrymeela is a Christian community, we hold worship twice a day. These worships are attended by the staff and the volunteers and anyone else who wishes to do so. Our worship sessions are somewhat different than the kind of thing most people are used to. They last about fifteen minutes and could include a poem reading, a song, an African chant, a meditation or even a game of musical chairs! Our aim is to make it an enjoyable and different experience for the groups. In the worships I lead, I like to touch on the moral side of things more than the spiritual side, as the young people who come here consider anything related to religion to be a no-go area. This is understandable when you think about the roots of all the troubles in Northern Ireland. This is where *Chicken Soup for the Teenage Soul* comes in. I use different readings from the book at different worships, and no matter what I choose to base my worship on there is always something appropriate to read. The reading that I use the most is the poem called "Please Listen." I think it is an amazing piece, and I can totally relate to it. I like to use it in the worships with young people. A lot of the youth groups that come to Corrymeela include teens who have been labeled as "problem children." Most of the time this just isn't the case. These kids have simply learned to put up walls as a defense mechanism because they are not "listened" to, and deep down they are hurting. This poem gets the listener thinking about how important it is to really be listened to and understood, and the young people can definitely relate. That is what makes Corrymeela so unique and special—we listen, and 99 percent of the time, the groups come back again and keep coming back.

People of all ages have been able to relate to the readings from *Chicken Soup for the Teenage Soul*. Best of all, the pieces are written by regular people so they strike a universal chord. It is truly an inspiring book and one of the most popular ones to read during worship time. It leaves the listeners with something to think about, and they often come back to worship asking, "Can you read something out of that book again?" Truly amazing. Thank you.

Peace,

~Jen Ashton
Chicken Soup for the Teenage Soul Letters

Eskimo's Gift

Howling winds whistled through the electrical outlets, making an eerie sound in my tiny apartment. Crystallized snow as far as the eye could see was the norm in Churchill, Manitoba — polar bear country. The blizzard whipped around the old army barracks, converted to apartments. I was a nursing instructor teaching Eskimo teenagers a nurses' aid course.

One day after class in September, I'd said to beautiful sixteen-year-old Anita, "I'd sure like to get a pair of mukluks and some mitts. Do you know where I can get some for winter?"

"Yes, my mother... she make you some," she beamed.

"Really!" I replied, delighted. Sure enough, a month later, she brought me a beautiful pair of mukluks, made with sealskin uppers and moose hide soles, along with a pair of sealskin mitts. They were not exactly fashionable, but beautifully beaded and I wore them with pleasure. They didn't cost much either, not like the expensive leather knee-high boots in my closet, bought on the spur of the moment in Montreal before I came to this howling wilderness. As I emptied my wallet, the salesman guaranteed they would keep me warm, but they were unsuited for this weather.

I heard Anita's tinkling laughter just outside my door, like wind chimes in a soft breeze. She was early. I'd wondered if anyone would show up tonight.

A hesitant knock. Anita, a sloe-eyed, raven-haired beauty walked in and sat down on the floor. She shivered and I did too. Her ebony eyes twinkled. She was serene even at her age and I was drawn to her bubbling personality and simplicity as she spoke.

It was then I noticed her tattered sneakers, frayed and yawning open at the toe. But she never mentioned her frozen feet. She sat cross-legged, her toes peeking out at me. I thought, "How can she stand it in this cold? Her feet must be frozen!"

But she chattered on and on about her childhood, when everyone in the north cared for everyone else. She told me that when an animal is shot, enough is left for the next hunter, just in case they didn't get anything. She learned caring at an early age.

When the other students were a "no show," she told me about her wonderful faith in God. "He answer prayers," she grinned.

It was then I sensed a nudging in my spirit: Give her those boots in your closet.

I ignored the idea. After all, they were much too expensive for such a young girl. She wouldn't appreciate them. Mukluks were much more serviceable up here because the soft soles easily slithered over the crystallized snow. So I continued to rationalize as I thought about my precious boots.

But the nudging persisted and I had no rest until I stood up and opened the closet. There they were, sitting there unused and useless. Fashionable. Warm with sheepskin lining. Beautiful. I loved them. I bit my lip as I remembered that God loves a cheerful giver and I handed them to her.

"I think these are yours," I said.

"Thank you. I pray that Jesus give me boots!" she exclaimed in her staccato English.

She pulled them over her feet. They were a perfect fit. Of course. They were hers after all. For a fleeting moment I wanted to switch the mukluks for those beautiful boots, for she had no idea of their value. But I resisted.

The wind continued to howl outside and we continued to share with one another the significance of faith in God. When she left and plodded out across the snow, I stared out at the mounting storm, and a thrill permeated my spirit knowing Anita's feet were as warm as my heart.

~Arlene Centerwall
Chicken Soup for the Christian Soul 2

Chapter
11

CHRISTIAN Teen Talk

Not Really Gone

*Love is stronger than death even though
it can't stop death from happening,
but no matter how hard death tries,
it can't separate people from love.*

~Anonymous

85

Sometimes

The guardian angels of life sometimes
fly so high as to be beyond our sight,
but they are always looking down on us.
~Jean Paul Richter

Sometimes I question you,
And wonder whether you're listening.
I can't see you, or touch you, or even feel you,
So how do I know if you're really there?

Sometimes I get mad at you,
When I see bad things happen to good people.
I wonder why you wouldn't save them.
It makes me wonder if you're real.

Sometimes when I pray to you,
I can sense that you are there with me,
Watching over me as your child,
Blessing me with your grace.

Sometimes when I can see you clearly,
When I see little babies or kind smiles,
Generous people and the beauty of nature,
It makes me believe with my whole heart.

Sometimes my questions about you don't matter,
Even though there are never definite answers.
I have faith in your love.
Forgive me, God, for ever questioning you.

~Jenny Sharaf
Chicken Soup for the Christian Teenage Soul

86

Beyond the Grave

I can clearly remember the happy weekends my family and I spent at my abuelita Susana's apartment in the South Bronx. We are a big Dominican family and loved getting together in my grandmother's home. As soon as you walked in, you would be enveloped in the delicious smells coming from the kitchen. You could practically taste the rice, beans and pernil in the air. If one of her five grandchildren had a birthday, there'd be a freshly baked cake with icing and sprinkles on the dining room table. If it was Easter Sunday, you could count on getting a huge Easter basket filled with toys, plush teddy bears and lots of candy. As an eight-year-old child, going to her home was magical. She was a great cook and homemaker, but an even greater human being.

She had a calm and welcoming demeanor that could put anyone at ease. She was warm and nurturing, always caring for others, but not enough for herself. We don't know when she was diagnosed with lung cancer, but when we found out, it was too late. She died the same year she told the family of her illness. By then, all we could do was comfort her and each other and enjoy what little time we had left together. She died in the hospital five days after her sixty-second birthday.

We all missed her dearly. Family and close friends crammed into her apartment for a velorio, to pray for her and mourn her loss. That was the first and only time I ever saw my father cry. Tex didn't grieve aloud, like everyone else. Silent tears streamed down his face, but I knew inside he was raging with grief. I understood that she had died, but, at such a young age, I couldn't fully grasp the impact of a loved one's death.

A couple of months after her death, I became very sick with a respiratory illness that just wouldn't go away. My mother was worried and prayed for my health.

One night she dreamt of my grandmother. In her dream, my grandmother rang the doorbell of our apartment. My mother opened the door in surprise.

"Susana, what are you doing here? You're not supposed to be here. You're dead."

"I didn't come to see you," Susana said. "I'm here to see Yahaira."

She went past my mother, entered my bedroom and closed the door behind her.

The next day I approached my mom in the living room.

"Mami, can I have a candle?"

"Why do you want a candle, Yary?" My mother frowned.

"It's for Abuelita Susana. I want to pray for her."

My mother remembered her dream from the night before and agreed to buy me the candle. Within the week, my respiratory illness had disappeared.

Since then I have maintained my "special bond" with my abuelita. Every once in a while, I make sure to light a candle in her name and pray. When I reach out to her in my time of need, I feel her presence and her love. It's been fifteen years since her death, and still it comforts me to know that she can hear me and feel my love for her.

My mother retells this story every time the family gets together. For us, it's proof that family, love and faith know no limits. Love has no boundaries and can be felt across distance and time. Even from beyond the grave.

~Yahaira Lawrence
Chicken Soup for the Latino Soul

87

Hi Daddy

The bitterest tears shed over graves are for
words left unsaid and deeds left undone.
~Harriet Beecher Stowe

October 29, 2003

Hi Daddy,

Sorry I haven't written to you in a while. A lot of things have been going on. I miss you so much. How have you been? Is heaven everything they say it is? I know it's probably that and more. I can't wait till I can come join you again. I miss you so much—just being here for me to hold your hand and you calling me "princess." But one day we can do this again.

But it will be even better because Jesus will be with us. I keep going in your office to see all your things and your awards that you have gotten over the years. You accomplished so much. I am proud you were my daddy; I would not have chosen anyone else. I like to go into your closet, too and just touch and smell all your clothes... it gives me so many memories that I miss so much. Sitting at this table I see your writing on a little piece of paper telling me and mom what e-mail and address in Iraq to write to you ... CSM JAMES D. BLANKENBECLER, 1-44 ADA. I love to just look at your handwriting so much. I have your military ring on right now. It's kind of big for my little finger, but it makes me feel you're holding my hand when I have it on....

It's been on since we found out the news. I have your driver's license with me, too, so I can just look at you whenever I want. You have a little smile this time. When we went to get them done in El Paso, I asked you to just smile this time... and you did it just for me. I also was looking at your car keys and that little brown leather pouch you always had on your key chain. It made me cry a lot when I picked it up.

Everything reminds me of you so much. When we pass by Chili's I remember you sitting across from me eating your favorite salad. You always told the waiter to take off the little white crunchy things... because you hated them. And when we drive by billboards that say "An Army of One," it makes me remember you in your military uniform, how you always made a crunching sound when you walked, and how you shined your big boots every night before you went to bed. I miss seeing that all the time.

Little things that I took for granted when you were here seem priceless now. One thing that I regret is when you wanted to open my car door for me, I always got it myself. I wish I had let you do it. And when you wanted to hold my hand, I would sometimes pull away because I didn't want people to see me holding my daddy's hand... I feel so ashamed that I cared what people thought of me walking down the parking lot holding your hand. But now I would give anything just to feel the warmth of your hand holding mine.

I can't believe this has happened to my daddy... the best daddy in the whole world. It feels so unreal, like you're still in Iraq. You were only there for seventeen days. Why did they have to kill you? Why couldn't they know how loved you are here? Why couldn't they know? You have so many friends that love you with all their hearts and you affected each and every person you have met in your lifetime. Why couldn't they know? When I get shots at the hospital, I won't have my daddy's thumb to hold tight. Why couldn't they know I loved when you called me "princess"? Why couldn't they know if they killed you I would not have a daddy to walk me down the aisle when I get married? Why couldn't they know all this? Why? I know that you are gone now, but it only means that I have another angel watching over me for the rest of my life. That's the only way I can think of this being good. There is no other way I can think of it.

All the kids at my school know about your death. They even had a moment of silence for you at our football game. A lot of my teachers came over to try to comfort me and Mom. They all ask if they can get us anything, but the only thing anyone can do is give me my daddy back... and I don't think anyone can do that. You always told me and Mom you never wanted to die in a stupid way like a car accident or something like that. And you really didn't die in a stupid way... you died in the most honorable way a man like you could—protecting me, mom, Joseph, Amanda and the rest of the United States.

In the Bible it says everyone is put on this earth for a purpose, and once they accomplished this you can return to Jesus. I did not know at first what you did to go home to God so soon. But I thought about it—you have done everything. You have been the best husband, father, son and soldier in the world. And everyone knows this.

One of my teachers called me from El Paso and told me that when her dad died, he always told her, "When you walk outside, the first star you see is me."

She told me that it is the same for me and you. I needed to talk to you last night, and I walked outside and looked up... and I saw the brightest star in the sky. I knew that was you right away, because you are now the brightest star in heaven.

I love you so much, Daddy. Only you and I know this. Words can't even begin to show how much. But I tried to tell you in this letter, just a portion of my love for you. I will miss you, daddy, with all of my heart. I will always be your little girl and I will never forget that...

I love you Daddy. I will miss you!!
P.S. I have never been so proud of my last name.

Sunrise—June 27, 1963
Sunset—October 1, 2003

~Jessica Blankenbecler
Chicken Soup for the Military Wife's Soul

Here to Stay

C ancer. Even the sound of it gives me chills, and it always has. I always felt bad for those who had it or knew someone who had it, but it never seemed real to me. That is, until sixth grade. Then it became very real, and it changed my life forever.

My best friend James was diagnosed with cancer that year. I was so scared. He found out about it near the beginning of the school year, and he was only given a five percent chance of making it through Christmas. James proved them wrong, though, because he did live through Christmas. In fact, he lived through all of sixth and seventh grade.

Toward the end of seventh grade, James was still receiving some chemotherapy, but he had hair. He no longer wore a hat to hide his baldness, and he was happy. But by the end of June, we were all in tears. He had relapsed.

James fought the disease with all of his might, but it spread to his bone marrow. Three bone marrow matches were found in the national registry, but James would have to be in remission before the transplant could happen. Unfortunately, in early September, the doctors said that James's body wasn't responding to the treatments he was receiving. They started him on a new round of chemo, and we prayed that it would work.

James's body never did respond to the treatments. That's when the doctors gave him four to six months to live. When he called me and told me, I started crying. It was the only time that I ever let him hear me cry. He was so strong, though. He told me it was going to be okay. I don't know how he could have done that, but James was always strong and never let anything get him down, not even cancer.

About a week before Thanksgiving, the doctors gave James a slim chance of making it through the week. I was nervous the whole time, but Thanksgiving came and went, and James was still here.

In mid-December, however, James had a reaction to his platelet injection. He wasn't expected to make it through the night, but as usual he beat the odds. The doctors were almost sure he would be gone by Christmas, but he stayed with us into the New Year.

After that, he progressively got worse. He was in a lot of pain, and things were not looking good. On January 7th, James passed away. It was the saddest day of my life. I couldn't sleep for two days. I kept repeating the same thoughts: I will never see him again. I will never hear his voice again. I will never see his smile again.

But I was wrong. That night I was on my bed crying when I heard something.

"Brittany," a voice said. "Brittany, look up." The voice was all too familiar. When I looked up, James was sitting on the edge of my bed. He looked the same as he always had, but he was sort of glowing.

"James?" I asked. "Is that you?"

"No," he said, sarcastically. "It's Santa Claus. Of course, it's me." I laughed, and he smiled. "That's what I like to see, Brittany. No more tears."

"But you're gone," I told him.

"No, I'm not," he said. "I'm right here."

I haven't seen James since that night, and I know some people think I'm a little nuts when I tell this story, but that's okay. James gave me the greatest gift that night. So much of what drives me is being afraid of losing—losing my parents, losing my friends and, most of all, losing the love that keeps me going. That night I learned. I experienced firsthand that no matter what, love never leaves us.

~Brittany Lynn Jones
Chicken Soup for the Christian Teenage Soul

Unbreakable Bond

y mother always told me that I was my "father's daughter." By that she meant that we looked alike and shared similar traits—Dad and I were both stocky, intellectual, quick-tempered and funny. Being the firstborn and only child for nearly seven years, I developed a strong bond with my father. We would rub each other's feet and be goofy together, and he always told me that he loved me and that he was proud of my academic performance and artistic endeavors. We understood one another and sensed that we were always on each other's side.

Dad had always been a healthy and energetic man. He had a big appetite, lifted weights and rarely got sick. With his dark hair, green eyes, olive complexion and round belly, he was an image of vigor and joviality. His temper, humor, outspokenness and hearty laugh made him a powerful presence.

Dad was diagnosed with hepatitis C during my freshman year of high school. Doctors told him he had contracted the liver-eating disease as a teenager and that it had lain dormant in his body up until then. The doctors also said Dad would need a liver transplant to survive.

Dad's deterioration was rapid and heart-wrenching. His skin grew pale, he lost about seventy pounds, his physical activity was drastically restricted and his diet was altered. His barely functioning liver caused him to be in pain most of the time. Toward the end of Dad's battle, the toxins produced by the liver caused encephalitis, which made him an incoherent insomniac who could barely control his own actions. He died on April 27, 1998. My grandfather died from cancer two months later, leaving my mom orphaned and widowed—and leaving me with only one parent and one grandparent.

I never thought I would be able to handle life without Dad. His death was a tragic event in my world—but it was not the end of it. I think about Dad every day, and I am still trying to work through my emotions three and a half years after the fact.

Nonetheless, I have managed to go on with my life. Writing about his death is the ultimate testimony to that statement, because I have aspired to be a writer since I was a small child. I know that by actively pursuing my dream, I am doing what Dad wants me to be doing—I am going after what I want in life.

It saddens me to think there are so many events that he did not and will not get to participate in; he never saw me graduate from high school, and he will not be there to walk my sister and me down the aisle when we get married. But even if he cannot be there physically, I know that he is always with me. Every beautiful sunset that I witness and every piece of good fortune that I am graced by reminds me that I have angels watching over me, and there is one in particular who is always whispering, "I'll go wherever you will go."

~Lauren Fritsky
Chicken Soup for the Teenage Soul IV

Let's Go Dancing in the Rain

It is not known precisely where angels dwell—
whether in the air, the void, or the planets.
It has not been God's pleasure that we should be informed of their abode.
~Voltaire

Spring break of 1999 was perfect—I got to spend the entire time with my friends just vegging and hanging out. Of course, there was that English project due the day I got back, which I put off until the Sunday before. I was sitting at my computer furiously making up an essay when my little sister walked in from softball practice eating a snow cone and laughing with a sticky smile.

"Whatcha working on?" she asked lightheartedly.

I smiled at her appearance and told her that it was just an English essay. I turned back and continued clacking away. From behind my shoulder she tried to start a conversation.

"So..." she began. "You know a kid in your grade named Justin? Justin Schultz?" She licked at a drip on her snow cone.

"Yeah, I know him," I replied. I had gone to elementary school with Justin. He had to be the greatest guy I knew. He never stopped smiling. Justin had tried to teach me to play soccer in the third grade. I couldn't get it, so he smiled and told me to do my best and cheer everyone else on. I'd kind of lost touch with him in the last year, but I told my sister yes, anyway.

"Well," she said, trying to keep her messy snow cone under control. "His church group went skiing this week." She paused to take a lick.

Lucky guy, I thought.

My sister swallowed the ice chips and continued, "So he went skiing and today he died."

I felt the blood drain from my face in disbelief. My hands froze on the keyboard, and a line of Rs inched across the screen. My jaw slowly dropped as I tried to process what she'd said. Breathe, something in my head screamed. I shook my head and whipped around to look at my sister.

She was still innocently munching on her snow cone, staring at it determinedly. Her eyes rose to mine and she leaned back, a little startled. "What?" she asked.

"Y-you're joking, right? Who told you that? I don't believe it. How? Are you sure?" I spit out a long string of questions.

"Claire," she stopped me. She began a little slower this time. "A girl on my softball team was house-sitting for them. Justin's parents called her today and told her, and she told me. Sorry, I didn't think you knew him." She sat very still waiting for my response.

Every memory I had of Justin flashed through my mind. I inhaled slowly. "No. No! NO!" I tried to scream. No words came out. I sat up clumsily and shakily ran from the room with my sister behind me yelling, "Wait! I'm sorry..."

I called one of our mutual friends right away. She told me between sobs that no one knew why he died. The thirteen-year-old was as healthy as a horse. He fell asleep on Saturday night in the hotel room, and when his roommate tried to wake him up Sunday morning, Justin wasn't breathing. I didn't want her to hear me cry, so I quickly got off the phone.

I went to school the next day and put on the same strong mask. The principal gave an impersonal announcement about Justin's death that morning and almost immediately I could hear sobs throughout the classroom. That was the worst week of my life. I tried to be a shoulder for others to cry on, but inside I was the one crying.

On Wednesday evening my friend gave me a ride to Justin's viewing. What surprised me when we walked into the room was that Justin's parents weren't crying. They were smiling and comforting everyone. I asked them how they were holding up, and they told me that they were fine. They told me they knew that he wasn't hurting now, that he was with God and would wait for them in heaven. I cried and nearly collapsed. Mrs. Schultz stepped forward to hug me, and I cried on her beautiful red sweater. I looked into her eyes and saw her sympathy for a girl who'd lost her friend.

I went home that night with a deep sadness in my heart for Justin. I wrote a letter to him that I planned on giving him at his funeral. In the letter I wrote to him about how sad everyone was, how much we missed him, how wonderful his parents were and the things he'd never get to do on Earth. I closed it with:

> *Somehow I've always believed that once in heaven, tangible things really don't mean that much anymore. Well, before you get too used to your new life, take these things with you. The smell of grass thirty minutes after it's cut. The feel of freshly washed sheets. The heat of a small candle. The sound a bee makes. The taste of a hot Coke just poured and swirling with ice — hot, but partially cold. The feel of raindrops on your soaked face. But if you take nothing else with you, take your family's embrace.*

I paused and stared into my candle. I rearranged my pen in my hand and continued writing.

> *Tell you what, Justin. When I die, let's go dancing in the rain.*

I smiled through tears and slid my letter into an envelope.

The next day was Justin's funeral. At the last minute, my ride had to cancel because of a schedule conflict, and I was left to sit alone in my house crying. I glanced down at my letter and smiled, "How am I going to get this to you now, Justin?" I laughed through my tears and kept crying.

Sometimes strange thoughts pop into my head, as if from somewhere else. Sitting on my bed fingering a tissue, one of those thoughts told me how to get it to him: Smoke is faster than dirt. I was startled by this, but after thinking about it, I realized I was supposed to burn the letter, not bury it. I cried for an hour as I carefully burned the letter. I'd burn a corner, then blow it out under the running water in the sink, afraid of the flames. Eventually, the letter was gone and the white smoke streamed from my window. I waved it away and prayed to God that Justin would someday read my words in the smoke.

That night I dreamt about death and awoke at 2:38 A.M. to hear rain tapping on my window. Rare are the visible words from heaven, but those precious raindrops were my answer. I had told Justin that I wanted to go dancing in the rain. The slow rhythm on my window told me that Justin had heard me. In that moment, I knew that he felt no pain and that we would see each other again. And on that day, we will go dancing in the rain together.

~Claire Hayenga
Chicken Soup for the Teenage Soul on Tough Stuff

Karen, Do You Know Him?

I was an intern in pediatrics, fresh out of medical school. A lot of facts and figures were crammed into my brain, but my clinical experience was somewhat limited. But that's what it means to be an intern.

One of my most memorable first patients was a young lady named Karen. She had been referred to our city hospital from a small community in North Carolina because of symptoms of weakness and anemia. I knew when I first met Karen that I was dealing with someone out of the ordinary. She was not the least intimidated by the title "Doctor" or the white coat, and she always spoke what was on her mind. During our first interview, Karen wanted to know my credentials down to a T, and wanted me to know that she knew that I was, indeed, "just" an intern. She was fourteen years old and full of life.

Unfortunately, our evaluations revealed that she had a type of leukemia that was somewhat unusual, and not as responsive to different treatment modalities as were other types of leukemia. In fact, the prognosis for her surviving even one year was unlikely.

Chemotherapy was initiated, and Karen was never shy in telling us how sick we were making her with the medicine. She never spoke in a mean way, but simply in a way that always made her feelings known. If we had difficulty with an IV, she would readily point out our incompetence. However, she would just as readily forgive us and compliment us when an IV was maintained in her fragile veins on the first try.

Remarkably, within three months Karen went into remission, becoming free of her disease. She continued to come in for routine chemotherapy. During those short visits, Karen and I became friends. It was almost uncanny how, during random rotations, I would turn up as her physician. Always when she would see me coming, she'd gasp, "Oh no, do I have to have Dr. Brown?" Sometimes she was kidding, sometimes she wasn't, but she always wanted me to hear her.

About a year after her original diagnosis, her disease returned. When this type of leukemia returns, it is almost impossible to regain remission because all of the therapeutic modalities have already been spent. However, once again—remarkably if not miraculously—Karen went into remission. I was now a second-year resident, a little more competent and quite a bit more attached to this family. I continued to see Karen and her family over the next year and a half. She proceeded in her high school career and remained an outspoken, fun-loving teenager.

I was now in my chief residency year, spending my last month on the inpatient ward prior to completing my training. Karen came in once again with an exacerbation of her disease; she was extremely ill. There was involvement of every organ of her body, including her brain, and literally no other chemical agent to be tried. There was nothing we could do. Karen was made comfortable, given IV fluids and medication for pain. After long discussions, Karen's doctors and family decided that the goal would be to keep her comfortable and pain-free. No unnecessary heroic measures would be performed to prolong the inevitable. In fact, there were no heroic measures left.

Karen soon slipped into a coma. After viewing the CT scan and seeing the diffuse brain involvement, it was easy to see why. We expected each day to be her last. Her eyes were fixed and nonresponsive, her breathing shallow. Her heart was still strong, as we knew it would be. However, the disease was ravaging her blood system and brain, and there was evidence of opportunistic pneumonia involving both lungs. We knew that she would soon die.

I began to have a tremendous dread of Karen dying while I was on call. I did not want to pronounce her dead. It came to the point where I hoped that her death would come on nights that I was away from the hospital because I feared that I would not be any emotional support for the family, or that I would even be able to perform my duties as a physician. This family had come to mean so much to me.

It was a Wednesday night, and Karen had been in a coma for four days. I was the chief resident on call for the wards. I spoke with the family and peeked in on Karen. I noticed her breathing was very shallow and her temperature quite low. Death could be imminent. I selfishly hoped to myself that maybe she'd wait until tomorrow to die. I went about my chores until about 3:00 A.M., when I finally tried to get some sleep. At 4:00 A.M. I received a STAT page to Karen's room. This puzzled me somewhat because we were not going to make any heroic interventions. Nevertheless, I ran to her room.

The nurse greeted me outside the room and grabbed my arm. "Karen wants to talk to you." I literally thought this nurse was crazy. I couldn't imagine what she was talking about — Karen was in a coma. At this point in my life, my scientific, Newtonian way of thinking ruled my thoughts, primarily because this is the approach we are trained in day in and day out in medical school. I had neglected other, more important spiritual aspects of my being, ignoring the instinct that knows what reason cannot know.

I went into the room, and to my amazement, Karen was sitting up in bed. Her mother was on the left side of the bed, her father on the right. I stood next to the father, not saying anything, not knowing what to say. Karen's eyes, which had been glazed over for four days, were now clear and sharp. She simply stated, "God has come for me. It is time for me to go." She then went around to each of us at the bedside and hugged us tightly, one at a time. These were strong hugs, hugs that I kept thinking were impossible. I could only visualize her CT scan and the severe degree of brain damage. How could this be?

Then Karen lay down. But she popped back up immediately, as if she had forgotten something. She went around the bed to each of us again, with her penetrating eyes fixing our stares. No hugs this time. But her hands were strong and steady, squeezing our shoulders as she spoke. "God is here," she said. "Do you see him? Do you know him?" I was scared. Nothing in my experience could explain what was happening here. There was nothing else to say, so I mumbled, "Yes. Goodbye. Thank you." I didn't know what to say. The entire time, I kept visualizing that CT scan. Then Karen lay back down and died—or I should say, she quit breathing and her heart stopped. Her powerful spirit went on living.

It was years before I could tell that story, even to my wife. I still cannot tell it without feeling overwhelming emotions. I know now that this experience is not something to be understood through the limited viewpoint of the scientific realm. We are, in essence, spiritual beings in a spiritual universe, not primarily governed by Newton's laws, but by the laws of God.

~James C. Brown, M.D.
A 5th Portion of Chicken Soup for the Soul

92

The White Butterfly

I was lucky: I got to take the afternoon city bus home from high school. Since both my parents worked and my mom's job was closer to my sister's grade school, they decided that I would take the public bus home from school every day.

The bus stop was smack dab right in front of my private, Catholic high school, so all of my affluent classmates could see us "bus riders" waiting for our slow transportation home. At around 2:45 every afternoon, the bus came by and picked up the waiting ragtag group of high school students. The ride was usually a fun one, filled with lots of teenage chatter and gossip. As the bus dropped off each of my bus mates, I hoped the smelly homeless man or the crazy lady with the big hat wouldn't take the empty seat next to me. Otherwise, it would mean holding my breath or pretending to read one of my homework assignments for the rest of the ride to my stop.

I would reach up to ring the bus bell, letting the driver know my stop was coming, and the big smoggy monster of a bus would pass in front of my house and lurch its way to the bus stop that was only a half-block from my front doorstep. As soon as the bus passed my house, I could always see the small figure of my grandmother, Boya, as all her grandchildren called her instead of abuela, already standing at the steps leading from our front yard to the sidewalk. My grandmother had lived with us since I was about seven years old, which had been great until recently when I started feeling smothered and annoyed at what I had previously treasured—my beloved grand-mother's attention and coddling.

When I would see her waiting for me on the steps, I would auto-matically roll my eyes, frustrated that my seventy-something-year-old grandmother still treated me—a mature fifteen-year-old young woman—like a little kid who needed to be watched like a hawk. Ridiculous, I thought.

After giving her a hug and a kiss, I would tell her, in Spanish, "Boya, you don't have to wait out here for me, you know. It's only half a block. Nothing is going to happen to me. I can take care of myself."

She would shake her head and say, "You never know. There are lots of crazy people out there. Somebody might kidnap you."

I was always in awe of how paranoid she was. At my young age, I never imagined that someone could be so distrustful of everything. I just rolled my eyes (making sure she didn't see for fear of getting the chancla thrown at me) and followed her into the house, hoping she had made one of my favorite dishes for dinner.

Some days, the bus would pass by, and I wouldn't see her in the front yard. I would get excited, thinking that maybe she had gotten caught up watching her favorite telenovela and lost track of time, or maybe she had finally realized I was not a kid anymore and had given up babysitting me. As I jumped off the bus and onto the sidewalk, I would happily start my short path home. Before I could take even one step, there she would be, like clockwork, standing down the block, her small body somehow looking bigger on the sidewalk in front of my house—the sergeant standing guard. All I could do was give one of my big, annoyed-teenager sighs, roll my eyes and shake my head as I slowly made my way down that dangerous half block.

Over the next seven years, my grandmother stood watch as my sister and I grew up and graduated from high school, then moved out of the house to go to college. She even saw me graduate from college, the first woman in our family to do so.

One month after my college graduation, my beautiful, tough, amazing boya lost her short battle against pancreatic cancer. Seeing her succumb to such a horrible illness was both heartbreaking and overwhelming.

As my family tried to heal the tremendous hole that her death left in all of us, I began thinking back to my bus trips home from school and her constant vigil over me. Every time I visited my parents on the weekends, I would think of my boya as I drove up to their house, always expecting to see her come down the steps to welcome me home. Of course, my guardian was no longer there, and I could only dream of those days of walking half a block toward her smile, her hugs or even to her lectures.

One day, my cousin, Wendy, and I were leaving a restaurant, and I suddenly heard her say, "Hi, Boya." When I gave her a puzzled look, Wendy pointed to the white butterfly that was fluttering around us. "That's Boya," Wendy said. "Haven't you ever noticed that the white butterfly is always around, especially when you're thinking about her?"

I had not. Yet, after that day, I began seeing the white butterfly almost on a daily basis. No matter where I was—at work, at home, out shopping or running errands—the white butterfly was always nearby and would always make me stop and smile. I was comforted knowing that my boya had never left me—I just had not recognized her presence.

Even today, ten years after her death, the white butterfly still follows me wherever I wander. I see her everywhere I go, fluttering near me, watching over me as I continue my journey, making sure I always reach home safe and sound.

Gracias, Boya.

~Jennifer Ramon-Dover
Chicken Soup for the Latino Soul

93

Angels Among Us

Angels have no philosophy but love.
~Adeline Cullen Ray

There are things in life
That will make you cry,
And it's times like these
When you barely get by.

There are people in life
Who will make it hard,
There are times when you'll feel
Like you're on your guard.

But up in the sky,
The stars shine bright,
Over your sorrows
And all through the night.

Upon those stars,
The angels watch,
And guide us through
Life's toughest parts.

They make us laugh
And dry our tears,

They release our anger
And calm our fears.

There are angels among us
When you're feeling blue,
And when you feel alone,
They come to you.

They pick you up
And hold your hand,
They walk with you,
They understand.

So the sadder you get
And the worse you feel,
Always remember,
Angels are here.

~Kerri Knipper
Chicken Soup for the Christian Teenage Soul

CHRISTIAN Teen Talk

Love Is All You Need

There is no surprise more magical than the surprise of being loved.
It is God's finger on man's shoulder.
~Charles Morgan

The Surrogate Grandmother

All the way to the nursing home, I could hear Pam complaining.

"I don't like this idea. I hate being around old people, and I think nursing homes are gross."

I had suggested to my teen Girl Scout troop that each girl adopt an elderly lady in the nursing home as a grandmother. I thought it would be good for the girls to learn about the elderly and the hardships they have with ill health and loneliness. It would teach them, I hoped, to have compassion for others. Most of the girls thought it was a good idea, except for Pam.

"If anyone needs to learn about compassion, it's Pam," I thought. She was an only child and very spoiled. She seemed to care about nothing but her looks, clothes and boys.

"Phew! It stinks in here."

"Shhh," I told Pam. "It's not the most pleasant smell, I know. Just be grateful you're not in here all the time, like they are."

I turned away to talk to the administrator. After a few minutes, I went to the main sitting room to check on the girls. They had all found an elderly woman and seemed to be getting along fine. All except Pam. She was nowhere to be seen.

I started down the long hallway in time to see Pam enter a room. I stopped beside the door.

"Hello." The weak shaky voice had come from a small hump lying in a narrow bed. "I'm Hannah."

"Hi. I'm Pamela."

"My, you're a pretty girl, Pamela. I've never had anyone as pretty as you to visit me before."

"Really?"

I could tell Pam was very pleased over this comment.

"Really." The bright, little eyes looked Pam over. "You're not one of those feisty girls, are you?"

"Feisty?" Pam couldn't keep from smiling at the way Hannah had said the word. Like it was something bad.

"Yes. Feisty. In my day, bad girls were called feisty."

"They were?" Pam couldn't hide her surprise. "When was that, Hannah? Would you mind if I ask how old you are?"

Grinning wide and showing her toothless gums, Hannah proudly said, "I'm 104."

"A hundred and four?" Pam's mouth gaped opened. "You're really 104?"

Hannah chuckled. "I bet you didn't think anyone could live that long, right? Well, you drag that chair over here and sit a spell. It's been a long time since I've had anyone to visit with."

"Don't you have any family?" Pam asked.

"Oh no. They're all dead and gone. I'm the last member of my family left."

I walked in and introduced myself to Hannah and reminded Pam why we were there.

Pam looked at me and whispered. "She's 104!"

I explained to Hannah about the girls wanting to adopt an elderly lady as their grandmother.

A little reluctantly, Pam asked Hannah if she could adopt her.

Hannah smiled her big, toothless grin. "I would be right proud to be your grandma."

I took the girls to visit their surrogate grandmothers every week. I don't know who was enjoying it more, the girls or the grandmothers. At first, Pam was quiet, but over the weeks, I could see a change in her.

"She's amazing!" Pam told the other girls. "Do you know, she can remember when there was trouble with Indians! Some of the things we study about in American history—she witnessed."

"You've come to really love her in these last few months, haven't you?" Pam's best friend asked.

"You know, I really have. She's the most interesting person I know. And the stories she tells! She's so interested in everything that's going on. She's crippled with arthritis and completely bedridden, but she never complains."

I could see the affection between Pam and Hannah grow with each visit. Pam would brush Hannah's long white hair while listening to stories about the way Hannah and other young ladies in her day dressed and wore their hair. In turn, Pam told Hannah all her thoughts and fears, and Hannah would share her wisdom, born of long experience, with Pam. They laughed together often.

Pam brought little gifts that made Hannah's eyes light up. Hannah's favorite was the milk-chocolate drops that Pam sneaked in. Smiling, Hannah would let them melt in her mouth.

On our way to visit one day, I noticed Pam was carrying a big bouquet of lilacs.

"Those are beautiful, Pam."

"I'm taking them to Hannah. They're her favorite flower."

When we arrived, Pam rushed into Hannah's room. "Hannah?"

I heard her call out Hannah's name and went into the room. The bed was made up with white, starched sheets as though no one had ever been in it.

"Can I help you?" One of the attendants walked into the room.

"Yes, we're looking for Hannah," I told her.

"Oh dear, didn't anyone tell you? Hannah passed away last night."

"Passed away?" Pam whispered.

"Yes, her heart stopped. She went very peacefully."

"Pam, I'm sorry." I put my arm around her.

Throwing the lilacs on the floor, Pam turned to me. "It's all your fault!" she yelled. "I didn't want to adopt an old person. Then, I met Hannah. I loved her, and now she's gone. It's not fair."

I put my arms around her and let her cry. She had never lost anyone before.

"Hannah wanted you to have this." The attendant held an old, worn Bible out to Pam. With it was a note, addressed to: "My Granddaughter, Pamela." The note simply said, "Love never dies."

I attended Hannah's funeral with Pam. She never said a word through the whole service. She just held Hannah's Bible.

I wasn't surprised that Pam started skipping our scout meetings on the days we visited the nursing home. I didn't know what to say to her. Maybe it hadn't been such a good idea after all, I thought.

A few months later, at one of our regular meetings, Pam asked, "Can I go back to the nursing home with the rest of you next week?"

"Of course you can, but are you sure you want to?"

Pam smiled and said, "Yes. No one can ever take Hannah's place, but I know there are other grandmothers, just as wonderful, waiting to be adopted."

"Yes, I bet there are. What a good idea, Pam."

She had learned and in doing so, she had reminded me: Love is always a good idea.

~Pat Curtis
Chicken Soup for the Mother's Soul 2

The Rest of the Story

J ennifer would have caught my attention even if she hadn't stopped to talk that afternoon. The first couple of weeks in my writing class are always a bit unsettling. The students are a blur of unfamiliar faces, most of them freshmen trying to acclimate themselves to their new environment. When Jennifer approached me with a question after the second day, I was grateful for the chance to connect at least one name with a face.

Her writing wasn't perfect, but her effort was. She worked hard and pushed herself to excel. She was excited to learn, which made me enjoy teaching her. I didn't realize then how much she would also teach me.

One Friday afternoon, a few weeks into the semester, Jennifer stopped by after class. She wasn't clarifying an assignment or asking a question about a paper I'd returned.

"I didn't make it to career day yesterday," she said quietly. "I was at the health center the whole day." I gave her a sideways look, startled. "I'm fine now," she reassured me with confidence. "It was just a virus." Then she was gone.

Two nights later, her father called to tell me that Jennifer would be missing a few classes. She had been hospitalized with meningitis. I heard from him again a few days later, and again after that. Her condition had worsened, he said, and it appeared she might not finish the semester at all.

Jenny remained hospitalized, ninety miles away from home. Her mother stayed by her side, camped out in the corner of a cramped hospital room, sleeping night after night on a chair. In the middle of the night, while Jenny slept, her mother sneaked out—but just to duck down the hall for a quick shower.

Grandparents, ministers and long-standing friends all made their pilgrimages to the hospital room. Jenny's condition grew worse, not better. I was terrified when I saw the pale, emaciated girl who had only ten days earlier radiated life and warmth in my classroom. When her grandparents arrived, she spoke the only words during our visit. "This is my college writing teacher," she announced proudly, in a tiny voice. I remembered what her father had said in his first phone call: "School means everything to Jenny."

A week later, Jenny herself called me to tell me she was on the road to recovery. "I'll be back," she insisted. "I have no doubt," I told her, choking back tears. But around the same time, news reports announced the meningitis-induced death of another student at another school. Jenny sank back into her hospital bed.

Then, five weeks later, I walked into my classroom to find Jenny in her seat, smiling as she talked to the students around her. I caught my breath as her rail-thin body approached my desk, and she handed over all of her missed assignments, completed with thought and excellence. The strength of her will to overcome shone out of her pale, weak, eighteen-year-old face. It would be a few more days, though, before I learned the rest of the story.

Jenny's suitemates, Maren and Kate, were just getting up the Sunday morning that Jenny was dragging herself into the bathroom they shared. She had a horrendous headache and had been throwing up all night. Forty-five minutes later, as the two were leaving for church, she was still there. Maren had a bad feeling about Jenny and asked her Sunday school class to pray for her. When they returned to the dorm three hours later, Jenny was still violently ill. Concerned that she was becoming dehydrated, they decided to take her to the emergency room.

The two girls lifted Jenny up and carried her out to the car, then from the car to the hospital. They spent the next seven hours at their friend's side, tracking down her parents, responding to doctors and trying to comfort a very sick eighteen-year-old through a CAT scan, a spinal tap and myriad other medical tests. They left the hospital when Jenny's parents arrived but were back the next morning when the doctors confirmed that the meningitis was bacterial. By noon, they had the whole two-hundred-member campus Christian group praying for Jenny.

I credit these two young students with the miracle of Jenny's life. That same semester, just an hour away on another college campus, two students found a friend in a similar condition—motionless and deathly ill. Instead of getting him to a hospital, they took a permanent marker and wrote on his forehead the number of shots he had consumed in celebration of his twenty-first birthday. Their friend died of alcohol poisoning. Jenny finished the semester with a 4.0.

I remember being asked as a college freshman who I considered a hero. I didn't have an answer then. Since that time, I've learned that I may have been looking for heroes in the wrong places. Ask me now who I admire, and I'll tell you about a couple of ordinary college students I know.

~Jo Wiley Cornell
Chicken Soup for the College Soul

96

Many Times Over

You can't live a perfect day without doing something
for someone who will never be able to repay you.
~John Wooden

I t was a cold day in early December. I was pretty bored just sitting around the house. There was nothing on TV, my friends weren't around, and I'd read every magazine I had on skateboarding, snowboarding and every other hobby of mine. I was about to go stir-crazy when my Aunt Mary, who had stopped by to visit, asked me if I'd like to go grocery shopping with her.

"Perfect opportunity to get a new magazine," I thought. There was one problem, though. I'd run out of allowance money. So I decided to ask my mom, in the nicest, sweetest voice I could, if I could have five dollars from my upcoming allowance to buy a magazine that I had been wanting really badly. To my relief, Mom agreed to the deal, and my aunt and I took off shopping.

As we were walking into the grocery store, a poor, homeless woman sat outside the doors asking customers for money donations. "Wow," I thought. "And I thought I was having a bad day, because I was bored." I checked on the five dollars in my pocket as I thought about the magazine that was waiting inside the store. My aunt went to do her shopping, and I headed for the magazine racks. As I flipped through the new magazines, looking for the one with the article my friend had told me about, I kept flashing on the woman sitting out in the cold without a home to keep her warm. Before I knew it, I had put the magazines back and was heading in the direction of the homeless woman. I realized that she needed the money a lot more than I needed a new magazine.

As I passed the produce section, I saw my aunt picking out vegetables, so I stopped to tell her that I'd meet her at the checkout counter. Before she could question me about where I was going, I was off and running toward the store entrance.

I stepped out into the cold air and looked to my right. Sure enough, the woman was still where she had been when we came in. I reached into my pocket, pulled out the five dollars and handed it to the woman. The look of appreciation on her face was worth more than five dollars. She was so grateful that she stood up and gave me a big hug. "Thank you, young man," she said with a shaky voice. "I can't believe that you ran all the way back here to give me your money."

"No problem," I assured her. "And, hey—Merry Christmas," I said, as I smiled and turned to go find my aunt.

When I arrived back at my house, my mom said there was some mail for me. Much to my surprise, my uncle had sent me a Christmas card—with a twenty-dollar bill inside!

I've heard it said that if you give from the heart, unselfishly and unconditionally, it will be returned to you many times over. On that cold December day, I realized how that isn't just a saying. Good deeds do come back to you.

~Nick Montavon
Chicken Soup for the Soul Christmas Treasury for Kids

97

A Different Kind of Friend

Someone to tell it to is one of the fundamental needs of human beings.
~Miles Franklin

I never thought that one of my very best friends would be twelve years older than me. But it's true. I, the girl who used to laugh at the idea, have a mentor. Two years ago, when I was a sophomore in high school, my former youth leader, Judy, came up to me in church.

"Hey, Sarah," she said, "I've been praying about this, and I'd really like to start meeting with you weekly—doing a Bible study, talking, just getting to know each other on a deeper level."

I was touched beyond words. This tall, slim, beautiful woman the girls in my youth group wanted to emulate had just asked me if I wanted to hang out with her! "Wow—I'd love that!"

"Great! Are you free for dinner sometime this week?"

And so it began.

Judy surprised me with her realness. Whenever we met, she didn't compel me to spill all my problems. Instead, she waited until I felt like sharing whatever was on my heart, and when I did (it didn't take long), she never once made me feel like a patient she was counseling. She came down to my level and showed me how she solved similar problems in her life when she was my age. She does that to this day. She listens to me... really listens. She supports me, no matter what.

During my junior year, I went through a difficult situation and, surprisingly, when I talked to Judy about it, begging her to understand my point of view, she didn't give me the whole, "Well, this is what you could have done differently" speech. She took my side and let me know that I was doing just fine with how I handled it. I needed to hear that she supported me. I needed to hear that an adult understood that sometimes a teenager can be right.

Judy also treats me like an equal. I spent the night at her house once, and we lounged around in our PJs watching reality shows and talking about deep issues. And not just my personal issues... hers, too. She doesn't mind talking with me about her struggles, and because of that, I feel like I can share mine.

Judy is one of my most precious sources of encouragement. I constantly receive sweet notes that simply say, "I hope you're having a good week! You mean so much to me!" She encourages me in other ways, too. Once the question, "Who is a person you look up to and admire in your life?" came up in our Bible study book. She wrote my name in the blank and listed several character qualities she admires about me. That encouragement went straight to my heart and stayed there.

I left my high school when I was a junior, and the change tore me up inside. For a while, I thought I was depressed, and even when I told her that, she let me know that I had made a good decision to leave and that life would only get better (she was right—it did), and that she was behind me the whole way.

Judy's got it all—she's real, she's supportive, she's encouraging, and she treats me equally. But the quality I love most about her is that she genuinely loves me. It's not often you meet a person who knows all your flaws and still seems only to notice the good. That's what I've found in Judy. I have few of what I would call "best friends," and she is undoubtedly one of them.

~Beth Marshall
Chicken Soup for the Teenage Soul: The Real Deal Friends

98

A Forgiving Heart

Thursday afternoon was turning out to be anything but beautiful. The day started right as Trevor began his morning on his knees in prayer. The day became more challenging until finally school was out, and Trevor went home.

The door slammed, and the sound of footsteps clomping up the stairs caught his mother's attention. "Trevor?"

"Yes, Mom." Although detecting that "I'm miserable" sound in his voice, his mother didn't say anything, knowing Trevor would soon come to talk. She was right. Ten minutes later, Trevor walked into the kitchen and plopped down in a chair.

"Mom, do you remember that boy, Robby, that I told you about?"

His mom nodded.

"Well, we got into a fight today."

"Oh, Trevor."

"Wait, Mom, it's nothing like that. I sat next to him in third period. He kept pushing my books onto the floor and poking at me. I just sat there and said nothing. After the bell rang, I walked out into the hall and he pushed me. When I turned, he said, 'You must think you're real cool 'cause you're on the football team.' I turned and started to walk off. He shouted, 'Are you too good to fight me?' I responded, 'I don't want to fight you.' He stood in front of me and, with a bunch of other kids standing around watching, he said, 'If I hit you, you won't fight back?' As I turned away from him, he hit me. I just looked at him. He waited for me to hit back, but I just said, 'Feel better?' and walked off. He didn't follow me."

"You did the right thing," Trevor's mom said. "God will take care of the rest."

By Saturday morning, Trevor was less bothered by what had happened with Robby. In fact, Robby had been extremely quiet on Friday and didn't even look at Trevor.

Trevor told his mother, "I'm going over to Steve's to see if he wants to go canoeing."

Halfway to Steve's house, Trevor saw a Chevy with its flashers on. As he passed by, he noticed a person working under the hood. Trevor turned around and pulled up next to the car. Getting out of his truck, he walked up and asked, "Do you need help?"

The guy slowly turned. It was Robby.

Trevor swallowed hard as he walked closer to the car. "What seems to be wrong?"

Robby stood there, amazed, then told Trevor what his car had done. Trevor was mechanically inclined, and the boys worked together for over an hour, not really saying much.

With the car finally running, Trevor said, "Well, see you around."

"Wait!" Trevor turned to see Robby's hand extended. "Thank you, Trevor."

"You're welcome." Trevor felt God leading him to add, "What are you doing today?"

Robby couldn't hold eye contact with Trevor when he said, "Nothing."

"Ever been canoeing?"

Robby looked at him with a smile. "I used to go with my dad when I was younger."

The two headed toward the river and were soon floating with the current. "Hey, I'm sorry about the other day, Trevor."

"Don't sweat it. It's no big deal."

Robby continued, "It's just, I see you in school and you seem so different, you know, happy all the time."

Robby told Trevor how his stepfather had beaten him after his real dad died. Robby said he used drugs as a way of escaping reality. His stepdad finally walked out, but the darkness and despair still surrounded Robby. He explained his plan of suicide that would have taken place that very afternoon.

Robby dug into his pocket and pulled out a note. It read, "I have reached the end; desperation and loneliness have won. I can't change my life and have given up trying. I doubt anyone will miss me. I write this not as a cry for help, because it's too late for me, but as a cry for hope, hope that someone will love the unlovable." Trevor looked up from the note to Robby, who was visibly shaken.

Trevor spoke in a broken voice, "Jesus loves the unlovable, Robby, and it's never too late for God." Trevor told Robby of the compassionate love of Christ and how it could change his life.

Over time, Robby's life changed dramatically. He gave his life to Christ and began to rely on God more and more. The two boys now share their faith with anyone who will listen and have put together a Bible study group at their school. They are always there for each other, even on the most challenging of days. They know there's nothing that canoeing down the river with a best friend can't cure.

~Gary Flaherty
Chicken Soup for the Christian Teenage Soul

The Day Our Dad Came Home

For where your treasure is, there your heart will be also.
~Matthew 6:21

I remember so clearly the day I found my dad. It was a few days away from my fourteenth birthday, and Mom had sent me to the store to buy a few things. As I approached the front of the store, I saw this man sitting on a Harley-Davidson motorcycle. He had dark hair, and he was wearing a black T-shirt and black jeans. I thought he was so handsome. I decided that I wanted to take him home to meet my mother. She was divorced with six children, and I was determined they would meet, fall in love and get married.

I walked up to him and said, "Hi, my name is Pam. What's your name?"

He smiled, and said, "Well, hello there, Pam! My name is Duke." I asked him if he was married, and he said, "No, but I think I'm a little too old for you."

I laughed and said, "Not for me silly! I want you to meet my mom."

He was so full of life. I thought he would be good for Mom — she needed some excitement in her life. She married my daddy when she was very young, and he was a truck driver who rarely came home. Daddy was an alcoholic so he spent all of his money at the bars, and everything was left up to my mom. She finally divorced him after he came home one day in a drunken rage.

My mother was a conservative and modest woman. She was raised in a Baptist church in a small Southern town. I just knew that today would be her lucky day.

I took Duke to my house, telling him how beautiful Mom was and how I just knew they would fall in love. He smiled at my excitement, but Mom stopped us in our tracks as we walked inside. I said, "Mom, this is Duke, and he is going to take you on a date!" He stood there, snapping his fingers and looking so cool!

Mom quickly asked him to leave and walked to the door to show him the way out. He turned to look at me and said, "Don't worry. I won't give up."

After he left, Mom gave me a lecture for bringing a stranger to our home. "What were you thinking? He looks like some kind of crazy man. I bet he parties all the time."

Well, the crazy man did not give up, just as he promised. He kept coming back and finally, Mom gave in to his handsome ways. They went on a date a few days later, and on a beautiful day in April my mother married Duke. He became Dad to Brenda, Denese, Ruth, Johnny, Jody and me. He would never allow anyone to refer to us as his stepchildren. We were his children, and he was adored by our entire family.

He was such a positive influence for us. I can't recall ever hearing him say anything derogatory about anyone. He encouraged us to believe in ourselves and that we could accomplish anything we desired or dreamed of achieving. "Just set your goals and go for it!" he would tell us. He took really good care of my mom and all of us.

A few years later, Dad started having some problems, so he made a doctor's appointment to have a biopsy on his throat. The results were not good—Dad had throat cancer. His prognosis was maybe six months. The doctors had to insert a feeding tube into his stomach, and he would never be able to eat or drink again. He would never again be able to have his cup of coffee in the mornings as he sat and watched the birds playing on the many feeders that he'd made for them.

A couple of weeks passed, and we noticed Dad getting weaker—he was sleeping all the time. Dad was giving up, and we had to encourage him to fight. My sisters and I took turns feeding him, and we had to give him morphine around the clock for the pain. Our emotions were like a roller coaster—we wanted to cry, but we couldn't. We had to stay strong for Dad and Mom.

Early one morning, I slipped into Dad's room and sat down beside him. I started singing, "Good morning to you, good morning to you. Good morning, dear Dad, good morning to you."

He smiled weakly and sang, "Good morning, dear daughter."

I took his hand in mine and whispered, "Do you remember singing this song to me when I was a little girl?" And I sang to him the song about the rubber tree and the ant that had high hopes. It was the song he sang to us whenever we were having a difficult time. He nodded and smiled up at me.

In April, my sister and I were giving Dad a bath. Dad turned his head and said, "Pam?"

I whispered through a broken voice, "Yes, Dad. I'm here."

He said, "Thank you for finding me that day. I didn't know I was lost until you found me."

I laid my head on his chest and as tears fell from my eyes, I said, "Oh, Dad. It was you that found us."

Dad held on until the next morning. His wife and all six of his children were by his bed. I held Dad's hand. The room was crowded as Dad slipped away to heaven.

I will always remember the first day I saw him. He didn't just happen to be at that store. I know in my heart that God had placed Duke right where we needed him the most. My dad had seen a woman with six children, and he had fallen in love with all of us. He said, "I'll do whatever it takes to take care of them," and he kept his promise. Dad never thought of himself, only of those he loved. He filled the gap for the children who had always longed to have a loving daddy.

The other day when I was getting a little discouraged, I found myself humming the song about the ant. And when I got to the chorus, I swear I thought I heard Dad singing, "...because, he's got high hopes."

~Pamela D. Hamalainen
Chicken Soup for the Girl's Soul

Love's Power

*Too often we underestimate the power of a touch, a smile, a kind word, a
listening ear, an honest compliment, or the smallest act of caring, all of which
have the potential to turn a life around.*
~Leo Buscaglia

Does Mom hear that train whistle? Pam wondered. Her
mother and grandmother were having a loud argument as
they rode in the front seat of the car. Pam's mom had been
cross all morning. "I'd better not say anything," Pam thought.

As the noise got louder, Pam could see the locomotive fast
approaching the crossing. Her mother was oblivious to the danger
and hadn't even slowed. "Mom!" she cried, trying not to scream.

"In a minute," her mother snapped.

And then Pam did scream, "Mom, look!"

It was too late. The train careened into the car, cleanly shearing
off the front seat. Pam and her sister were left unhurt in the backseat
as mother and grandmother were dragged beneath the train for a full
quarter of a mile down the track.

The tragedy occurred in the summer between Pam's seventh and
eighth grade years. The eighth-grader who returned to school that
fall was not the same girl who had left. In the seventh grade, Pam had
been a student who teachers enjoyed having in their classes. Bright
and eager to learn, she'd never been a discipline problem and had
always seemed to enjoy school. That Pam had ceased to exist. The
Pam that came back to school in September was a sullen, angry and

inattentive person who was very difficult to have around. It became commonplace for her to be disciplined for her rudeness and disrespectful behavior. She was obviously a very troubled young girl.

As a guidance counselor, Rose was worried about Pam. Rose was usually successful at reaching troubled kids, but so far she hadn't been able to help Pam. Week after week went by, and Rose's frustration grew. No less frustrated was Ken, Pam's science teacher. Great with kids of almost any age, Ken was disturbed by the fact that he couldn't get through Pam's shell. The three of us met frequently to discuss Pam. By November her behavior had worsened. All of us were worried, but we felt like our hands were tied. It's difficult in this day and age to reach out to a student without being accused of some indiscretion or outright perversion.

The week after Thanksgiving, Ken showed me a newspaper article and picture of his high school science teacher who was retiring. It was a long article which traced the life experiences of this man who had been Ken's mentor. Ken had enjoyed a very special relationship with this man who, long ago, had served as Ken's inspiration. In reading the article, Ken became determined to meet with Pam and discuss some personal feelings with her, regardless of the political incorrectness of doing so.

"I can't help but think about where I would be today if Mr. Smith hadn't reached out to me," Ken fumed. "I am so sick of this walking on eggshells when kids need help!" We talked about it for a bit. Ultimately, Ken took Pam's school picture from her student file and decided to go ahead and hang the consequences of overstepping "politically correct" boundaries.

At the end of science class, Ken gave Pam a note for her study hall teacher requesting that Pam come to see him that afternoon. Pam came in with a big chip securely fastened on her shoulder, expecting to be reprimanded for some new transgression. She slumped down in a seat in the first row with a sullen face. Ken moved a chair over next to her and opened his folder on the desk that they now shared.

The folder contained pictures. Pam said nothing and looked suspiciously at the desktop. "This," he said, "is my mother. I love her.

She's always been there for me. I can't even imagine my life without her. It must be hard for you." When Pam just looked away, he moved on to the next picture, his mentor. He explained his affection for that man and told her how without that person in his life, he would not be who or what he was today. "He was a great teacher," Ken said. "He inspired me. I loved him, too. But it was a different kind of love than I have for my mom."

There were more pictures in the folder. One was of Ken's two little girls and his wife; another one was of Christ. The love he had for his family was easily expressed as he talked with Pam. The picture of Jesus prompted him to explain how he loved the Lord and how that love differed from any earthly love. Pointing to the pictures, Ken said, "All of these are people that I love."

The final picture in the file was of Pam herself. Holding her picture, he said very gently, "This is someone else I love. I haven't told you until now. I know it's awkward for a teacher to tell a student something like this. But I think you need to know. What happened last summer convinced me that you should know." Tears sparkled on Pam's lashes. "You're a terrific person. I love you for that. And I love you for your love of learning and many, many other things. And I love you unconditionally." The sullen look had been replaced by an expression of pain and hurt as tears streamed down Pam's cheeks. It was the first time Ken had seen anything but anger from her in a long time. Ken retrieved a box of Kleenex from the front of the room and slid the box across to her. They just sat quietly until she seemed ready to leave.

The change in Pam began that afternoon. Day by day, week by week, she began to gain ground again. Rose, Ken and I watched with delight as she progressed. By Easter she was doing very well. She was nearly the delightful girl she had been before that traumatic accident. I congratulated Ken on his success. I was convinced it was the power of Ken's love that had inspired Pam's journey back to her former self.

Rose didn't agree with me. She believed it was the power of the Holy Spirit moving through Ken that inspired him to share his feelings with Pam and thus heal her. Only God knows for sure, as He smiles down on a living photo album of the children He loves.

~Harry Randles
Chicken Soup for the Christian Woman's Soul

A Day That Changed Us All

Dear *Chicken Soup for the Teenage Soul*,

On April 20, 1999, in a school across the country from mine, one of the biggest tragedies of my lifetime occurred: Two teenage boys entered Columbine High School in Littleton, Colorado, and killed thirteen people. The news devastated and scared me. The thought of a student coming into my own school and shooting people terrified me. I wasn't directly impacted by what happened at Columbine, but the tragedy affected me deeply.

I found solace in discussing the tragedy with my dad. He spent hours talking with me about my thoughts and feelings and he encouraged me, as he does so well, to think of ways that I could come to terms with what had happened. He asked me what I thought would make me feel better, and how we could show the students and those in the community that people around the world love them. I thought about it long and hard until I knew in my heart what I wanted to do. I realized I wanted to help the students—to give them something that could make them feel better and ease their pain, however slightly. I told my dad that I had found a great deal of comfort in reading the stories in *Chicken Soup for the Teenage Soul*. The stories in the book, I explained, helped me realize that we all have within us the power to overcome any obstacle. I wanted each of the students at Columbine to have a copy of *Chicken Soup for the Teenage Soul* to help them cope with this horribly painful ordeal.

My father immediately got on the phone to the publisher of the *Chicken Soup for the Soul* series, and explained to them that we wanted to purchase two thousand copies of *Chicken Soup for the Teenage Soul II* for the students at Columbine. The publisher contacted Kimberly Kirberger, the coauthor, right away and told her what we wanted to do. She immediately called my house and said how deeply moved she was by what we were doing. She told us that she, the other coauthors of Teenage Soul, and the publisher, without hesitation, had decided to match our purchase of two thousand books and donate two thousand *Chicken Soup for the Teenage Soul Journals* as well. I was ecstatic to say the least, not because I was proud of what I was doing, but for what these books would do for the Columbine students at such a traumatic time.

From that point on, everything else seemed to fall into place. So many people were willing to help out in any way they could. First, we needed a place to store the books once they arrived in Littleton, until they could be distributed. We were so fortunate to meet a very special woman from Media Play who was gracious enough to provide a storage place for the books. She made sure there were PTA members and other volunteers available to help stuff the books with letters written by myself and the Chicken Soup for the Soul team, and to help pass the books out to the students. And throughout the entire process, Darren Martin also helped in whatever ways he could.

I was not able to be in Littleton when the students received their books, but a few days later the letters and e-mail started pouring in. After reading all the amazing words about how happy they were to receive the books, I was able to picture in my mind their excitement on that day. I was overwhelmed by it all. It's difficult to find words to describe how incredible it was to receive all those letters, but it was a feeling I will treasure forever. I received letters not only from students of Columbine, but from parents and even a school bus driver. His was particularly touching because he told me that on the day the books were given out the mood of the students seemed to change. Faces brightened up just a bit. One morning with a bus full of students he looked in his rearview mirror and saw a sea of Chicken Soup books being read and teenagers beginning to regain those smiles they had before the shooting. He was so moved that he couldn't help but get choked up by what he saw.

Later, in September 1999, I received another phone call from Kimberly Kirberger. She was going to be in Colorado in October for book signings and was hoping my father and I could join her there. Without thinking twice about it, I told her we would make it.

We flew to Colorado to meet Kim and attend her book signing in Littleton. She was awesome! We got to know each other over dinner, and I don't think I have met a sweeter person than Kim. I was also able to meet a few of the Columbine students I had kept in contact with who were at the book signing. To be able to talk to them in person was something I really wanted to do and was important to me. They were extremely nice and outgoing—their lives were heading in the right direction now. It was the perfect culmination to everything that had happened.

Throughout the whole experience I became closer to those around me, including my family, friends and God. I received a tremendous amount of support from them and without it I would have had a really difficult time dealing with the Columbine shooting. One is never okay with something as tragic as this, but the love and support helped me tremendously, and I am very grateful for that.

I look at life differently now, knowing how precious it is and how quickly things can be turned upside down. I pray often that a tragedy such as Columbine never happens again.

Thank you so much, *Chicken Soup for the Teenage Soul* for creating these amazing books and giving teenagers more hope, inspiration, love and encouragement.

God bless,

~Jackie Morgenstern
Chicken Soup for the Teenage Soul Letters

~Share with Us~
~More Chicken Soup~
~About the Authors~
~Acknowledgments~

Share with Us

We would like to know how these stories affected you and which ones were your favorites. Please e-mail us and let us know.

We also would like to share your stories with future readers. You may be able to help another reader, and become a published author at the same time. Please send us your own stories and poems for our future books. Some of our past contributors have launched writing and speaking careers from the publication of their stories in our books!

Your stories have the best chance of being used if you submit them through our web site, at:

www.chickensoup.com

If you do not have access to the Internet, you may submit your stories by mail or by facsimile. Please do not send us any book manuscripts, unless through a literary agent, as these will be automatically discarded.

Chicken Soup for the Soul
P.O. Box 700
Cos Cob, CT 06807-0700
Fax 203-861-7194

More for Christian Teens

Chicken Soup for the Christian Teenage Soul
0-7573-0095-2
Chicken Soup for the Teenage Soul
1-55874-463-0
Chicken Soup for the Teenage Soul II
1-55874-616-1
Chicken Soup for the Teenage Soul III
1-55874-761-3
Chicken Soup for the Teenage Soul on Tough Stuff
1-55874-942-X
Chicken Soup for the Teenage Soul Teen Letters
1-55874-804-0
Chicken Soup for the Soul for the Teenage Soul
on Love & Friendship
0-7573-0022-7
Chicken Soup for the Teenage Soul IV
0-7573-0233-5
Chicken Soup for the Teen Soul: Real-Life Stories by Real Teens
0-7573-0682-9
Chicken Soup for the Soul: Real Deal School
0-7573-0255-6
Chicken Soup for the Soul: Real Deal Friends
0-7573-0317-X
Chicken Soup for the Soul: Real Deal Challenges
0-7573-0407-9
Chicken Soup for the Christian Soul
1-55874-501-7
Chicken Soup for the Christian Family Soul
1-55874-714-1
Chicken Soup for the Christian Woman's Soul
0-7573-0018-9
Chicken Soup for the Christian Soul II
0-7573-0320-X

Teens Talk Tough Times

Being a teenager is difficult even under idyllic circumstances. But when bad things happen, the challenges of being a teenager can be overwhelming, leading to self-destructive behavior, eating disorders, substance abuse, and other challenges. In addition, many teens are faced with illness, car accidents, loss of loved ones, divorces, or other upheavals. This book Includes 101 of our best stories about the toughest teenage times — and how to overcome them.

Teens Talk Relationships

The teenage years are difficult. Old friends drift away, new friends come with new issues, teens fall in and out of love, and relationships with family members change. This book reminds teenagers that they are not alone, as they read the 101 best stories from Chicken Soup's library written, by other teens just like themselves, about the problems and issues they face every day — stories about friends, family, love, loss, and many lessons learned.

Teens Talk Growing Up

Being a teenager is hard — school is challenging, college and career are looming on the horizon, family issues arise, friends and love come and go, bodies and emotions go through major changes, and many teens experience the loss of a loved one for the first time. This book reminds teenagers that they are not alone, as they read stories written by other teens about the problems and issues they all face every day.

*C*heck out our
great books for

Teens Talk Getting In... to College

These days, colleges are deluged with applications, and the application process has become something traumatic that students and parents experience together. This book isn't about how to get into college — it's about providing emotional support from kids who have been there. Story topics include parental and peer pressure, the stress of grades and standardized tests, applications and interviews, recruiting, disappointments, and successes.

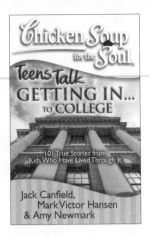

Teens Talk High School

This book focuses on issues specific to high school age kids, ages fourteen to eighteen. This book covers topics of interest to older teens such as sports and clubs, religion and faith, driving, curfews, growing up, self-image and self-acceptance, dating and sex, family relationships, friends, divorce, illness, death, pregnancy, drinking, failure, and preparing for life after high school. High school students will refer to this book all four years of their high school experience, like a portable support group.

Teens Talk Middle School

This "support group in a book" is specifically geared to middle school students ages eleven to fourteen — the ones still worrying about puberty, cliques, discovering the opposite sex, and figuring out who they are. Stories cover regrets and lessons learned, love and "like," popularity, friendship, tough issues such as divorce, illness, and death, failure and rising above it, embarrassing moments, bullying, and finding something you're passionate about.

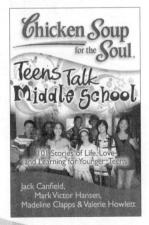

Teens

This is the first Chicken Soup book to focus specifically on stories of faith, including 101 of the best stories from Chicken Soup's library on faith, hope, miracles, and devotion. These true stories written by regular people tell of prayers answered miraculously, amazing coincidences, rediscovered faith, and the serenity that comes from believing in a greater power, appealing to Christians and those of other faiths, and everyone who seeks enlightenment and inspiration through a good story.
978-1-935096-14-6

Check out our great books for

This is Chicken Soup for the Soul's first book written just for Catholics. From the once-a-year attendee at Christmas Mass, to the devout church volunteer and daily worshipper. 101 spirit-filled stories written by Catholics of all ages, this book covers the gamut, including fun stories about growing up Catholic to serious stories about sacraments and miracles. Whether the reader is a cradle Catholic, a convert, simply curious, or struggling, these stories bestow happiness, hope, and healing to everyone in all stages of life and faith.

978-1-935096-23-8

CHRISTIANS

Chicken Soup for the Soul®

Our 101 BEST STORIES

Christian Kids

Stories to Inspire, Amuse, and Warm the Hearts of Christian Kids and Their Parents

Jack Canfield
& Mark Victor Hansen
edited by Amy Newmark

This is the first Chicken Soup book, with 101 great stories from Chicken Soup's library, created specifically for Christian parents to read themselves or to share with their children. All of the selected stories are appropriate for children and are about raising Christian kids twelve and under. Christian parents will enjoy reading these heartfelt, inspiring, and often humorous stories about the ups and downs of daily life in today's contemporary Christian families.

978-1-935096-13-9

Check out our great books for

Everyone loves Christmas and the holiday season. We reunite scattered family members, watch the wonder in a child's eyes, and feel the joy of giving gifts. The rituals of the holiday season give a rhythm to the years and create a foundation for our lives, as we gather with family, with our communities at church, at school, and even at the mall, to share the special spirit of the season, brightening those long winter days.

978-1-935096-15-3

CHRISTIANS

Who Is
Jack Canfield?

J ack Canfield is the co-creator and editor of the *Chicken Soup for the Soul* series, which *Time* magazine has called "the publishing phenomenon of the decade." Jack is also the co-author of eight other bestselling books including *The Success Principles™: How to Get from Where You Are to Where You Want to Be*, *Dare to Win*, *The Aladdin Factor*, *You've Got to Read This Book*, and *The Power of Focus: How to Hit Your Business and Personal and Financial Targets with Absolute Certainty*.

Jack has recently developed a telephone coaching program and an online coaching program based on his most recent book *The Success Principles*. He also offers a seven-day *Breakthrough to Success* seminar every summer, which attracts 400 people from fifteen countries around the world.

Jack is the CEO of the Canfield Training Group in Santa Barbara, California, and founder of the Foundation for Self-Esteem in Culver City, California. He has conducted intensive personal and professional development seminars on the principles of success for over a million people in twenty-three countries. Jack is a dynamic keynote speaker and he has spoken to hundreds of thousands of others at more than 1,000 corporations, universities, professional conferences and conventions, and has been seen by millions more on national television shows such as *The Today Show*, *Fox and Friends*, *Inside Edition*, *Hard Copy*, *CNN's Talk Back Live*, *20/20*, *Eye to Eye*, and the *NBC Nightly News* and the *CBS Evening News*.

Jack is the recipient of many awards and honors, including three honorary doctorates and a *Guinness World Records Certificate* for having seven books from the *Chicken Soup for the Soul* series appearing on the *New York Times* bestseller list on May 24, 1998.

To write to Jack or for inquiries about Jack as a speaker, his coaching programs, trainings or seminars, use the following contact information:

Jack Canfield
The Canfield Companies
P.O. Box 30880 • Santa Barbara, CA 93130
phone: 805-563-2935 • fax: 805-563-2945
E-mail: info@jackcanfield.com
www.jackcanfield.com

Who Is
Mark Victor Hansen?

ark Victor Hansen is the co-founder of *Chicken Soup for the Soul*, along with Jack Canfield. He is also a sought-after keynote speaker, bestselling author, and marketing maven.

For more than thirty years, Mark has focused solely on helping people from all walks of life reshape their personal vision of what's possible. His powerful messages of possibility, opportunity, and action have created powerful change in thousands of organizations and millions of individuals worldwide.

Mark's credentials include a lifetime of entrepreneurial success. He is a prolific writer with many bestselling books, such as *The One Minute Millionaire*, *Cracking the Millionaire Code*, *How to Make the Rest of Your Life the Best of Your Life*, *The Power of Focus*, *The Aladdin Factor*, and *Dare to Win*, in addition to the *Chicken Soup for the Soul* series. Mark has had a profound influence in the field of human potential through his library of audios, videos, and articles in the areas of big thinking, sales achievement, wealth building, publishing success, and personal and professional development.

Mark is the founder of the *MEGA Seminar Series*. *MEGA Book Marketing University* and *Building Your MEGA Speaking Empire* are annual conferences where Mark coaches and teaches new and aspiring authors, speakers, and experts on building lucrative publishing and speaking careers. Other MEGA events include *MEGA Info-Marketing* and *My MEGA Life*.

He has appeared on *Oprah*, *CNN*, and *The Today Show*. He has been quoted in *Time*, *U.S. News & World Report*, *USA Today*, *New York Times*, and *Entrepreneur* and has had countless radio interviews, assuring our planet's people that "You can easily create the life you deserve."

As a philanthropist and humanitarian, Mark works tirelessly for organizations such as Habitat for Humanity, American Red Cross, March of Dimes, Childhelp USA, and many others. He is the recipient of numerous awards that honor his entrepreneurial spirit, philanthropic heart, and business acumen. He is a lifetime member of the Horatio Alger Association of Distinguished Americans, an organization that honored Mark with the prestigious Horatio Alger Award for his extraordinary life achievements.

Mark Victor Hansen is an enthusiastic crusader of what's possible and is driven to make the world a better place.

Mark Victor Hansen & Associates, Inc.
P.O. Box 7665 • Newport Beach, CA 92658
phone: 949-764-2640 • fax: 949-722-6912
www.markvictorhansen.com

Who Is
Amy Newmark?

my Newmark was recently named publisher of Chicken Soup for the Soul, after a thirty-year career as a writer, speaker, financial analyst, and business executive in the worlds of finance and telecommunications.

Amy is a graduate of Harvard College, where she majored in Portuguese, minored in French, and traveled extensively. She is also the mother of two children in college and has two grown stepchildren.

After a long career writing books on telecommunications, voluminous financial reports, business plans, and corporate press releases, Chicken Soup for the Soul is a breath of fresh air for Amy. She has fallen in love with Chicken Soup for the Soul and its life-changing books, and found it a true pleasure to conceptualize, compile, and edit the "101 Best Stories" books for our readers.

The best way to contact Chicken Soup for the Soul is through our web site, at www.chickensoup.com. This will always get the fastest attention.

If you do not have access to the Internet, please contact us by mail or by facsimile.

Chicken Soup for the Soul
P.O. Box 700
Cos Cob, CT 06807-0700
Fax 203-861-7194

Thank You!

Our first thanks go to our loyal readers who have inspired the entire Chicken Soup team for the past fifteen years. Your appreciative letters and emails have reminded us why we work so hard on these books.

We owe huge thanks to all of our contributors as well. We know that you pour your hearts and souls into the stories and poems that you share with us, and ultimately with each other. We appreciate your willingness to open up your lives to other Chicken Soup readers.

We can only publish a small percentage of the stories that are submitted, but we read every single one and even the ones that do not appear in a book have an influence on us and on the final manuscripts.

As always, we would like to thank the entire staff of Chicken Soup for the Soul for their help on this project and the 101 Best series in general.

Among our California staff, we would especially like to single out the following people:

- D'ette Corona, our Assistant Publisher, who is the heart and soul of the Chicken Soup publishing operation, and who put together the first draft of this manuscript

- Barbara LoMonaco, our Webmaster and Chicken Soup for the Soul Editor, for invaluable assistance in obtaining the

fabulous quotations that add depth and meaning to this
book

- Patty Hansen for her extra special help with the permissions
for these fabulous stories and for her amazing knowledge of
the Chicken Soup library

- and Patti Clement for her help with permissions and other
organizational matters.

In our Connecticut office, we would like to thank our able editors,
Valerie Howlett and Madeline Clapps, for their assistance in setting
up our new offices, editing, and helping us put together the best
possible books.

We would also like to thank our master of design, Brian Taylor at
Pneuma Books, for his brilliant vision for our covers and interiors.
Finally, none of this would be possible without the business and cre-
ative leadership of our CEO, Bill Rouhana, and our president, Bob
Jacobs.